Female Fans, Gender Relations and Football Fandom

This book assesses the transformation of football fan culture from a gender perspective. Referring to the notions of homosociality, hegemonic masculinity and performative perspectives on gender and fandom, it investigates the processes of women entering the world of football fandom.

Drawing on multidimensional qualitative and quantitative research, the book analyses different aspects of female fandom, such as women's socialisation to be a fan, building their sense of fan identity, ways of performing fandom, and gender. Also, it explores the response of male fans by shedding light on the sense-making process of a growing number of female fans in the stands and its consequences for prevailingly male football culture. This study stands out for its richness and diversity of empirical material used in order to make a significant contribution to our understanding of social dynamics related to the changing nature of female football fandom.

The book is fascinating reading for researchers and students in a broad range of areas, including gender studies, sociology of sport, football, women's studies and Central Eastern European studies. It is also a valuable resource for scholars, and football and club authorities who have an interest in understanding the development of female football fandom and its impact on the male fandom community.

Honorata Jakubowska is Professor of Sociology and Chair of the Department of Sociology of the Individual and Social Relations at Adam Mickiewicz University in Poznań, Poland.

Dominik Antonowicz is Professor of Sociology and Chair of the Department of Science and Higher Education Research at Nicolas Copernicus University in Toruń, Poland.

Radosław Kossakowski is Professor of Sociology and Chair of the Scientific Council of Sociology at the University of Gdańsk, Poland, where he is also Director of the Institute of Sociology.

Routledge Research in Sport, Culture and Society

Deleuze and the Physically Active Body
Pirkko Markula

Capitalism, Sport Mega Events and the Global South
Billy Graeff

The Nordic Model and Physical Culture
*Edited by Mikkel B. Tin, Frode Telseth, Jan Ove Tangen
and Richard Giulianotti*

Sport and Mediatization
Kirsten Frandsen

Social Activism in Women's Tennis
Generations of Politics and Cultural Change
Kristi Tredway

Sport, Welfare and Social Policy in the European Union
Nicola R. Porro, Stefano Martelli and Alberto Testa

Disability, the Media and the Paralympic Games
Carolyn Jackson-Brown

Sport, Film and National Culture
Edited by Seán Crosson

Female Fans, Gender Relations and Football Fandom
Challenging the Brotherhood Culture
Honorata Jakubowska, Dominik Antonowicz and Radosław Kossakowski

For more information about this series, please visit: www.routledge.com/sport/
series/RRSCS

Female Fans, Gender Relations and Football Fandom

Challenging the Brotherhood Culture

Honorata Jakubowska,
Dominik Antonowicz and
Radosław Kossakowski

Routledge
Taylor & Francis Group

LONDON AND NEW YORK

First published 2021
by Routledge
2 Park Square, Milton Park, Abingdon, Oxon OX14 4RN

and by Routledge
52 Vanderbilt Avenue, New York, NY 10017

Routledge is an imprint of the Taylor & Francis Group, an informa business

British Library Cataloguing-in-Publication Data
A catalogue record for this book is available from the British Library

Library of Congress Cataloging-in-Publication Data
A catalog record has been requested for this book

ISBN: 978-0-367-36552-3 (hbk)
ISBN: 978-0-429-34700-9 (ebk)

Typeset in Times New Roman
by Wearset Ltd, Boldon, Tyne and Wear

Contents

vi *Contents*

Acknowledgements

This book results from a research project funded by the National Science Centre in Poland (project number: 2016/21/B/HS6/00846).

The research project would not have been successful without the respondents that agreed to share their fandom experiences and the help of people working in Lech Poznań, Legia Warszawa and Lechia Gdańsk.

We would like to thank Simon Whitmore and Rebecca Connor from Routledge for their professional support in the publishing process, as well as the reviewers of the book proposal for their helpful comments on how to improve the publication.

Additionally, Dominik and Radosław would like to thank their families for their unconditional support.

Introduction

The main aim of this book is to investigate the role and position of female supporters[1] in the football fandom culture. Football fandom is male-dominated and found by many studies to be one of the main sources of reproducing hegemonic masculinity (Redhead 1993; King 1997; Hughson 2000). Thus, the conducted research project on which this book is based has addressed three fundamental research questions: (1) How are female supporters as 'a new type of fan' becoming integrated into the football fandom culture? (2) How have a growing number of female supporters been changing the male-dominated communities of football fans? (3) To what extent is the growing number of female supporters an intentional development caused by both football clubs and football authorities or does it stem from a wider cultural transformation in which women are beginning to perform social roles traditionally assigned to males?

By addressing these research questions, the analysis presented in the book contributes to the discussion about changing football fandom culture under the influence of a growing number of women attending football matches (Dunn 2014; Pfister, Lenneis and Mintert 2013; Pope 2017). Contrary to previous investigations, the process of women entering the world of football fans and their status in this world are analysed from three different, albeit connected, perspectives, namely: (1) female supporters themselves; (2) male supporters; (3) football clubs and football authorities.

In Poland, similar to other countries, one can see an increasing number of female fans in the stands. Unfortunately, systematic data on these changes has not been published; however, all research participants, both fans and the clubs' authorities, have confirmed the presence of this phenomenon. The commercial research report from 2019, based on the data collected passively from all stadiums of teams in the *Ekstraklasa* (Polish national league) in 2018/2019, states that women constitute 22% of fans in the stands (*Nie tylko mężczyźni* [Not only men] 2019). Polish female fans have established a few female-only groups, such as 'Female Elite' (GKS Katowice), 'Żółto-Czerwone Dziewczyny' [Yellow-Red Girls] (Korona Kielce) and 'Fanatical Girls' 1920' (Ruch Chorzów). There are also groups such as 'czaROWnice' [Witches] (Energetyk ROW Rybnik) and Ultra Girls (Wisła Kraków) whose activity has decreased in recent years. Moreover, the presence of female supporters can be identified in various other contexts. For example, the website of Legia Warszawa contains a female section called 'Legionistki', where girls presented in pictures usually hold club emblems. As well as clubs' websites and fanpages on social media, there is also, for example, the website 'Polskie fanatyczki' [(female) Polish fanatics], which offers special clothing for female fans.

The process of stadiums' 'feminisation' (Pope 2017) is sociologically fascinating and inspiring in terms of empirical investigation. The ingress of women into the world of men has most often been studied in regard to politics and the labour market. The world of football fandom – which is the focus of this book – remains considerably different from other areas of social life (for example politics and the labour market) for several reasons. First, the sense of brotherhood and togetherness plays an important role among supporters, particularly in the community of ultra supporters. It also implies that such a community is based on mechanical solidarity and a hierarchical and punitive structure. Second, the fandom culture has a strongly homosocial nature and the discursive practices of stigmatisation of the opponents concerning their 'feminisation', including assaulting homosexuals and objectifying women, are quite common among 'diehard' fans. In this perspective, the stands are perceived as 'permission zones' (Ben-Porat 2009), 'enclaves', where some behaviours, including sexist and homophobic ones, are largely accepted. Moreover, fandom is also entertainment by nature. Hence, gender equality does not seem (from the fans' perspective) to be a key issue in comparison to its meaning in other fields of social life. Therefore, analysis of football fandom and its gendered nature can provide knowledge that will not only develop sports (football) studies, but also contribute to gender studies.

In 'Western' sociology, female football supporters have recently received attention (Dunn 2014; Pfister, Lenneis and Mintert 2013; Pope 2017; Toffoletti 2017), but even in the UK – which is the cradle of football studies – the number of papers published on this subject is still 'insignificant' (McDowell 2016) compared to the amount of research focused on male fans. Therefore, in this book, we want to contribute to reducing this gap, at least partially.

Furthermore, it also offers new insight into existing knowledge on female fans for several reasons. The publication goes beyond the dominant British and 'Western' perspective in research on football fans by referring to Poland – one of the biggest post-communist countries from Central Eastern Europe and the sixth most populous member of the EU. The geopolitical and cultural situation provides a new context for the analysis of gender differences and fandom culture, and the study of football fandom in Poland can be seen, to some extent, as representative of the region of Central Eastern Europe. In particular, the situation of female fans will be investigated in the context of Polish women's emancipation in other social domains, placing the analysis at the forefront of studies on the transformation of gender roles.

Although the vast majority of publications on female fans are based on empirical studies, their scope has usually been limited. Unlike these publications, our book is found on a large research project that uses mixed qualitative and quantitative methods, the main ones being: (1) an online survey for football fans; and (2) in-depth interviews with female and male fans, and football authorities, as well as the following complementary methods: (a) analysis of fanzines; (b) participatory observations; (c) analyses of merchandising offers; (d) netnography of fans' forums and profiles of female groups in social media. Due to rich and diverse empirical data, female fandom has been analysed from many perspectives and the points of view of different stakeholders. The conducted research has taken into account the presence of female supporters in various sections of football stadiums – those for VIPs, regular fans and ultra supporters. We assume that female fans might be driven to different parts of the stadium ('subworlds' of the fandom community) for various reasons, and their experience of fans' attitudes and behaviour, as well as their reception in football stands, can be distinctively different.

Moreover, one can see that, in the majority of cases, male authors write about male fans and female authors write about female fans. This book, however, has been written by authors of both genders: one woman and two men, who have also conducted all the empirical research that this book is based on. The research strategy of including researchers of both genders can be perceived as innovative in fandom research and can contribute to the development of gender-sensitive methodologies and analysis within football research. We are convinced that mixed-gender teams have allowed different aspects of female fandom and its male perception to be noticed and have made us attentive to various issues. The both-gender perspective has helped to keep an analytical balance when it comes to the interpretation of some – both female and male – statements referring to the gender issue. Without a doubt, the 'double-gender check' provides a more distanced, more reflexive and more nuanced approach. It seems that this methodology is an excellent tool to enable us to fully understand that values prevailing in fandom culture affect women and men differently.

The book consists of four parts. Part I, 'Female fandom: theoretical and empirical investigation', comprises two chapters. Chapter 1 presents the existing state of the art of female fandom based on research conducted in Europe and beyond our continent. In Chapter 2, we examine the main theoretical concepts that have been used as the framework of our analysis. On the one hand, they refer to masculinity (of fandom), including the concepts of hegemonic masculinity and homosociality, and on the other hand, a performative perspective, which is useful for analysing both gender and fandom.

Part II, 'The local context of development of female fandom', introduces the reader to the wider socio-political Polish context. In Chapter 3, we discuss the history of football fandom in Poland, which is, in fact, a male story. Beyond football, as the second main context, we present the main socio-cultural changes that have influenced women's status and gender relations in Poland today. Chapter 4 describes the methodology of the conducted research. Taking into account the scale of the research project, its complex nature and the multiplicity of methods used, we are convinced that this chapter is necessary to reveal the scale of the research project to the readers and to present in a detailed way the methods whose results are analysed in further parts of the book. Moreover, it can also, as we hope, provide some directions for further research on (female) fandom.

Part III, 'Performing female fandom in the male reservoir', studies the rocky path that female fans have taken to enter the football fandom culture and break the homosocial boundaries that make it inaccessible to them. It examines highly nuanced and multifaceted sociological characteristics of Polish female fans as well as the ways they perform their fandom. By doing so, it covers a range of different aspects, including various roles and identities as football fans, their self-images (expressed through different channels, such as profiles on social media), dominant patterns of behaviours inside and outside football grounds and dominant forms of fans' activities. More specifically, Part III aims to address pivotal issues related to female fandom, starting with how women perform their roles as women and as fans in the football stands. Are there situations in which female fans must hide or down-play their gender to be recognised as regular fans? In other words, here we study whether there is any identity conflict between being a fan and being a woman and whether there is a potential conflict that forces women to construct their scripts about being a fan and their own specific ways to perform football fandom.

Part III is divided into six chapters. Chapter 6 analyses the process of women's socialisation into the fandom culture. Chapter 7 examines women's attendance at home and away matches, and this is followed by Chapter 8 explaining the main reasons for this. The next two, Chapters 9 and 10, discuss the ways in which women demonstrate fandom as fans and customers during and beyond matches. The part ends with reflections concerning the perception of football stands as a space for women.

Part IV, 'Female fans in the eyes of others: male and football stakeholders' perspective', consists of Chapters 12 and 13: the first explores the response of male fans to the growing numbers of females in the stands at football matches, and the second focuses on the recognition of female fans by clubs' managers and football authorities. At the end, we present the main conclusions drawn from the conducted research project.

Note

1 In the book we use the terms 'fan' and 'supporter' interchangeably. In English literature they have different meanings as 'supporter' is associated with a more traditional style of supporting, and 'fan' with a more modern one (see Giulianotti 2002). However, in Polish there is only one word referring to supporting a football club, namely *kibic*. There are some different terms like 'hooligan', 'ultras' and 'picnic', which emphasise different kinds of activity (respectively: fighting, performances, consuming sport) but *kibic* comprises all people engaged in watching sport and supporting teams/clubs/athletes. The female term – used very rarely – is *kibicka*.

References

Ben-Porat, A. 2009. 'Not just for men: Israeli women who fancy football'. *Soccer & Society* 10(6): 883–896. doi: 10.1080/14660970903240030.
Dunn, C. 2014. *Female Football Fans. Community, Identity and Sexism.* Basingstoke: Palgrave Macmillan.

Giulianotti, R. 2002. 'Supporters, followers, fans, and flaneurs: A taxonomy of spectator identities in football'. *Journal of Sport and Social Issues* 26(1): 25–46. doi: 10.1177/0193723502261003.

Hughson, J. 2000. 'The boys are back in town: Soccer support and the social reproduction of masculinity'. *Journal of Sport & Social Issues* 24(1): 8–23. doi: 10.1177/0193723500241002.

King, A. 1997. 'The lads: Masculinity and the new consumption of football'. *Sociology* 31(2): 329–346. doi: 10.1177/0038038597031002008.

McDowell, M. L. 2016. 'Female football fans: Community, identity and sexism'. *Soccer & Society* 17(4): 650–651. doi: 10.1080/14660970.2015.1095468.

'*Nie tylko mężczyźni kibicują klubom Ekstraklasy. Co piąta osoba chodząca na mecze to kobieta*' ['It's not just the men who are supporting the clubs of the Ekstraklasa. Every fifth person who goes to matches is a woman']. 2019. *Wirtualne media*, 28 September. Accessed 3 January 2020. www.wirtualnemedia.pl/artykul/nie-tylko-mezczyzni-kibicuja-klubom-ekstraklasy-co-piata-osoba-chodzaca-na-mecze-to-kobieta_2.

Pfister, G., Lenneis, V. and S. Mintert. 2013. 'Female fans of men's football: A case study in Denmark'. *Soccer & Society* 6: 850–871. doi: 10.1080/14660970.2013.843923.

Pope, S. 2017. *The Feminization of Sports Fandom: A Sociological Study*. New York: Routledge.

Redhead, S. 1993. *The Passion and the Fashion: Football Fandom in New Europe*. Avebury: Ashgate Publishing Limited.

Toffoletti, K. 2017. *Women Sport Fans: Identification, Participation, Representation*. New York: Routledge.

Part I

Female fandom

Theoretical and empirical investigation

1 Researching female fandom

In this chapter, we will situate our study against previous works on female football fandom. Through the decades, research on fandom has been mostly focused on men. The omission of female fans could be the result not only of their much smaller presence in stadiums but also of the fact that male scientists have dominated fandom research. 'The practice of conducting observational research on football "hooligans" was deemed only appropriate for male sociologists' (Richards 2015, 395). As a result, female researchers willing to investigate the male-dominated communities of football supporters face methodological challenges that have been undertaken recently by several authors (Poulton 2014; Richards 2015; Pitti 2019).

Being a fan (a supporter) – for most researchers – is tantamount to being a male fan. Fandom studies have been characterised by 'gender blindness', as described by Marcus Free and John Hugson (2003). The analysis of many ethnographies of football supporters has led these authors to the conclusion that a significant proportion of research misses the gender-related context. Even the most 'classical' studies on this topic (see, for example, Dunning, Murphy and Williams 1988) disregard the matter of gender. Investigations into fandom lack in-depth analysis not only of the relations between male and female fans, but also of the process of emerging and constituting of masculine identity. Other researches also confirm that the topic of gender identity in the male domain of football has not been studied very often (see Spaaij 2008; Kossakowski, Antonowicz and Jakubowska 2020).

Thus, it is not surprising that the analysis of female fans has remained on the margins of fandom research. As Kim Toffoletti and Peter Mewett (2012) state: '[S]tudies of women fans (or studies of fans that include some reference to women) are slowly accumulating', however 'it remains very much an under-researched area' (p. 3). Fortunately, recently, many studies dedicated to women fans have been introduced in broadly understood football/fans studies. However, the appearance of research on female fans should not be considered an exploration of a completely new phenomenon that has recently appeared in football as women have always been present in sport. The works of, for example, Carrie Dunn (2014), Stacey Pope (2017), Kim Toffoletti (2017), and many other scholars across the globe (mentioned later in this chapter), confirm that studies of female fans in football (as well as in other sports) are growing in terms of numbers and importance. However, the existing state of the art reveals that there is a knowledge gap concerning female fandom in Central and Eastern Europe, which we want to address in this book.

The chapter is structured as follows. First, the emergence of female fans and different forms of female fandom are elaborated in depth. The next part, based on empirical research conducted by other authors around the world, describes the relation between male and female fans, and the strategies for reproducing and challenging gender order in the stands. In the last part, major findings on how female fans perceive their identity are presented.

The emergence of female fandom and its different forms around the world

The institutionalised modern sport 'was created in the late nineteenth and early twentieth century by and for white middle-class men to bolster a sagging ideology of "natural superiority" over women' (Dworkin and Messner 2002, 17). Men have organised and managed sport, including football, since its modern beginnings; men have also been key actors in playing sports. For some people, sport has been perceived as being 'naturally' divided in terms of the roles played by men and women, with the public sphere being seen as an arena of men's activity and the private sphere being associated with female duties. Features seen as necessary to practise sport, such as physical strength, aggression, willingness to compete and risk appetite, have also been traditionally assigned to men (Messner 1992). Football fandom has fitted in this male world not only because of the competitive nature of matches, but also due to rivalry, sometimes directly, between the fans. However, one should note that despite the cultural and habitual limitations, female fans were not absent from football stadiums in the early days.

Analysing female fandom in the United Kingdom, where the first institutionalised form of football, as well as the first patterns of fandom, were detected, Robert Lewis (2009) remarks:

> [D]espite the restrictions placed on women's leisure time in this period [1880–1914 – ed. authors], it is clear from evidence that a small but significant number of women could and did attend professional football matches throughout the period, and participated as consumers in this new leisure industry.
>
> (p. 2162)

The author recalls studies mentioning, for example, the case of 2,000 female fans attending a match of Preston North End F.C. in 1885.[1] However, in the following years, due to 'rough' crowds, women had been discouraged from attending matches in bigger numbers. They would have preferred to attend matches sitting (the alternative was standing in densely crowded terraces), which was difficult due to the prices of these tickets. The data reveal that the infrastructure of stadiums was adapted mainly to one type of fan, that is, men, who largely ignored the lack of comfort in the stands. At the same time, it did not encourage those who gave thought to the conditions in which matches were watched. As Stacey Pope (2017) notes, stadiums in the late nineteenth century and first decades of the twenty-first century were not closed to women; however, they were 'natural' reservoirs for working-class men. Football matches and socio-cultural situations around them allowed men to escape from 'paid work, as well as from demasculinising domestic constraints' (p. 25).

It is fair to say that the post-Hillsborough (1989) situation strongly influenced football and fandom based in the UK in a multidimensional way. The trans-formation of terraces into stands (King 2002) facilitated the influx of women who might have been afraid of attending matches in the 1980s due to hooligan violence. Football fandom has become a space for the expression of identity for women in the same way as for men. As a result, women have started to form an integral part of the fandom community even if there are fewer of them than their male counterparts. This process can be referred to, after Stacey Pope (2017), as the 'feminisation of sports fandom'.

According to Pope, a greater presence of women in sports (fans) crowds has been possible for two main reasons: the emancipation of women in society in general (more space for activities historically associated almost exclusively with men, for example the labour market and politics) and the transformation of sport itself – with the creation of an open and inclusive environment for women. As a consequence, the proportion of women attending Premier League matches has reached 30% (GlobalWebIndex 2018).

In other countries, the popularity of football has spread equally fast. The data from different countries allow a wide and differentiated image of female fandom to be presented. One should not forget that women's presence in an ultras culture, which is the most spectacular form of expressing support in most European coun-tries (except the UK region), and it attracts the most ardent fans. In Italy, the 'homeland' of the ultras culture (Doidge 2015; Doidge, Kossakowski and Mintert 2020), an organised style of fandom appeared in the 1960s. Although it has been strongly masculine, some female groups are an active part of this movement. Ultras groups were an attractive platform for young people with radical, non-conformist attitudes and some young women perceived them as a space in which to 'address their invisibility and oppression in Italian society'(Cere 2012, 48). The presence of women in the ultras structure was also a result of their demand to be recognised as 'real' football fans. Women were visible in ultras groups in the 1970s playing roles of active members rather than just the *donna del capo* [the leader's woman] (Cere 2012, 49). In recent times, more than 30 organised female ultras groups have been detected in Italy, as well as the national association of female fans. As Alessandro Dal Lago and Rocco De Biasi (1994) show, although the ultras environment in Italy is firmly masculine and men take most of the leading positions, women can participate as members of ultras groups, and they can even act as spokeswomen.

In Germany, the presence of women in contemporary ultras groups is also visible. In some cases – as in St Pauli's fandom – well known for its leftist, pro-gressive agenda, women are very active, and they have an important influence on the local fandom community and political engagement (Totten 2016). In the case of some other clubs, women were forced out of attending matches at the time when there was a high level of violence in the stands. Some of them tried to keep up with the harsh conditions, using some 'male' features as one female fan of Bayer Leverkusen states:

> I didn't used to see many women. And if I did, then they used to be real "tough butches". They were drinking real hard and they were well tough and quick to get into a fight. They really had to prove themselves to be accepted.
>
> (Sandvoss and Ball 2018, 282)

Other female fans in Germany established their groups. The provocative names of particular women-only groups, for example 'tits abroad' and 'hooli-geese', can be considered a tool for counteracting the sexist attitude of male fans, a tool for neutralising sexism and the sign of irony female fans introduce in their situations (Sülzle 2004).

The passion of the fandom can express itself differently, as examples from many countries show. In Spain, one very popular form of fans groups is *peñas*. They have a clear sociable character: '*Peñas* are groups of friends and supporters that meet to watch matches involving their football teams' (Llopis-Goig 2013, 2). Mostly, they are arranged and managed by men, as in many cases their main gathering places are Spanish bars. As Ramon Llopis-Goig states:

> Historically, the small numbers of women who have attended matches have come from the higher social classes, and they went to the stadium, usually, as a simple companion or 'ornament' of men. Fundamentally they were considered to be passive spectators. If they showed any interest in being present at matches, their husbands were often suspicious of their motives.
>
> (2013, 4)

This was a consequence of the fact that football in Spain, and sport in general, was always a 'business' for men. For example, at the beginning of the twenty-first century authorities from some clubs provided extra tickets for men to bring their wives to the stadiums, which illustrates that men had a decisive voice on the role of women in the stands. Elsewhere, Llopis-Goig (2007) analyses popular football chants in which women are perceived only in the context of being admirers of male football players. Interestingly, in the context of the data referred to, the biggest Spanish clubs – Real Madrid and FC Barcelona – allowed women to be members of the *socios* structure just in the first few decades of the twentieth century. However, in the structures of fans groups – the *peñas* – women were practically invisible.

Spanish female fans 'feel uncomfortable in traditional *peñas* due to the strong male ethos and masculine undertones associated with such *peñas*' (Llopis-Goig 2007, 180). Therefore, they established women-only *peñas* to enjoy football with no obligation to follow male rules. The first one was founded in 1984 in Valencia, followed by groups from other parts of the country (for example the *Peña La Tentación Blanca* – Real Madrid). Setting up female-only fan groups can be perceived as a better strategy to express fandom than an attempt to reorganise existing, traditional groups, particularly when some 'transformations' are impossible:

> a woman cannot go into a bar alone in which there is a men's *peña*. She can turn up with her husband, but not alone. She cannot turn up alone and have a coffee. This is why the women's *peñas* have appeared.
>
> (One of the respondents; Llopis-Goig 2007, 183)

The independent women's groups demonstrate not only courage and the will to promote their own sense of fandom, but also reflect the general transformations of women's lives in contemporary Spain.

Italy and Spain could be perceived as regions with a high level of masculine dominance in the football stands that place some limits on women being an active part of the fandom. However, it is not only the southern parts of Europe that are characterised by such phenomena. For example, the situation in the Nordic countries (which lead the way when it comes to gender equality; see, for example, Gender Equality Index 2019) is quite similar, which can be illustrated by research conducted in Denmark. The number of women participating actively in the fandom culture is not very high even under friendly circumstances.[2] An analysis of websites conducted by Pfister, Lenneis and Mintert (2013) revealed that 'women were among members of the governing boards in most official fan groups. In contrast, women have no access to the small but very visible "firms" of casuals and hooligans, although some may accompany them sporadically' (pp. 856–857). Although the number of women watching football on Danish TV ranges from 10 to 30%, the number of female supporters in the stands rarely exceeds 10% (Mintert and Pfister 2015), which was also confirmed by observation of participants conducted at the Brøndby Copenhagen stadium (Pfister, Lenneis and Mintert 2013).

In terms of institutionalised structure, the first women-only group was established in Denmark in 2001 by female fans of Lyngby FC (although women were active in Lyngby fans' organisations before). In 2012, the 'Pink Lions' group was established by female fans of FC Copenhagen. Both these groups are exceptions rather than the rule, which demonstrates how masculine the fandom environment is even in such a well-emancipated society.

Women-only fan groups have also been created in other countries. The 'Ladies of Besiktas' group was created by female supporters of one of the biggest clubs in Turkey. The main idea behind it was to reconcile 'the three seemingly contradictory concepts of "women", "football" and "fandom" in Turkey. Their main fight is directed against the gender inequality and violence inside the stadia' (Erhart 2011, 83). 'Ladies of Besiktas' is a huge, supralocal organisation as it has branches in 12 Turkish cities, in Germany, the US and even in Japan. The group's motto is: 'Despite being women we won't keep quiet. We'll scream out our love [for Besiktas]' (Erhart 2011, 91). Female fans of Besiktas do not follow the 'male' practices of fandom; they have developed their own ways of performing fandom, for example with the omission of the use of sexist and homophobic chants during matches. The group from Besiktas inspired others, as evidenced by the establishment of the GFB Angels of Fenerbahce and the Female Fans of Trabzonspor. The foundation of most female fan groups is based on two main aspects: love for a club (active fans founded all groups) and a need to overcome obstacles resulting from male rules of behaviour (for example, by blowing whistles to mute male vulgar language). At the same time, one can perceive their emergence as one of the indicators of women's emancipation, mainly in countries where their rights are strongly limited.

Resistance to vulgar, sexist behaviour and language from male fans is one of the key aspects of female fandom in other countries, including outside Europe, as illustrated by the case of Zimbabwe. Manase Chiweshe (2014) shows different strategies used by female football fans in Zimbabwe to find their places in the stands. The development of female ways of supporting is based – similarly to some European cases – on resistance to male dominance, male language and their attitudes.[3] Although many of Chiweshe's interlocutors adopt 'masculine' ways of supporting, using sexist and offensive language, some of them prefer to position themselves in sitting sections where the audience is more 'civilised' while others have just given up attending matches as they could not accept the level of misogynistic and sexist language. But, crucially, most individual narratives provide the testimony that football is an 'identity issue' for respondents. Female fans in Zimbabwe love their team, even if they have to confront a hostile male environment.

Female fans from Iran face a problem in an entirely different sense. They have been banned from attending matches due to religious rules (in September 2019, Sahar Khodayari, an Iranian female fan, died after an act of self-immolation outside the court facing prison for trying to enter a stadium). As Kim Toffoletti states when investigating the meaning of the movie *Offside* (which presents the case of Iranian female football fans trying to get access to matches), the situation of women from Iran is perfectly described by the 'long-distance love' metaphor, as they are structurally, but maybe more importantly culturally, separated from their football passion (Toffoletti 2014, 83). However, they share similar emotions to men – they go crazy because of football, thereby being 'authentic' fans.

The Iranian case shows the importance of the cultural context, and it is crucial to consider this as well as a broader social environment when it comes to evaluating the history of female fandom in a particular region. For example, in Japan, the 'boom' for fandom appeared in the mid-1990s after the launch of the J. League. Its success was connected to the commercial character of a whole initiative:

> A meticulously styled corporate identity for almost all of the teams, consisting of uniforms, cute mascots, team songs, slogans and cool merchandise

goods, was a deliberate attempt to attract Japan's most important consumer group of the 1990s, young females, who had repeatedly shown their power to move entire leisure markets.… Huge numbers of young women flocked into the football stadia, enthusiastically buying the accompanying merchandise goods, which turned into the most important revenue source of the first two years.

(Manzenreiter 2008, 248)

Most of the new female fans were attracted by football players rather than a particular team, thereby turning male players into a kind of commodity. As Wolfram Manzenreiter underlines, the history of female fandom in Japan is related to broader social circumstances: 'phenomenon corresponds with the gender-specific role division of bourgeois society: men appear as actors on the pitch, in the back office or in the media, whereas women fulfil supporting roles in the stands or behind the scenes' (2008, 248). This was also the reason why most female fans only partially challenge male dominance in football. Moreover, in contrast to the countries mentioned, Japanese female fans do not express a need to establish their fan groups to create women-only spaces for supporting.

Conquering the men's land

The history of female fandom is – de facto – the history of struggling for recognition, and the struggle to make football culture and stadiums more open for women. Since its industrial early stages, football has been an 'arena of masculinity' (Kreisky and Spitaler 2006) where men can build, adhere to and express their identity: '[F]ootball is an invention by men for men, and today, the majority of players and fans are men' (Pfister, Lenneis and Mintert 2013, 850). Without a doubt, identity (and its gender dimension) is spatialised and, as Linda McDowell (1999) shows, over decades, in capitalist societies the binary structure of public and private life (workplace and home) have determined the cultural and social (as well as the political in terms of legal acts referring to it) construction of femininity and masculinity. As a result, some spaces have become 'natural' for women and others for men, and any attempt made by women to enter 'male' space has led to inevitable resistance or even a backlash. Sport in general and especially football have belonged to the public sphere and men have perceived it as another (beyond workplaces and pubs) space in which to express their 'non-female' identity. The stadiums' atmosphere was built around male 'qualities': hardness, aggression and 'uncivilised' behaviour, and women were not welcome to challenge them. Considering the notion of 'topophilia' in the context of sport spaces – stadiums (see Bale 1993) – it is obvious that it is mostly masculine topophilia. Over the years, men recognised stadiums as a place for their identity and community.

Over decades, the fandom identity evolved around traditionally male traits and codes, making 'authentic' and 'real' only those types of attitudes and behaviours that men perceived as appropriate. All identity features that are passionately related to football – a sense of belonging, feeling of unity, identification, and so on – male fans treat as distinctive for them. In this context, questioning women's rights to share the same feelings can be perceived as one of the strategies of defending a 'natural' and traditional sense of place. By raising the 'authenticity' aspect in discussion, men reproduce social borders and hierarchy in the structure of fandom. Some researchers reproduced this way of thinking; for example, Anthony King perceived women as 'new, consumer fans' in contrast to traditional 'lads', even though women had attended football matches long before the Premier League was established in 1993 (for more see King 2002).

Men retain the power in stadiums both symbolically and practically, and the masculine character of fan groups could be a serious problem for introducing women. For example, in some Swedish and Polish clubs, women are banned from travelling with male ultras to away matches (Radmann and Hedenborg 2018; Antonowicz, Jakubowska and Kossakowski 2020). The research in Poland also shows that male ultras marginalise female fans in terms of their significance and status as 'real' fans. Moreover, male fans use symbolic violence – abusive chants and slogans directed at women (for example 'a fan whore'; see Radmann and Hedenborg 2018, 249). As a consequence, women (as well as children, old people, etc.) gain the status of 'marginalised subjectives' (Cauldwell 2009). Even if they manage to enter stadiums in growing numbers, men introduce particular strategies to re-establish and maintain 'appropriate' order on the football field. Honorata Jakubowska (2013) lists three such strategies: (1) sexualisation of women; (2) stripping women from the status of 'real' fans; (3) prejudice related to women's appearance in sports spaces. The first mechanism is based on assigning them sexual roles instead of the role of football fans. For example, when big football tournaments are organised the attention is drawn to the prostitutes whose numbers increase in the host cities and 'hot fans' in the stands instead of female fans passionate about football. Second, women are sometimes perceived through the lenses of family roles – they bring children to family sectors and look after then there. If they support the team, their role is to calm and 'civilise' the behaviour of male partners. Polish women who want to be perceived as an 'authentic' fan tend to avoid 'female' terms and they use only the male form of the word 'fan' (or supporter) when they describe their status.[4] Moreover, women's engagement is frequently boiled down to admiration of the physical appearance of football players. Although some researches confirm the existence of the latter phenomenon (Crawford and Gosling 2004; Manzenreiter 2008; Robinson and Trail 2005), seeking sexual or emotional relations with players is just one, and not necessarily the dominant, aspect of female fandom.

A case of Japanese female fans, previously mentioned, suggests that women can be more focused on the consumer aspect of fandom, and they consume sport in a different way to men. However, as Sveinson, Hoeber and Toffoletti (2018) state: 'The idea that women fans consume sport for different reasons than men is problematic for two reasons' (p. 737). First, men perceive women's experience as unauthentic, assuming that the main reason for women attending matches is the attraction of players while it is not possible to indicate a single reason attracting women to being a football fan. Second, female fans perform and consume fandom in extremely diverse (gendered) ways. 'The results in the literature are quite inconsistent, in terms of the reasons for male and female attendance at sports events.... This is a result of the differences in the sport branches and sport levels included in the studies' (Gencer 2015, 83).

However, taking into account the male dominance of the stands, it should be noted that men are the ones who can guarantee or deny women the 'cultural ticket' to fandom (Pfister, Lenneis and Mintert 2013). This 'ticket' opens the gate to the 'permission zone' (Ben-Porat 2009) where norms of behaviour that are largely unacceptable outside football grounds, such as body gestures, offensive banners, rough language and so on, can be nearly freely expressed. In many countries, 'permission zones' allow male-dominated groups to express misogynistic views, celebrate their domination over women and degrade opponents with sexually saturated chants (it is worth underlining that similar language frames exist on many websites and online forums dedicated to fans' lives; see Cecamore *et al.* 2011). In these 'zones', female fans have to accept that rivals are portrayed as 'whores', 'bitches' or just women, who are – by definition – inferior people. Sometimes, as the aforementioned 'Ladies of Besiktas' (Erhart 2011), 'Female Vikings' and 'Pink Lions' groups demonstrate, women do not accept the rules of the male 'permission zones' and establish their own 'zones' (Pfister, Lenneis and Mintert 2013). Otherwise, as in the case of England, female fans tend to 'downplay' their gender identities to reinforce their fan identities (Jones 2008) and get the 'cultural ticket'. The strategies for dealing with those circumstances vary as much as cultural contexts.

> Women are very different, and they are in the fan groups for different reasons: they like the atmosphere and the team spirit.... Some are the girl-friends of male fans, some love football, others love the fireworks, very few will participate in fights.
>
> (Pfister, Lenneis and Mintert 2013, 858)

Studying women's strategies at football stadiums, Jones (2008) specifies an additional two strategies (in addition to downplaying gender identity) incorporated by women to respond to the sexism of (male) fandom. The first is the expression of disgust at abuse and sexist content and different forms of rejecting negative, in their opinions, forms of fandom. The second strategy refers to the acceptance of gender stereotypes existing in the stands along with the argument that 'femininity was inconsistent with "authentic" fandom and that abuse was a fundamental part of football' (p. 516). In the first case, abuse is acknowledged as a problem, and women's reactions towards it create some 'resistant femininity'. The 'downplaying' strategy means that women are still aware of sexist and misogynistic behaviours, but they think that it is as big a problem as outsiders find it. Indeed, women sometimes perceive racism as more problematic and urgent to eliminate than sexism. The last strategy found by Jones concerns women who accept the traditional way in which fans behave as well as the language they express. Women agree that the gender order in the stands is built around hegemonic masculinity and sexism is a part of the game. Kevin Dixon (2015) reached similar conclusions on English female fans. He underlines that

> given that the goal of many female fans was to fit into the practice as authentic supporters, one of the strategies that female fans have adopted to overcome gender discrimination is to position themselves as 'similar to' males and to adopt the associated style of masculine communication.
>
> (p. 646)

The researches in Zimbabwe (Chiwashe 2014, 2017) concerning the strategies for dealing with the male definition of the situation reveal that some women ignore the vulgar language and focus only on football as it is more important and any abuse cannot keep them away from it. As they say: 'We are here for the football. Forget about the singing' (Chiwashe 2017, 83). Other women accept language as a part of the fandom culture, as illustrated by the words of one of them:

> The vulgar songs do not bother me at all because it is part of football. We sing about prostitutes because they exist and there is nothing special about that. If you feel offended then you can always go and watch from the expensive seats.
>
> (Chiwashe 2014, 216–217)

In this case, female fans are immersed in the extreme masculinising culture, accept it and play their roles along with its principles. The third women's strategy is based on refraining from going to the stadiums even though they love football and their team; however, they feel that the 'stadium is not for us' (Chiwashe 2017, 85).

In Denmark, there are also female fans who behave in the 'male' style: they shout, swear, insult the referee, sing chants and wear the club's jerseys, and they, 'at least those in the fan sections, do not "beautify" themselves; high heels and miniskirts are out of place in the stadium' (Pfister, Lenneis and Mintert 2013, 858–859). Some Danish women sing sexist songs, perceiving them as fun rather than offensive, while other female fans accept their exclusion from the most aggressive male groups.

> The prevailing code of behaviour stipulates that doing femininity is quite out of place in the football stadium and that traditionally masculine behaviour like shouting, swearing, cursing, drinking beer, etc. is not reserved for men but is regarded as the proper behaviour for female fans as well.
>
> (Lenneis and Pfister 2015, 175)

Conquering men's land or men's territory requires many strategies on the part of women, and even then the outcome is uncertain as women need to challenge the symbolism of machismo (see Kossakowski, Antonowicz and Jakubowska 2020). Depending on the cultural context, it is either easier (in commercialised frames) or more difficult (in traditional, religious states) for them to be incorporated. The research conducted so far, and the use of the constructivist approach, allows it to be revealed that the notion of an 'authentic' fan is based on social and culturally constructed expectations (Lennis and Pfister 2015, 162) and 'existing for ages' discourses. Being a social construct, 'authentic' fandom identity is not essentially fixed, and its foundations and frames can be challenged and transformed, even if its discursive deconstruction can lead only to limited changes in performing fandom.

The identity of female fans

Men can control discourse and gender order on the terraces, but it is hard to imagine that they can radically influence the sense of identification that particular individuals feel. This is an area where women can embody their football passion as it is mostly based on deep, emotional and privately experienced space. One can refer here to the concept of social identity that is quite popular in fans' research (see Stott, Hutchison and Drury 2001; Kossakowski and Besta 2018) and explains that people adopt the identity of the group with which they have built emotional bounds, and (if this identity becomes salient and is activated) the norms and beliefs related to this group turn into important factors driving people's behaviours.

In respect to gender, as men dominate on the stadium terraces, it seems obvious that the fans community is identified as important mainly for them. And men derive a stronger social identity than women from the sports community (James and Ridinger 2002). Moreover, men are socialised earlier into the sport due to different paths of sports (football) socialisation; therefore, male fans' identity is perceived as more intense. As women face more obstacles to being introduced into the frame of such a community, the feeling of identification with the group is harder to achieve. However, as research on female fans is growing, it seems to be necessary to evaluate how the social identity of fans' community influences the personal experience of women. Some qualitative researches demonstrate that women describe their fandom identity by using narratives and description that are commonly recognised in the fandom community. When it comes to the meaning of football and clubs for women, their statements seem to be no different from those expressed by men.

For example, Katherine Sveinson and Larena Hoeber (2014) have analysed how female fans from Canada define fans' characteristics. As the crucial ones, the interviewed fans listed: love of the team/game and the importance of team colours and positive fanship (the last two being related to loyalty); and as secondary characteristics, attendance at matches and the possession of knowledge. The two primary categories seem to essentially embrace emotional and personal attachment to football and the club while being a positive fan includes supporting the team but without rough or offensive language and behaviours. Secondary categories are not considered essential to be a 'real' fan, although some researches demonstrate that knowledge about sport is a determinant of being an 'authentic' fan, particularly in the eyes of men (Crawford and Gosling 2004). These two characteristics are becoming interlocked over time as gaining experience of fandom translates into growing knowledge.

Research from Denmark shows that being a fan of the local club is part of self-concept and identity for women. It creates space for daily routine as the club takes an intrinsic role in existence. Wearing the club's jersey is something usual, and female fans have even got married in the stadium. One Danish study confirms that women's interest, dedication and loyalty are not different from those of their male counterparts (Mintert and Pfesiter 2015). Similar motifs and identity discourses are revealed among female fans from Israel, for example: 'I am proud to be a fan of Hapoel FC. I don't hide it. Every day I wear a red item'; 'I'm proud of the club and I love its badge'; 'This is part of me'. 'At work, everybody knows that I support Haifa FC. My car is covered with stickers. I'm absolutely proud' (Ben-Porat 2009, 892).

As previously mentioned, the identity dimension can be perceived as independent, to a large extent, of male rules imposed in the stands. For this reason, a female fan can create a strong system of values and personal beliefs related to her club:

> She does not need male mediation concerning her fan identity. She is responsible for the dilemmas and tensions that stem from football. It is possible to suggest that the socio-economic profile of the female fan explains, at least in part, her extended relative autonomy.... Besides the issues related to her status in the stadium, she does everything else by herself.
>
> (Ben-Porat 2009, 892)

And it works even in countries where the level of misogyny and homophobia at stadiums is unacceptable for women, and some of them decide to cultivate the fans' identity outside of the stadium (Chiwashe 2014).

In her research, Stacey Pope (2017) used Richard Giulianotti's taxonomy (2002) when considering the level of engagement and identification. She proposed two categories of fans: 'hot', for whom 'being a football fan was an extension of their sense of self or way of adding to their identities' (Pope 2017, 211), and 'cool', referring to fans for whom the club is not central to their life but who still attend matches. Next, Pope placed all 50 interviewed female football fans of Leicester City FC in the relevant category. Most of them, that is, 41, were characterised as 'hot' and only nine as 'cool'. The following reference seems to be typical for 'hot' fans: 'Football's always been my life. Like I said, playing it, watching it ... I like lots of different sports but football's always been the one, if you like... the love of my life. That's me; that's part of me' (Pope 2017, 212). 'Hot' fans display some of the symptoms typical for 'football addiction' (Griffiths 2014): salience (being dominated by the issue of football through the week; planning family life according to the season's schedule), mood modification (bad mood after defeat, euphoria after victory) or conflict (conflict about football with a partner not engaged in football; conflict with co-employee supporting 'enemy' club).

The examples presented demonstrate that on an identity level, female fans are not different from male fans. However, it is crucial to underline that to achieve this, women need to sacrifice more. For many of them, football is also a means of escaping from other social identities they have: being a partner, employee, mother or daughter. Some researches show that, historically, women had to combine different duties: for example, cooking and watching football (Gantz and Wenner 1991). This demonstrates that being a fan for women means taking on not only masculine social norms in the stadium but also unhidden social expectations pressuring them to perform certain social roles.

The analysis of female fans' identity narratives can be regarded as an important part of the response to the question about ways to be a 'real' and 'authentic' fan. And as previous researches show, female fans were regarded as non-authentic, sobbing, ignorant, screaming or even ridiculous (King 1997; Crawford 2003; Pope 2017). They are frequently seen through the lenses of family roles and addressed as girlfriends, wives, sisters or mothers of 'authentic' – male – supporters (Damato 2013). This means that in many cases women are perceived in the context of different (family) social roles, totally unrelated to football.

Additionally, the presence of female fans in stadiums is evaluated in the context of commercialisation and 'bourgeoisification' of contemporary football (Dixon 2015). As history shows, the transformation of contemporary football influences the socio-demographic change of stadiums' terraces, as it should not be forgotten that women had attended football matches from their modern beginnings in the nineteenth century (Lewis 2009). But the contemporary transformations of 'modern football' invite questions about the role women can play, and its significance, in the field of fandom.

Notes

1 Women were also present at the beginning of modern football in Germany. For example, at the first final of the national championship in 1903, women were seen in the stands and they stood out from their male counterparts due to their big hats (Cecamore *et al.* 2011, 31).

2 In Denmark all official fan groups are affiliated to the national umbrella organisation, namely the Federation of Danish Football Fan Clubs (Danske Fodbold Fanklubber [DFF]), which prohibits any kind of discrimination based not only on gender, but also on ethnicity and sexual orientation as well.

3 It should be noted also, however, that the history of football (and fandom as well) in Zimbabwe encompasses the colonial heritage of the country – as football was a tool used for controlling the black population by colonial authorities (who stated that physical activity would 'civilise' aggressive instincts).

4 In Polish, nouns have male and female forms. The word 'kibic' means male fans, while 'kibicka' means female fans. However, in many cases related mainly to some professions and positions (dominated by men), only the male form is used. For example, one can say 'pilot' (pilot), 'dziekan' (dean), 'minister' (minister). Although female forms can be used, they are not popular or accepted by a large part of society, including women themselves. On the other hand, some professions dominated by women don't have male forms, for example 'niania' (nanny).

References

Antonowicz, D., H. Jakubowska and R. Kossakowski. 2020. 'Marginalised, patronised and instrumentalised: Polish female fans in the ultras' narratives'. *International Review for the Sociology of Sport* 55(1): 60–76. doi: 10.1177/1012690218782828.

Bale, J. 1993. *Sport, Space, and the City*. London: Routledge.

Ben-Porat, A. 2009. 'Not just for men: Israeli women who fancy football'. *Soccer & Society* 10(6): 883–896. doi: 10.1080/14660970903240030.

Cauldwell, J. 2009. 'Girlfight and Bend it Like Beckham: Screening women, sport, and sexuality'. *Journal of Lesbian Studies* 13: 255–271. doi: 10.1080/10894160902876697.

Cecamore, S., K. Fraesdorf, R. Langer and A. Power. 2011. *Sports Fandom: What Do Women Want? A Multi-sport Analysis of Female Fans*. Neuchâtel, Switzerland: International Centre for Sports Studies.

Cere, R. 2012. '"Forever ultras": Female football support in Italy'. In *Sport and Its Female Fans* edited by P. Mewett and K. Toffoletti. New York: Routledge, 46–60.

Chiweshe, M. 2014. 'One of the boys: Female fans' responses to the masculine and phallocentric nature of football stadiums in Zimbabwe'. *Critical African Studies* 6(2–3): 211–222. doi: 10.1080/21681392.2014.940077.

Chiweshe, M. 2017. *The People's Game: Football Fandom in Zimbabwe*. Bamenda: Langaa RPCIG.

Crawford, G. 2003. 'The career of the sport supporter: The case of the Manchester Storm'. *Sociology* 37 (2): 219–237. doi: 10.1177/0038038503037002001.

Crawford, G. and V. Gosling. 2004. 'The myth of the "puck bunny": Female fans and men's ice hockey'. *Sociology* 38: 477–493. doi: 10.1177/0038038504043214.

Dal Lago, A. and R. De Biasi. 1994. 'Italian football fans: Culture and organization'. In *Football, Violence and Social Identity*, edited by R. Giulianotti, N. Bonney and M. Hepworth. London: Routledge, 73–89.

Damato, K. 2013. 'Female fan avidity in the National Football League'. *Sport Management Undergraduate*. Paper 62.

Dixon, K. 2015. 'A woman's place recurring: Structuration, football fandom and sub-cultural subservience'. *Sport in Society* 18(6): 636–651. doi: 10.1080/17430437.2014.982541.

Doidge, M. 2015. *Football Italia: Italian Football in an Age of Globalization*. New York: Bloomsbury.

Doidge, M., R. Kossakowski and S. Mintert. 2020. *Ultras: European Football Fandom in the Twenty-first Century*. Manchester: Manchester University Press.

Dunn, C. 2014. *Female Football Fans: Community, Identity and Sexism*. Basingstoke: Palgrave Macmillan.

Dunning, E., P. Murphy and J. Williams. 1988. *The Roots of Football Hooliganism*. Abingdon: Routledge.

Dworkin S. L. and M. A. Messner. 2002. 'Just do ... what? Sport, bodies, gender'. In *Gender and Sport: A Reader*, edited by S. Scraton and A. Flinton. London: Routledge, 17–29.

Erhart, I. 2011. 'Ladies of Besiktas: A dismantling of male hegemony at Inönü Stadium'. *International Review for the Sociology of Sport* 48(1): 83–98. doi: 10.1177/10126 90211427986.

Free, M. and J. Hugson. 2003. 'Settling accounts with hooligans: Gender blindness in football supporter subculture research'. *Men and Masculinities* 6(2): 136–155. doi: 10.1177/1097184X03255849.

Gantz, W. and L. A. Wenner. 1991. 'Men, women, and sports: Audience experiences and effects'. *Journal of Broadcasting & Electronic Media* 35(2): 233–243. doi: 10.1080/08838159109364120.

Gencer T. R. 2015. 'Spectator motives and points of attachment: Gender differences in professional football'. *The Anthropologist* 19(1): 77–85. doi: 10.1080/09720073.2015.11891641.

Gender Equality Index 2019. Accessed 3 January 2020. https://eige.europa.eu/gender-equality-index/2019.

Giulianotti, R. 2002. 'Supporters, followers, fans, and flaneurs: A taxonomy of spectator identities in football'. *Journal of Sport and Social Issues* 26(1): 25–46. doi: 10.1177/0193723502261003.

GlobalWebIndex 2018. Accessed 3 January 2020. https://blog.globalwebindex.com/chart-of-the-week/premier-league-fans/.

Griffiths, M. 2014. 'Fanatical about football? Watch out, you could be an addict'. *The Conversation*, 3 July. Accessed 7 July 2019. http://theconversation.com/fanatical-about-football-watch-out-you-could-be-an-addict-28240.

James, J. D. and L. L. Ridinger. 2002. 'Female and male sport fans: A comparison of sport consumption motives'. *Journal of Sport Behaviour* 25(3): 260–278.

Jakubowska, H. 2013. 'Stadion z perspektywy płci'. ['The stadium from a gender perspective'] In *Futbol i cała reszta. Sport w perspektywie nauk społecznych [Football and All the Rest. Sport from Social Sciences' Perspective]*, edited by R. Kossakowski, K. Stachura, A. Strzałkowska and M. Żadkowska. Pszczółki: Wydawnictwo Orbis Exterior, 57–70.

Jones, K. 2008. 'Female fandom: Identity, sexism, and men's professional football in England'. *Sociology of Sport Journal*, 25: 516–37. doi: 10.1123/ssj.25.4.516.

King, A. 1997. 'The lads: Masculinity and the new consumption of football'. *Sociology* 31(2): 329–46. doi: 10.1177/0038038597031002008.

King, A. 2002. *The End of the Terraces: The Transformation of English Football.* Leicester: Leicester University Press.

Kossakowski, R. and T. Besta 2018. 'Football, conservative values, and a feeling of oneness with the group: A study of Polish football fandom'. *East European Politics and Societies* 32(4): 866–891. doi: 10.1177/0888325418756991.

Kossakowski R., D. Antonowicz and H. Jakubowska. 2020. 'The reproduction of hegemonic masculinity in football fandom: An analysis of the performance of Polish ultras'. In *The Palgrave Handbook of Masculinity and Sport*, edited by R. Magrath, J. Cleland and E. Anderson. Cham: Palgrave Macmillan, 517–536.

Kreisky, E. and G. Spitaler. 2006. *Arena der Männlichkeit: Über das Verhältnis von Fußball und Geschlecht [Arena of Masculinity. The Relationship between Football and Gender]*. Frankfurt/Main: Campus.

Lenneis, V. and G. Pfister. 2015. 'Gender constructions and negotiations of female football fans. A case study in Denmark'. *European Journal for Sport and Society* 12(2): 157–185. doi: 10.1080/16138171.2015.11687961.

Lewis, R. 2009. '"Our lady specialists at Pikes Lane": Female spectators in early English professional football, 1880–1914'. *The International Journal of the History of Sport* 26(15): 2161–2181. doi: 10.1080/09523360903367651.

Llopis-Goig, R. 2007. 'Female football supporters' communities in Spain: A focus on women's peñas'. In *Women, Football and Europe: Histories, Equity and Experiences*, edited by J. Magee, J. Caudwell, K. Liston and S. Scraton. Oxford: Meyer and Meyer Sport, 175–189.

Llopis-Goig, R. 2013. 'Avoiding hegemonic masculinity through women's *peñas*: A case study of female football supporters' communities in Spain'. Paper presented at FREE conference, Copenhagen, June 2013.

Manzenreiter, W. 2008. 'Football in the reconstruction of the gender order in Japan'. *Soccer & Society* 9(2): 244–258. doi: 10.1080/14660970701811156.

McDowell, L. 1999. *Gender, Identity and Place: Understanding Feminist Geographies*. Cambridge: Polity Press.

Messner, M. 1992. *Power at Play*. Boston: Beacon Press.

Mintert, S. and G. Pfister. 2015. 'The FREE project and the feminization of football: The role of women in the European fan community'. *Soccer & Society* 16(2–3): 405–421. doi: 10.1080/14660970.2014.961383.

Pfister, G., V. Lenneis and S. Mintert. 2013. 'Female fans of men's football: A case study in Denmark'. *Soccer & Society* 14(6): 850–871. doi: 10.1080/14660970.2013.843923.

Pitti, I. 2019. 'Being women in a male preserve: an ethnography of female football ultras'. *Journal of Gender Studies* 28(3): 318–329. doi: 10.1080/09589236.2018.1443803.

Pope, S. 2017. *The Feminization of Sports Fandom: A Sociological Study*. London and New York: Routledge.

Poulton, E. 2014. 'Having the balls: Reflections on doing gendered research with football hooligans'. In *Reflexivity in Criminological Research: Experiences with the Powerful and Powerless*, edited by K. Lumsden and A. Winter. Basingstoke: Palgrave Macmillan, 77–89.

Radmann, A. and S. Hedenborg. 2018. 'Women's football supporter culture in Sweden'. In *Female Football Players and Fans. Intruding into a Man's World*, edited by G. Pfister and S. Pope. London: Palgrave Macmillan, 241–258.

Richards, J. 2015. '"Which player do you fancy then?" Locating the female ethnographer in the field of the sociology of sport'. *Soccer & Society*, 16(2–3): 393–404. doi: 10.1080/14660970.2014.961379.

Robinson M. J. and G. T. Trail. 2005. 'Relationships among spectator gender, motives, points of attachment, and sport preference'. *Journal of Sport Management* 19: 58–80. doi: 10.1123/jsm.19.1.58.

Sandvoss, C. and E. Ball. 2018. 'Gender, play and identity: A longitudinal study of structure and agency in female football fandom'. In *Female Football Players and Fans. Intruding into a Man's World*, edited by G. Pfister and S. Pope. London: Palgrave Macmillan, 279–308.

Spaaij, R. 2008. 'Men like us, boys like them: Violence, masculinity, and collective identity in football hooliganism'. *Journal of Sport and Social Issues* 32(4), 369–392. doi: 10.1177/0193723508324082.

Stott, C., P. Hutchison, and J. Drury. 2001. '"Hooligans" abroad? Inter-group dynamics, social identity and participation in collective "disorder" at the 1998 World Cup finals'. *British Journal of Social Psychology* 40(3): 359–384.

Sveinson, K. and L. Hoeber. 2014. 'Female sport fans' experiences of marginalization and empowerment'. *Journal of Sport Management* 30(1): 8–21. doi: 10.1123/jsm.2014–0221.

Sveinson, K., L. Hoeber and K. Toffoletti. 2018. '"If people are wearing pink stuff they're probably not real fans": Exploring women's perceptions of sport fan clothing'. *Sport Management Review* 22(5): 736–747. doi: 10.1016/j.smr.2018.12.003.

Sülzle, A. 2004. *Das Fußballstadion – eine der letzen Männerdomänen? Ethografische Anmerkungen zur Geschlechterkonstruktion bei jugendlichen Fußballfans* [The football stadium – one of the last male domains? Ethnographic comments on gender construction in young football fans] Accessed 24 September 2019. www.fk12.tu-dortmund.de/cms/ ISO/Medienpool/Archiv-Alte-Dateien/arbeitsbereiche/soziologie_der_geschlechterver- haeltnisse/Medienpool/AIM_Beitraege_dritte_Tagung/almut_suelzle.pdf#page=1&zoo m=auto,-274,848.

Toffoletti, K. 2014. 'Iranian women's sports fandom: Gender, resistance, and identity in the football movie offside'. *Journal of Sport and Social Issues* 38(1): 75–92. doi: 10.1177/0193723512468758.

Toffoletti, K. 2017. *Women Sport Fans: Identification, Participation, Representation*. New York: Routledge.

Toffoletti, K. and P. Mewett. 2012. *Sport and its Female Fans*. New York: Routledge.

Totten, M. 2016. 'Football and community empowerment: How FC Sankt Pauli fans organize to influence'. *Soccer & Society* 17(5): 703–720. doi: 10.1080/14660970. 2015.1100436.

2 Theorising female fandom

The desk research conducted has allowed us not only to recognise the existing state of knowledge on female fans in Europe and on other continents but also to distinguish the main theoretical approaches that are appropriate for analysing women's entrance into a male-dominated fandom. This chapter presents the theoretical concepts that have inspired our research and explains, to a large extent, the phenomenon observed in football stadiums in Poland. First, to analyse the male-dominated football fans' world into which women enter, we refer to the concepts of 'hegemonic masculinity' (Connell 1987), 'homosocial bonding' (Lipman-Blumen 1976) and 'brotherhood' (Kossakowski, Antonowicz and Jakubowska 2020). Second, when focusing on fans' experiences, we use the concept of 'performative sport fandom', as developed by Osborne and Coombs (2013), to address the question of how women perform their gender and fandom roles and, at the same time, how male fans react to these performances. It will also allow the complexities of fans' experiences, behaviours and reactions to the gender scripts to be described.

Hegemonic masculinity

The concept of 'hegemonic masculinity' has been widely recognised in gender studies and social sciences (Messerschmidt 2012). Introduced by Connell in 1987 (see also Connell 1995, 2000; Connell and Messerschmidt 2005), it has been used in numerous analyses of gender order and masculinities, as well as being discussed and reviewed as a theoretical approach. The notion of hegemonic masculinity represents the dominant position in the hierarchical gender order consisting of different types of masculinities and femininities. Statistically, hegemonic masculinity is not dominant. It does not have to be related to the everyday life of a significant number of men, and it should be not reduced to individual experiences. It represents, rather, normative ideals, models of masculinity, the most desirable form of being a 'real' man. On the one hand, it forces other men to position themselves in relation to it, and on the other, it legitimates the subordination of women to men (Connell and Messerschmidt 2005).

Masculinity itself is defined by Connell (1987) as 'simultaneously a place in gender relations, the practices through which men and women engage that place in gender, and the effects of these practices on bodily experience, personality and culture' (p. 71). Therefore, it indicates the social position of individuals, the practices and characteristics perceived as 'masculine' and the socio-cultural effects of these practices embodied mainly by men (Schippers 2007). Masculinity is not something possessed by an individual, but rather the set (or configuration) of practices recognised as masculine produced over time and space. These practices reproduce gender order and power relationships (Demetriou 2001). Connell distinguishes three structures of gender relations, those of labour, power and cathexis (i.e. desire and sexuality), as well as three institutions related to them: labour market, state and family. Each of these institutions is characterised by gender regimes that influence gender relations within them, while gender order refers rather to the 'macro-politics of gender' (Connell 1987, 20). Therefore, hegemonic masculinity is reproduced both by everyday individual practices and social structures.

From this perspective, hegemonic masculinity is understood by Connell (1987) as 'the configuration of gender practice which embodies the currently accepted answer to the problem of the legitimacy of patriarchy, which guarantees (or is taken to guarantee) the dominant position of men and the subordination of women' (p. 77). It is 'centred around authority, physical toughness and strength, heterosexuality and paid work' (Pilcher 1999, 12, as cited in Pope 2013; see also Sisjord and Kristiansen 2009). According to Connell, not only are women subordinated to men, but also other forms of masculinity are subordinated to the hegemonic one. Demetriou (2001) proposes to name hegemony over women – external hegemonic masculinity and hegemony over other men – internal hegemonic masculinity, emphasising at the same time that they are interconnected or inseparable (p. 341). As one of the most important contributions of Connell's theory, one can indicate the recognition that 'all masculinities are not created equal' (Kimmel 1997) and that there is not one masculinity, but multiple masculinities.

The concept of 'hegemonic masculinity' created in the 1980s has been not only widely used but also subjected to criticism, including self-criticism (see, for example, Demetriou 2001; Flood 2002; Hearn 2004; Connell and Messerschmidt 2005; Messerschmidt 2012). For example, Flood (2002, after Beasley 2008) states that the notion of 'hegemonic masculinity' is used by Connell in at least three different meanings: (1) as a political mechanism – a hegemony; (2) as a dominant form of manhood; and (3) as a description of some groups of men analysed in empirical studies. Demetriou (2001) accuses Connell of presenting hegemonic masculinity and non-hegemonic masculinities as a dichotomy, clearly separated and differentiated sets of practices, while empirical studies reveal that they are not as such inseparable. Moreover, he claims that Connell defines hegemonic masculinity mainly by its relations to other masculinities instead of relations towards women, although Connell sees the concept itself as a tool for subordinating women. To deconstruct Connell's *dualism*, Demetriou (2001) suggests perceiving hegemonic masculinity as 'a hybrid bloc that unites various and diverse practices to construct the best possible strategy for the reproduction of patriarchy' (p. 348).

This *hegemonic masculine bloc* embraces different kinds of men including that excluded from hegemonic masculinity in Connell's theory, and can be perceived as an answer to the actions taken by feminist and LGBTQ movements. In this context, hybridisation is 'thus a strategy for the reproduction of patriarchy' (Demetriou 2001, 349).

Messerschmidt (2012) in his article recalls the main criticisms of 'hegemonic masculinity', listing four of them:

> (1) concerns over the underlying concept of masculinity itself; (2) a lack of specificity about who represents hegemonic masculinity; (3) whether hegemonic masculinity simply reduces in practice to a reification of power or toxicity; and (4) the concept's unsatisfactory theory of the masculine subject.
>
> (p. 59)

Responding to the previous criticisms, Connell (together with Messerschmidt) has revised the concept, although its core has remained the same.

Connell and Messerschmidt (2005) note that several empirical studies have confirmed the existence of multiple masculinities and their hierarchical order. The conducted studies also reveal that certain masculinities are related to a larger extent to authority and power, and other masculinities are subordinated to them. Therefore, the concept of hegemony is appropriate to describe the hierarchical gender order. 'Cultural consent, discursive centrality, institutionalisation and the marginalisation or delegitimation of alternatives are widely documented features of socially dominant masculinities' (Connell and Messerschmidt 2005, 846). At the same time, the authors admit that Connell has proposed too simple model of gender relations and understanding of gender hierarchy. The other self-criticism concerns the use of the essentialist and the trait approach to describe masculinity.

As a consequence, Connell and Messerschmidt (2005, see also Messerschmidt 2012) suggest reformulating the concept of hegemonic masculinity in four areas: 'the nature of gender hierarchy, the geography of masculine configurations, the process of social embodiment and the dynamics of masculinities' (p. 847). First, the gender hierarchy should be analysed more deeply, taking into account not only dominant groups but also the agency of subordinated groups and their mutual influence on each other. Moreover, gender dynamics and other social dynamics should be considered. Second, the authors emphasise that it is necessary to study hegemonic masculinity not only at society-wide level but at three distinguished, albeit interrelated, levels: local (face-to-face interactions), regional (particular culture or society) and global (media, business, world politics). Third, Connell and Messerschmidt (2005) suggest that deeper and sophisticated analysis of the role of embodiment in the construction of hegemonic masculinity is needed. And finally, the considerations on hegemonic masculinity should acknowledge the possibility of its contestations and changes in the context of the dynamics of gender relations.

Women's agency, which should be taken into account as mentioned, can challenge the existing gender order, but it can also reproduce it and preserve hegemonic masculinity (Messerschmidt 2012).

> 'Emphasised femininity' is perceived as complementary to hegemonic masculinity, it is oriented to accommodating the interests and desires of men, characterised by a display of sociability rather than technical competence; its content is linked to the private realm, particularly marriage and childcare.
>
> (Sisjord and Kristiansen 2009, 232)

Other femininities are subordinated both to 'emphasised femininity' and masculinities and, as such, remain to a large extent invisible.

The concept of hegemonic masculinity has been widely used in sports studies to analyse the relations among athletes, coaches and members of sports organisations (for example Whisenant, Pedersen and Obenour 2002), as well as football fans. However, it should be noted that Connell's theory is used in an uncritical way to emphasise male domination in sport and its heteronormative nature. In the case of football fans, both the practices of male fans (for example Palmer and Thompson 2007; Chiweshe 2014) and women's experiences and reactions towards them have been studied (Jones 2008; Hoeber and Kerwin 2013). As regards football stadiums, social practices adhering to hegemonic masculinity are carried out mainly by those groups of fans that are marginalised and powerless in a wider social context (Jones 2008). However, as rightly noted by the author (Jones 2008), these practices should not only be linked to working-class men, because they are also undertaken by middle-class men who suspend their everyday politeness norms and express masculinity in a similar way that includes antagonistic chanting, shouts and swearing.

Hegemonic masculinity, as well as the homosocial bonds that will be discussed later, are based on the feeling of superiority over femininity and non-hegemonic forms of masculinities. As a consequence, female fans are perceived as 'others' in football stadiums, which is manifested among others by the use of the label 'female' before 'sports fan', which emphasises the otherness and marginalisation of women (Hoeber and Kerwin 2013). On the other hand, femininity is perceived by hegemonic fans in the frames of sexual attractiveness and conquest (Chiweshe 2014). Additionally, feminine labels are used to insult fans of the opposite team, referees, security and the police. Therefore, although football fandom has changed and different categories defined by Connell as 'subordinated' have appeared in the stadiums (Jones 2008), women are still not only denied the status of 'real' fans', but they are also instrumentalised (Antonowicz, Jakubowska and Kossakowski 2020).

As noted, in the reformulation of the hegemonic masculinity concept, Connell and Messerschmidt (2005) called for recognition of the agency of these groups. It is worth investigating whether and how female fans have managed to change football fandom and the gender order in the stands. At the same time, women as one of the marginalised categories can contribute to the maintenance and reinforcement of hegemonic masculinity (Messerschmidt 2012). In the case of football fans, women can adopt male fans' behaviours to gain the status of 'real' fans reproducing male domination (Jones 2008; Hoeber and Kerwin 2013).

Homosociality

The concept of hegemonic masculinity is closely related to the concept of 'homosociality', which also provides a valuable framework for the analysis of football fans from a gender perspective. The notion of 'homosocial' was introduced by Lipman-Blumen (1976), who defined it as 'the seeking, enjoyment and (or) preference for the company of the same sex' (p. 16). It should be distinguished from homosexual relations as it is not based on erotic and sexual desire. The term is used to describe male bonds that reproduce the gender order, male dominance, men's control over the available resources and their privileges (Kanter 1977; Kimmel 1994; Bird 1996; Flood 2008; Hammarén and Johansson 2014). Women assigned to the domestic sphere have not had opportunities to create this kind of bond in a public area and, as a consequence, their access to political, economic and occupational resources is limited.

According to Bird (1996), homosociality refers not only to segregation of women and men but also to the distinction between hegemonic and non-hegemonic masculinities. As such, it can also be defined as 'heterosociality' (p. 121), which is characterised by three features that maintain hegemonic masculinity: (1) emotional detachment; (2) competitiveness; and (3) sexual objectification of women. The role of heterosexuality is also emphasised by Flood (2008), who underlines the role of sexual activity and sexual storytelling in the creation of male status in a group of men and male bonding. Homosocial relations are built and reproduced through the exclusion of those who could pose a threat to them, which implies the exclusion of all non-masculine elements. By doing so, heterosexual men depreciate women due to their gender and homosexual men due to their sexual orientation, which does not fit into their heterosexual normative order. According to Demetriou (2001), subordination of gays is 'a part of the strategy for the reproduction of patriarchy through the institution of heterosexuality' (p. 344), while Jones, referring to Kimmel (2002), states that 'the homophobic feminisation of gay men reinforces the social construction of femininity as negative' (Jones 2008, 518).

Hammarén and Johansson (2014) state that the way the concept of homosociality has usually been used in empirical studies reinforces its perception as a part of hegemonic masculinity as defined by Connell (1987). The same authors suggest making a distinction between 'vertical' and 'horizontal' homosociality, although they can overlap each other. Vertical homosociality is related to hierarchical gender order, and it aims to maintain hegemony, usually the male hegemony. In horizontal homosociality, observed among women and men, relations 'are based on emotional closeness, intimacy and a non-profitable form of friendship' (Hammarén and Johansson 2014, 5).[1]

Beyond the notion of homosociality, one can also find in the literature on male bonds the notions of 'bromance' (Bray 2003; Chen 2012; Hammarén and

Johansson 2014) and 'fraternity' (Anderson 2008). 'Bromance' is created by combining two words, namely 'brother' and 'romance', and means close and intimate non-sexual relations between men. Although it seems similar to homosociality, it can be distinguished from this concept as not being focused on competition and hierarchy (Hammarén and Johansson 2014); however, it can also contain elements of rivalry and self-interest (Bray 2003). Nonetheless, 'bromance' is more often connected to close male friendship, which can be observed, for example, during common sports activities or when watching football matches. These situations create a space for men for asexual love and affection (Chen 2012). Because of the intimate character of this relation, it is assumed that only heterosexual men are involved in it. Thus, 'bromance', similarly to 'homosociality', maintains heteronormativity and homophobia (Chen 2012; Hammarén and Johansson 2014). The latter, as stated by Kimmel (2000), is 'one of the central organising principles of same-sex friendships for men' (p. 211).

The concept of 'fraternity' also describes male bonding, and, as the study of Polish football fans' narratives has revealed, is often used by them to name their relations (Kossakowski, Antonowicz and Jakubowska 2020). Fraternity has been perceived as maintaining hegemonic masculinity because of its selective recruitment system, distance from other masculinities and sexist culture. As the literature review reveals, it also appears as a theoretical context in the analysis of rape and other forms of sexual aggression towards women (Martin and Hummer 1989; Sanday 1990; Boswell and Spade 1996). Moreover, fraternity has usually been connected to homophobia, that is, intolerance of homosexuality. As noted by Martin and Hummer (1989), fraternities generally mean avoiding recruiting 'geeks, nerds and men that might give the fraternity a wimpy or gay reputation' (p. 460).[2]

Anderson (2008), describing the phenomenon of fraternity, notes that it has changed and one can observe within its frame not only hegemonic (or orthodox) masculinity, but also 'inclusive' masculinity. This kind of masculinity is more open to groups that have been previously excluded, that is, women and gays, and characteristics stereotypically attributed to them. The appearance of this kind of masculinity has not been observed among the Polish football ultras (Kossakowski, Antonowicz and Jakubowska 2020), whose fraternity is still based on the exclusion of homosexuality, the marginalisation of women and their sexualisation. However, it does not entail violence against them, as has been observed in other contexts (Martin and Hummer 1989; Boswell and Spade 1996). On the contrary, football ultras explain their violence against security, the police and fans of other clubs in the frame of chivalry and women's protection (Antonowicz, Jakubowska and Kossakowski 2020).

Male friendship has also been described as important for boys' and men's identity, 'a potential retreat from wider social changes' 'in the light of current transformations in gender relations, and what is still loosely termed a crisis of masculinity' (Thurnell Read 2012, 250). In the sports field, fans' fraternity can be perceived as a bastion of hegemonic masculinity when other fields of social life are feminised (Messner 1988).

Performing gendered fandom

As mentioned, hegemonic masculinity can be understood among others as a configuration of practices that reproduce gender relations and order. This understanding is not specific for hegemonic masculinity only; the perception of masculinity (masculinities) and femininity (femininities) as a set of practices or performative acts is widely recognised in the social sciences. On the one hand, it is related to Judith Butler's (1990) concept of performative gender, and on the other hand, to the concept of 'doing gender' (West and Zimmerman 1987). Contrary to Connell's theory, these theoretical perspectives are focused on women, although they use the more general notion of 'gender'.

As noted by Butler (1988), 'gender is in no way a stable identity or locus of agency from which various acts proceed; rather, it is an identity tenuously constituted in time – an identity instituted through a *stylized repetition of acts*' (p. 519). Gender is performed by movements, body gestures, types of body presentation including clothes, make-up, hairstyle, the vocabulary used and so on. 'Gender is not a thing we have, but rather something that we do at specific times and in specific circumstances' (Wood 2010, 60). The scripts of gender performances are not created by individuals but rather chosen by them from among the cultural scripts of being a man or a woman, that is, they behave in a way that is perceived as appropriate for their gender. According to Butler, individuals who 'fail to do their gender right are exposed to negative social sanctions' (Butler 1990, 140). Moreover, the 'reiterative' (repetitive) nature of gender performances reproduces gender patterns and norms.

The concept of performative gender assumes that gender should not be perceived as a social role or a set of characteristics, but as an outcome of interactions and practices (Hoeber and Kerwin 2013). Individuals 'do' or perform gender, which involves a 'complex of socially guided perceptual, interactional and micropolitical activities that cast particular pursuits as expressions of masculine and feminine "natures"' (West and Zimmerman 1987, 126; see also West and Fenstermaker 1995). Importantly, 'doing gender' is 'a situated doing', it is carried out in the presence (real or virtual) of others in a specific context. 'Our performances are not solo operations. They are always collaborative because however we express gender we do so in a context of social meanings that transcends our individual experiences' (Wood 2010, 60). Therefore, 'doing woman' and 'doing man' can have different natures depending on the context and particular interaction/s, that is, one person can perform gender in a different way being with his/her family, being at work or being in a football stadium. All these contexts can also have, at least partially, different expectations towards performing gender. Therefore, gender should be understood as an 'emergent feature of social situations' rather than the constant property of individuals (West and Zimmerman 1987, 126).

Moreover, to a large extent, doing gender is based on creating differences between women and men that due to the repetitive nature of performing acts become perceived as 'natural' and 'essential'. In this meaning, gender is also relational, constructed with relations to others that have also been emphasised by the concepts of hegemonic masculinity and homosociality. For this reason, the analysis presented in the following part of the book is focused not only on female fans but also on male fans' reactions towards women entering football stands in a growing number. Taking into account a relational perspective, it is assumed that male fans can change their way of doing masculinity to maintain their dominance of the stands.

The ways women do their gender can not only reproduce the normative feminine scripts but can also have a subversive or negotiated nature (Butler 1988). Ussher (1997), for example, proposes four types of performances or positions adopted by women. 'Being girl' is assigned to the archetypical position of woman and is performed by those women who 'want to *be* rather than merely *do* femininity' (Ussher 1997, 445). A woman who is 'doing girl' reflectively performs her gender, 'the feminine masquerade', knowing that this position can bring her some benefits. 'Resisting girl' means a rejection of some, but not all, features of (traditional) femininity such as body discipline and beauty ideals. 'Subverting girl' refers to those women who 'knowingly play with gender as a performance, twisting, imitating and parodying traditional scripts of femininity (or indeed masculinity) in a very public, polished display' (Ussher 1997, 458). The concept, like the previous ones, emphasises the relational and situational character of doing gender; moreover, it reveals the complexity of femininity and women's reactions towards the cultural scripts, as well as highlighting women's agency.

The concepts of 'performative gender' and 'doing gender' have been used in studies on sports fandom. For example, Pope (2013), based on Ussher's typology, suggests distinguishing two categories of female fans that represent 'masculine' femininities (the positions of 'doing girl' and 'resisting girl') and 'feminine' femininities (adapting the positions of 'doing girl' and 'being girl'). Dunn, in her book *Female Football Fans: Community, Identity and Sexism* (2014), perceives fandom as a performance emphasising that fan identity is not fixed, but fans can manage and present it in different ways, by, for example, choosing the matches to attend, the clothes that they wear or their behaviour in the stands (p. 64). Therefore, as the author states, it is important not to perceive female fans (or male fans) as a homogeneous group because 'all football fans choose to perform their fandom differently, and experience their fandom differently', although football fandom is still gendered and 'being female is a factor that affects football fandom, which results from the domination of men and male rules in the stands' (Dunn 2014, 110).

Osborne and Coombs (2013) proposed the concept of 'performative sport fandom', which on the one hand is based on identity and gender theories, and on the other hand perceives fandom itself as performative. Therefore, fans are not seen by their group affiliation but by their behaviours and experiences. Although the latter can be influenced by belonging to a particular group of fans, this approach allows differences to be recognised within particular groups. Perceiving gender as performative and identity as 'what one does' (Stets and Burke 2000, 234), Osborne and Coombs (2013) emphasise that (roles) performances are relational, contextual and negotiable. Moreover, both identity theory and performative gender theory draw attention to the internalisation of some social norms due to repetitive acts; however, the latter assumes greater subject agency and opportunities to contest or subvert the imposed cultural scripts consciously.

According to 'performative sport fandom' theory, 'individuals become sport fans through the performance of fandom. Those performances are socially constructed and vary based on context and audience' (Osborne and Coombs 2013, 677). They should not be analysed only regarding gender, but also race, sexual orientation and national identity, to perceive similarities and differences among the fans' performances. Moreover, it should not be limited to women, as gender theory has often been. Through their performances, sports fans produce sociocultural meanings of gender, race or sexual orientation. Therefore, their analysis allows exploration of the reproduction of gender (and other) scripts, the main barriers to challenging them and, if possible, ways to overcome them.

The conjunction of these theoretical perspectives provides an opportunity, on the one hand, to analyse the environment into which women enter (references to 'hegemonic masculinity', 'homosociality' and 'brotherhood') and, on the other, to study everyday practices of fans ('performative gender', 'performative sports fandom'). The practices of female fans can reproduce a heteronormative order in the stands but can also, at least to some small extent, challenge them. The practices of male fans should be analysed from the perspective of the process of feminising stands and wider socio-cultural changes concerning masculinities and femininities globally and in a particular society. The concepts of performative gender and fandom also provide an opportunity to see a multiplicity of performances rather than treating female fans as a homogeneous group. Moreover, an adaptation of Connell's (1987) concept to fans' research raises the question of whether fandom or – in a wider perspective – leisure can (or should) be perceived as the fourth institution of gender relations, beyond the labour market, the state and the family.

Notes

1 A different perception of 'homosociality' was proposed by Sedgwick (1985) in her analysis of British literature. The author is less focused on male domination, and male bonds as a tool of power, but rather on different forms of *desire*, that is, close and intimate but non-sexual relations between men. This understanding has not been developed within sports studies, contrary to Lipman-Blumen's concept, and will not be used in the book.
2 The notion of 'fraternities' has also been used to describe the clubs of male students from North American universities; however, this understanding is beyond the scope of the book.

References

Anderson, E. 2008. 'Inclusive masculinity in a fraternal setting'. *Men and Masculinities* 10(5): 604–620. doi: 10.1177/1097184X06291907.
Antonowicz, D., H. Jakubowska and R. Kossakowski. 2020. 'Marginalised, patronised and instrumentalised: Polish female fans in the ultras' narratives'. *International Review for the Sociology of Sport* 55(1): 60–76. doi: 10.1177/1012690218782828.

Beasley, Ch. 2008. 'Rethinking hegemonic masculinity in a globalizing world'. *Men and Masculinities* 11(1): 86–103. doi: 10.1177/1097184X08315102.

Bird, Sh. R. 1996. 'Welcome to the men's club: Homosociality and the maintenance of hegemonic masculinity'. *Gender and Society* 10(2): 120–132.

Boswell, A. and S. Z. Spade. 1996. 'Fraternities and collegiate rape culture: Why are some fraternities more dangerous places for women?' *Gender & Society* 10(2): 133–147.

Bray, A. 2003. *The Friend*. Chicago: The University of Chicago Press.

Butler, J. 1988. 'Performative acts and gender constitution: An essay in phenomenology and feminist theory'. *Theatre Journal* 40(4): 519–531.

Butler, J. 1990. *Gender Trouble*. New York: Routledge.

Chen, E. J. 2012. 'Caught in a bad bromance'. *Texas Journal of Women and the Law*, 21(2): 241–266.

Chiweshe, M. 2014. 'One of the boys: Female fans' responses to the masculine and phallocentric nature of football stadiums in Zimbabwe'. *Critical African Studies* 6(2–3): 211–222. doi: 10.1080/21681392.2014.940077.

Connell, R. W. 1987. *Gender and Power: Society, the Person and Sexual Politics*. Stanford: Stanford University Press.

Connell, R. W. 1995. *Masculinities*. Berkeley: University of California Press.

Connell, R. W. 2000. *The Men and the Boys*. Berkeley: University of California Press.

Connell, R. W. and J. W. Messerschmitt. 2005. 'Hegemonic masculinity: Rethinking the concept'. *Gender and Society* 19: 829–859.

Demetriou, D. Z. 2001. 'Connell's concept of hegemonic masculinity: A critique'. *Theory and Society* 30(3): 337–361.

Dunn, C. 2014. *Female Football Fans: Community, Identity and Sexism*. Basingstoke: Palgrave Macmillan.

Flood, M. 2002. 'Between men and masculinity: An assessment of the term "masculinity" in recent scholarship on men'. In *Manning the Next Millennium: Studies in Masculinities*, edited by S. Pearce and V. Muller. Perth, Australia: Black Swan.

Flood, M. 2008. 'Men, sex, and homosociality: How bonds between men shape their sexual relations with women'. *Men and Masculinities* 10(3): 339–359. doi: 10.1177/1097184X06287761.

Hammarén, N. and T. Johansson. 2014. 'Homosociality: In between power and intimacy'. *Sage Open*. doi: 10.1177/2158244013518057.

Hearn, J. 2004. 'From hegemonic masculinity to the hegemony of men'. *Feminist Theory* 5(1): 49–72. doi: 10.1177/1464700104040813.

Hoeber L. and S. Kerwin. 2013. 'Exploring the experiences of female sport fans: A collaborative self-ethnography'. *Sport Management Review* 16(3): 326–336. doi: 10.1016/j.smr.2012.12.002.

Jones, K. 2008. 'Female fandom: Identity, sexism, and men's professional football in England'. *Sociology of Sport Journal* 25: 516–537. doi: 10.1123/ssj.25.4.516.

Kanter, R. 1977. *Men and Women of the Corporation*. New York: Basic Books.

Kimmel, M. S. 1994. 'Masculinity as homophobia: Fear, shame, and silence in the construction of gender identity'. In *Theorizing Masculinities*, edited by H. Brod and M. Kaufman. London: Sage, 119–141.

Kimmel, M. S. 1997. 'Masculinity as homophobia: Fear, shame and silence in the construction of gender identity'. In *Toward a New Psychology of Gender*, edited by M. M. Gergen and S. N. Davis. New York: Routledge, 223–242.

Kimmel, M. S. 2000. *The Gendered Society*. New York: Oxford University Press.

Kimmel, M. S. 2002. 'Masculinity as homophobia: Fear, shame, and silence in the construction of gender identity'. In *Women, Culture and Society: A Reader*, edited by B. Balliet and P. McDaniel. Dubuque, IA: Kendall/Hunt, 200–215.

Kossakowski, R., D. Antonowicz and H. Jakubowska. 2020. 'The reproduction of hegemonic masculinity in football fandom: An analysis of the performance of Polish ultras'. In *The Palgrave Handbook of Masculinity and Sport*, edited by R. Magrath, J. Cleland and E. Anderson. Cham: Palgrave Macmillan, 517–536.

Lipman-Blumen, J. 1976. 'Toward a homosocial theory of sex roles: An explanation of the sex segregation of social institutions'. *Signs* 1(3): 15–31.

Martin, P. Y. and R. A. Hummer. 1989. 'Fraternities and rape on campus'. *Gender & Society* 3: 457–473.

Messerschmidt, J. W. 2012. 'Engendering gendered knowledge: Assessing the academic appropriation of hegemonic masculinity'. *Men and Masculinities* 15(1): 56–76. doi: 10.1177/1097184X11428384.

Messner, M. 1988. 'Sports and male domination: The female athlete as contested ideological terrain'. *Sociology of Sport Journal* 5(3): 197–211. doi: 10.1123/ssj.5.3.197.

Osborne, A. C. and D. S. Coombs. 2013. 'Performative sport fandom: An approach to retheorizing sport fans'. *Sport in Society* 16(5): 672–681. doi: 10.1080/17430437.2012.753523.

Palmer, C. and K. Thompson. 2007. 'The paradoxes of football spectatorship: On-field and online expressions of social capital among the "grog squad"'. *Sociology of Sport Journal* 24: 187–2005. doi: 10.1123/ssj.24.2.187.

Pilcher, J. 1999. *Women in Contemporary Britain: An Introduction*. London: Routledge.

Pope, S. 2013. '"The love of my life": The meaning and importance of sport for female fans'. *Journal of Sport and Social Issues* 37(2): 176–195. doi: 10.1177/0193723512455919.

Sanday, P. 1990. *Fraternity Gang Rape: Sex, Brotherhood, and Privilege on Campus*. New York: New York University Press.

Schippers, M. 2007. 'Recovering the feminine other: Masculinity, femininity, and gender hegemony'. *Theory and Society* 36: 85–102. doi: 10.1007/s11186–007–9022–4.

Sedgwick, E. 1985. *Between Men: English Literature and Male Homosocial Desire*. New York: Columbia University Press.

Sisjord, M. K. and E. Kristiansen. 2009. 'Elite women wrestlers' muscles: Physical strength and a social burden'. *International Review for the Sociology of Sport* 44(2–3): 231–246. doi: 10.1177/1012690209335278.

Stets, J. E. and P. J. Burke. 2000. 'Identity theory and social identity theory'. *Social Psychology Quarterly* 63: 224–237. doi: 10.2307/2695870.

Thurnell Read, T. 2012. 'What happens on tour: The premarital stag tour, homosocial bonding, and male friendship'. *Men and Masculinities* 15(3): 249–270. doi: 10.1177/1097184X12448465.

Ussher, J. M. 1997. *Fantasies of Femininity: Reframing the Boundaries of Sex*, New Brunswick: Rutgers University Press.

West, C. and S. Fenstermaker. 1995. 'Doing difference'. *Gender and Society* 9(1): 8–37. doi: 10.1177/089124395009001002.

West C. and D. H. Zimmerman. 1987. 'Doing gender'. *Gender and Society* 1(2): 125–151. doi: 10.1177/0891243287001002002.

Whisenant, W., P. Pedersen and B. Obenour. 2002. 'Success and gender: Determining the rate of advancement for intercollegiate athletic directors'. *Sex Roles* 47(9/10): 485–491.

Wood, J. T. 2010. *Gendered Lives: Communication, Gender, and Culture*. Boston: Wadsworth Publishing.

Part II

The local context of development of female fandom

3 History of football (male) fandom in Poland

Hegemonic masculinity, as discussed in the previous chapter, should be analysed, according to Connell and Messerschmidt (2005), in a particular local and regional context (see also Hoeber and Kerwin 2013). The former can refer to a specific social environment, such as fandom culture, and the latter to a particular nation and country. Taking into account this assumption to allow a better understanding of the process of Polish stadiums' 'feminisation', we want to familiarise the reader with the Polish context. Therefore, the next two chapters are devoted, first, to the history of Polish football fandom and its transformation and, second, to the socio-cultural changes of gender relations and women's status in Polish society.

Football fandom has been deeply embedded in local culture reflecting the social, political and cultural transformation of Poland (Antonowicz and Grodecki 2018; Kossakowski, Nosal and Woźniak 2020). Since it appeared as a social phenomenon, it has undergone deep changes not only echoing transnational trends in fandom culture but also being profoundly shaped by local factors such as politics, law and also the modernisation of sports facilities. The local environment has had a profound influence on the social norms and cultural practices of football fandom. Taking a bird's eye view, football fandom in Poland appears to have a particularly interesting and turbulent history, which helps us to understand its specific features and role in contemporary society. To structure the analysis, it is worth distinguishing three major phases of development during the unfolding of Polish football fandom. The first phase is marked by the emergence of football fandom as a form of subculture from an individual, spontaneous activity into a more organised social phenomenon with its distinct values and norms, while the second phase, spanning from the late 1980s until approximately the early years of the twenty-first century, is characterised by internal functional differentiation, the professionalisation of hooliganism and the rise of ultras. The last phase, which began with the announcement of Poland as co-host of Euro 2012, was driven by the rapid modernisation of the football culture and growing political sensitivity and consequently also engagement of the stands.

The history of Polish fandom is characterised by 'gender blindness' (Free and Hughson 2003). It is written by men and concerns male fans, although their gender is not emphasised and is taken for granted. To the best of our knowledge, the 'herstory' of Polish fandom has not been discovered thus far, nor subjected to investigation.

Rebellious beginning

Football has always been the most popular sport in Poland, and football matches have been well attended, with each game attracting thousands and top games even tens of thousands of spectators. Since the first league match in 1927, it has managed to attract large crowds of around 32,000 spectators (Hałys 1986), being by far the biggest form of entertainment for the social masses. Until the late 1970s, spectators gathered in the stands, watched and only spontaneously reacted to match situations. From the outset, football was primarily an entertainment for men. Although there are no statistical data regarding match attendances, all available sources (for example pictures, press releases, personal statements) suggest that stadiums used to be overwhelmingly populated by men. Football audiences have never resembled those at the theatre or the opera, as social norms have been far more relaxed, allowing fans to demonstrate spontaneous outbursts of emotion. Also, the profile of spectators has been very mixed, and gradually – particularly since the 1950s – football has come to be dominated by working-class masses for whom it was the main form of (outdoor) entertainment (Noga 2016).

The first organised support during a football match was reported by fans of Polonia Bytom in the middle of the 1960s, which was followed by fans from other big clubs such as Lechia Gdańska and Legia Warszawa (*Wszystko zaczęło się w Bytomiu* 2017). Despite patchy access to information from the other side of the Iron Curtain, Polish fans have been inspired by their Western counterparts (mainly Dutch and English) whom they encounter during European cups or whom they have watched on television. For example, it is believed that colourful football scarves, which became a trademark of 'diehards' (later also known as 'scarf boys'), were adopted after Feyenoord fans (Kossakowski 2017a).

Football in Poland was organised typically for countries of the communist bloc (Kossakowski, Nosal and Woźniak, 2020). Polish football clubs were affiliated to big state companies, which provided them with some form of institutional 'patronage'. This covered all sorts of 'services', including the financial support of clubs and giving players formal positions in factories that were 'fake employments'. Such practices were also deployed in the police and army, which also had to unfold patronage over football clubs and include football players on their payrolls. It was a part of the communist state that directly or indirectly kept control of almost every single aspect of social life (Bäcker and Hübner 1997). Those state enterprises (usually with a large number of employees) were central not only for clubs but surprisingly also for the development of the fandom culture. The first organised trips to away games were initiated by those factories, which also performed an important role in organising various aspects of their employees' social life. During the organised tours, besides watching the game, fans had the opportunity to sightsee host cities or visit other tourist destinations (Kossakowski 2017a, 2017b).

With the emergence of football fandom, various state institutions began to support and facilitate the passion of fans. State factories opened the first so-called 'fan clubs', organised meetings with players and facilitated various fans' activities – partly to address the growing interest in football (and other sports such as speedway) and partly to build boundaries between working masses and players. The latter, as early as in the 1970s, enjoyed the privileged position and higher status; it was not obviously a celebrity lifestyle but still they often became local heroes.

The away trips for matches, despite being organised 'top down' by factories, made a significant contribution to the development of the fandom culture. They provided an opportunity for most loyal (diehard) fans to integrate and consequently to distinguish themselves from the rest of the football crowd. Steadily but gradually, those groups also took a leading role in cheering during both home and away football games. At approximately the same time (in the early 1980s), Polish fans became heavily inspired by English football culture. This resulted in imitating the English fandom culture as exhibited in the appearance of flags in stadiums (many of them were simply a replica of UK flags) and following a specific fandom style based on the concept of hegemonic masculinity in which the role of violence prevailed (Taylor 1971; Marsh, Rosser and Harré 1978; Kerr 1994). As Anthony King (1997) aptly notes:

> One of the central elements of the lads' fandom is their 'pride'. This pride refers to the status of the club in football and particularly the team's success on the field, which is reflected on to the lads, as supporters.… The notion of pride is important in the lads' everyday lives as their masculinity is substantially defined through football.
>
> (p. 333)

So, together with official attempts to control the fandom culture, the latter began to evolve into an anti-system, rebel movement against the police, the oppressive state and its ideology. It should be acknowledged that football stadiums were one of the very few enclaves of relatively unrestrained expression in the communist regime. In the 1980s, the official communist propaganda tried to hide a growing number of violent incidents related to football. However, since the early 1970s, football violence has become an integral part of Polish football fandom. Football matches created a unique environment in an authoritarian socio-political system in which to manifest such anti-communist slogans as 'down with the commies' (*Precz z komuną*) and anti-system attitudes. Also,

> the environment of run-down and poorly maintained stadium infrastructure was conducive to the anarchisation of fan conduct during matches, while the anonymity of the crowd and an enormous wave of emotions stirred by sports rivalry created an exuberant atmosphere.
>
> (Antonowicz and Grodecki 2018, 494)

Nevertheless, the crowds gathered in stadiums and on away trips had some degree of freedom and anonymity. It was a unique situation in Poland under the communist regime that was used by football fans to both express their anti-communist views and, more frequently, to attack rival fans and police (see Zieliński 1993). One of the most memorable events that illustrated the use of such a unique space of liberty happened in 1983 during a European Cup tie between Lechia Gdańsk and Juventus when tens of thousands of Lechia fans spontaneously but loudly chanted the name of 'Lech Wałęsa' (who was present in the stadium), who was a charismatic leader of the democratic opposition movement '*Solidarność*' (Wąsowicz 2006).

In the early 1980s, such a spectacular demonstration of support for democratic opposition would never have happened elsewhere in Poland. The state found it hard to control tens of thousands of fans on match day. Political demonstrations such as the one in Gdańsk were rare, and the fandom culture was rebellious and driven by physical and symbolic violence. With the growing popularity of the fandom culture, the most loyal and diehard groups started to form their sub-culture with distinctive values and norms. It was built in the rebellious fashion inspired by the so-called 'English disease' (Stott and Pearson 2007), which, in the mid-1980s, was massively popular in Europe. Even the suspension of English football clubs after the Heysel disaster did not change anything. For many football fans in Europe, English hooligans served as role models, and Poland was no exception. Polish fans wanted to be as tough, antisocial and rebellious as their English counterparts. The fascination with English hooligans had far-reaching consequences for the football fandom culture. The idea of hard fans (commonly known as football hooligans) started to establish and execute social norms in the stadium. Due to their physical power, some form of organisation and also loyalty, they started to dominate the stands. As a consequence, hooligans' social and cultural practices, including abusive language, became the norm in the stands.

In other words, in the late 1970s and early 1980s, football fandom underwent the process of institutionalisation, transforming from the uncoordinated activity of watching the action on the pitch into organised support during home and away games. This was largely due to the emancipation of 'diehard fans' who took a leading role in developing football fandom into a rebellious subculture that was fundamentally different from the dominant culture. It rested upon unique sets of values, norms and internal organisation; it also developed its own specific artefacts (for example flags, scarves, fanzines, tattoos) and even its own hierarchy (the so-called 'league of hooligans'). The central role in the hooligans' culture was performed by a concept of a football 'hooligan' who embraced the essence of hegemonic masculinity (Connell 1987), and it also entailed any other forms of masculinity. Furthermore, it also had far-reaching consequences for establishing the fandom culture, which was built around the concept of loyalty demonstrated by toughness and bravery often perceived as directly related to a lower-working-class culture. Poland was no exception, as this was a common pattern. As Dunning, Murphy and Williams (1988) argued, fighting is an important source of meaning, status and pleasurable arousal. Correspondingly, there is a tendency for them to 'back down' less frequently than males from other areas and there are also occasions when they actively seek out fights and confrontations. Of course, males generally in our society are expected to defend themselves if attacked, but they are less likely than lower-working-class males to be initiators in this regard.

(pp. 209–210)

It automatically excluded other forms of masculinity as being inferior and less valuable (see Kossakowski, Antonowicz and Jakubowska 2020). Also, the hooligans' style of early fandom culture and its close ties with the vintage prison, culture (pol. *gitowcy*) had a massive influence on its character and dominant sets of values (Piotrowski 1999; Kowalski 2002). Moreover, one more characteristic started to prevail at the time – skinheads performed a leading role among diehard fans. Flags with Celtic crosses next to the English word 'hooligan' became one of the most frequent symbols exposed to diehard fans (Woźniak, Kossakowski and Nosal 2019). Their aim was to symbolise toughness, rivalry and the ability to confront enemies.

For the communist state, the football culture with its prevalence of hooligans became problematic as frequent public disruptions, fights between fans and ordinary vandalism undermined the authority of the communist state, the police and other paramilitary organisations (ZOMO and ORMO). Although the communist propaganda only obscurely reported on clashes, fights, incidents, casualties or any forms of organised violence on the streets or during football games, it was popular knowledge that diehard fans travelling on public transport caused havoc and sowed terror among the general public. There was only some patchy information made available (see Kossakowski 2017a), although numerous fanzines, hooligans' diaries and witness statements' leave no doubts that violence became an important part of football fandom at the time.

Some might say that hooligans represented a minority in the football stands, but the fact is they set social rules in the stands. They held symbolic power and authority among fans as the most loyal and devoted to the club. Among the greyish crowds attending football games, they stood out due to their colourful scarves, flags and loud chanting. They offered the spirit of liberty (and even anarchy) to a society that remained under strict political control. Many fans did not agree with the social practices carried out by diehard fans, but their impact on the fandom culture should not be underestimated. This was due to their dominant position in the stands and apostolic power to define the concept of fandom. Without doubt, in Poland, it was they who developed the football fandom culture through their social practices. However, the side effect was the rise of stadium hooliganism, which over time developed to become an integral part of Polish football. As mentioned earlier, the state's media tried to keep hooligan incidents at a low profile, but sometimes this was difficult. For example, during the cup final in 1980 the clashes between Lech and Legia fans unfolded into a regular war zone in the city of Częstochowa and caused dozens of casualties and a few deaths (Kossakowski 2017a).

To sum up, football fandom in Poland emerged as a mixture of the authoritarian state's operations and the popularity of the English football culture. Without doubt, it was dominated by working-class males and, as a consequence, it was rebellious by nature with explicit inclinations towards physical and symbolic violence. Also, the realities of the late 1980s were marked by the political and economic decline due to the institutional failure of the state, whose shortcomings and weaknesses were exposed by growing football violence. Of course, the hegemony and domination of young males among football fans must have had a far-reaching consequence on the masculine character of football fandom in Poland. It built a certain ideal type (Weber 2012) of the 'real' football fan that naturally influenced the profile of individuals attracted by the fandom subculture and also those not so much welcome on the stands.

Phase II – late 1980s and early twenty-first century

The eruption of football hooliganism

The institutionalisation of the football fandom subculture in the 1970s and 1980s made football one of the most popular sports in Polish society. The democratic and economic transformation that began in 1989 freed society from oppressive states but at the same time produced numerous other social, economic and political threats. The Polish economic transformation was the most neoliberal in the region, and its social cost was both high and largely unexpected. The transformation was a long and complex process that had far-reaching consequences for society (Rychard and Federowicz 1993; Morawski 1998; Kurczewska 1999); however, it did not affect the atmosphere in stadiums. On the contrary, football fandom became even more aggressive, violent and rebellious. Those features were left over from the communist era, which produced a strongly embedded feeling of freedom unconstrained by any legal regulations. This anarchical spirit did not fade away – on the contrary, it exploded with multiple power, as did the role of hooligans in the stands.

Stadiums often reflect the problems of society (Doidge 2015). In the 1990s, Poland faced a series of massive, previously unknown, social and economic problems, such as a high rate of unemployment, hyperinflation and mass structural poverty. This caused deep social frustration as the fall of the communist regime sparked high hopes in society of a better future. But prosperity did not benefit all, and those who were hit the most by the economic transformation were the least educated young males, who found themselves out of a job and also lacking social respect given that the main social role of men was that of the *breadwinner*. Antonowicz and Grodecki (2018) found that 'the hooligan problem was perceived as a natural part of the football show. The state, still in the initial stages of the transformation, neither commanded social respect nor had adequate institutional and legal instruments to enforce the existing law' (p. 497). There was no better place to relieve frustration than football stadiums.

And indeed, the rebellious nature of football fandom and its political sensitivity were good conditions in which many young males could demonstrate their anger and frustration. The clashes with the police became an integral part of football culture plunging Polish football even deeper into the mire. Moreover, football in Poland became a symbol of moral downfall, being corrupt to the core.[1] So it would be fair to conclude that for many years football matches in Poland were partly fixed and – to some extent – it was polysynthetic mystery.

Overall, this sketches a rather gloomy picture of Polish football – corrupt, underfunded, with ruined infrastructure and pervaded by fan violence. Football was entangled with various organised crime groups both on and off the pitch, and this had far-reaching consequences for the fandom culture. If in the 1980s football fandom showed some inclination towards violence, the 1990s were heavily dominated by violence. The crumbling state, troubled by a serious economic crisis, unemployment and public institutions that lacked respect and authority, paid little attention to sports events. The bankruptcy of the state's companies left clubs and their sports facilities in ruin. The side effect was the rise of stadium hooliganism, which over time developed to become an integral part of the sports events. The realities of the late 1990s included the political and economic decline of the institutionally inefficient state, whose shortcomings and weaknesses were exposed by stadium riots. Thus, the late 1990s are primarily marked as *the heyday of hooliganism* (Kossakowski 2017c; Antonowicz and Grodecki 2018) when the newly transformed state was helpless in addressing football hooliganism. Kossakowski and Besta (2018) characterised fans of this decade as follows:

> [T]he brutality of the fan world as well as the spread of extreme right-wing ideas in the structure of the fan movement has influenced the situation at Polish stadiums. So far, the hooligan groups, although quantitatively insignificant, have determined the strategies of the functioning of 'hard-core' fan terraces.
>
> (p. 10)

To add insult to injury, the state (austerity measures) decided to delegate the responsibility to football clubs, which became corporate organisations. They hired various newly established security agencies to provide security during football matches. As a result, sports events were frequently monitored by unprofessional, underpaid and inexperienced law enforcement agencies. It would not be an exaggeration to say that stadiums were almost totally left to football hooligans, who applied their rules and norms.

Ultras and hooligans

The 1990s saw one of the most significant changes in the fandom culture – its functional differentiation (Kossakowski 2017a, 2017b). In the 1980s and early 1990s, football fans were often described as 'an ordinary mob', which holds lots of truth. But in the mid-1990s the process of diversification began and from the rather homogeneous community two different groups started to emerge: ultras and hooligans, with specific tasks to perform.

The beginning of the ultras' activities in Poland dated back to the middle of the 1990s. In comparison to today's ultra activities, they were initially very 'amateurish', largely uncoordinated and bottom-up actions. Initially, the supporters of the biggest clubs displayed large, handmade flags and used pyrotechnic devices (white or orange smoke flares). Newspapers cut in small pieces were thrown upon command together with paper rolls from cash registers. Homemade smoke flares sometimes accompanied this. Kossakowski, Szlendak and Antonowicz (2018) found that flares were first used mostly by fans from the seaport cities (Szczecin, Gdańsk, Gdynia) taking advantage of their access to fishermen's supplies who had such equipment at their disposal. In the early days, ultras' 'performances' included simple but diverse elements (for example balloons, large flags on poles) that embellished the largely greyish reality in the football stands. Shortly after the ultras' performance arrived in Polish football, it came to function as a field for rivalry in terms of their content and form (scale). The overall effect could be described as 'spectacular chaos' but undoubtedly introduced new elements into football games. It was disturbing and perhaps irritating for regular football watchers, but it reflected the rebellious and often anarchical spirit of the stands. It was also an alternative to the growing violence and mindlessness of football crowds.

At approximately the same time, hooligan firms began to emerge with their specific activities – physical confrontations with other fans. One of the reasons for this development was the expansion of hooligans' activities outside sports stadiums and beyond match days. Slowly but surely, they began to resemble ordinary street gangs, which required a more 'professional' approach, and many fans – despite their radicalism and loyalty – were not interested in deliberately carrying out criminal activity. These two groups maintained strong links and sometimes some fans shared their activities between both hooligans and ultras. Hooligans always enjoyed a supreme position in the stands, and had the final say about almost everything that happened there.

Despite evolving into a more diverse community of fans, football fandom remained dominated by males. Although the rising role of ultras created some space and roles for those fans who did not want to engage in physical fights, the concept of 'hegemonic masculinity' remained strongly embedded in the fandom culture. The ethnographical investigation of graffiti, flags and fanzines presented a very bold message that football fans wanted to be seen as tough and fearless men with nationalistic and even racist views (as demonstrated by flags with the slogan 'white power'). Interestingly, from the very beginning Polish fans demonstrated right-wing political views. Not a single major fan group openly affiliated themselves with the left wing of the political scene (such as Livorno in Italy or St Pauli in Germany). This could be explained by the relatively strong conservatism of Polish society, which is the result of several factors, including the long struggle for national identity, the mass murders of intellectual elites during World War II, the cultural and civilisational backwardness of the communist era and the weak tradition of left-wing (though non-communist) political leaders. Kossakowski and Besta (2018) also add that the radical 'right wing' could be explained by the anti-communist nature of football fandom during the communist times and (later) the conflict with neoliberal governments (particularly shortly before Euro 2012). It did have an impact on the popularity of ring-wing political and even religious symbols and the reinvention of national heroes such as the Polish 'Cursed Soldiers', which helped to build a collective identity among football fans (Kossakowski, Antonowicz and Jakubowska 2020).

There is no doubt that conservative values are deeply entrenched in the Polish fandom culture. This must have had deep and far-reaching consequences for the perception of social roles performed by men and women. The authors mentioned did not investigate the gender aspect of ultras, focusing instead on other aspects. But for this study, it is important to examine the political views of football fans. The research published by Woźniak, Kossakowski and Nosal (2019) shows that football fans tend to lean towards the right of the political spectrum. This means that they associate with a traditional model of society with a clear-cut division between male and female roles in society, which in Poland is strongly advocated by the Roman Catholic Church. There is no empirical evidence that fans are more religious than the average individual in Polish society, but once a year thousands of Polish fans attend the Patriotic Pilgrimage of Fans to Jasna Góra Monastery (*Patriotyczna Pielgrzymka Kibiców na Jasną Górę*). Animosities between rivalry clubs are suspended for the duration of the event, which embraces the Holy Mass and the blessing of club scarves and numerous patriotic events on a small scale. Those fans are strongly rooted in the naturalistic model of a nation (see Greenfeld 1992) that pays strong attention to common history, tradition and territory and sees the supreme role of ethnic bonds and God. Polish fans use many patriotic symbols and slogans (for example God, honour, homeland) to underscore their attachment to traditional values (Woźniak, Kossakowski and Nosal 2019).

As Kossakowski, Szlendak and Antonowicz (2018) aptly noted,

> although the majority of the most committed fans forming the ultras move-ment are not religious or practising believers, they hold a set of values and display an inclination towards symbols, familiarised by the Polish popular class, which is deeply rooted in ritualised folk Catholicism.
>
> (p. 855)

Without going into a detailed analysis of Polish society (which is the subject of Chapter 4), the Polish fandom culture has always been deeply rooted in a traditional model society that attributes power and prestige to male roles and positions. Just like in the broader society, in the stands, males maintain their hegemonic position and adhere to it through social and cultural practices.

In the mid-1990s, the process of diversification of football fans might have been seen as slightly broadening the concept of fandom and also included non-militant activities. The evolution of ultras as a separate group of fans opened doors for those interested in non-violent activity, but it did not essentially affect the hegemony and domination of males. Ironically, the ultras' performance provided a new toolkit for demonstrating and fostering in almost every aspect stadium social and cultural practices, which have been analysed in depth by Kossakowski, Antonowicz and Jakubowska (2020).

Last but not least, the important dimension of changes in Polish football fandom refers to the professionalisation of fans' activity through grass-roots fans' associations. Their establishment was the result of legal requirements for organising away trips, and also football clubs sought to build relations with official representatives of their fans (see Grodecki 2019; Kossakowski 2019). On top of that, fans required some form of legal entity to provide help for bankrupt football clubs (for example Lechia Gdańsk, Chrobry Głógów, Stilon Gorzów, Szombierki Bytom, Hutnik Kraków, Widzew and ŁKS Łódź). This new situation required a fundamental transformation of football fandom from informal loosely coupled individuals who had been united by a common passion and collective support into a formal organisation with statutes, membership fees, statutory bodies and democratic procedures. Of course, the establishment of fans' associations was the outcome of the changing legal environment, not endogenous development, but it opened a completely new chapter in the history of football fandom in Poland. Fans had managed to accumulate a considerable amount of social capital based on mutual trust, which became their asset in numerous conflicts with football authorities, club managements and law enforcement agencies. At the same time, it became a window of opportunity for the expansion of fans' activities beyond the social context of football matches. In numerous cases (explored in depth by Kossakowski 2019) fans started to engage in various patriotic and charity-based actions, which required new fans with a different profile to young, physically strong and brave males. Football associations were undoubtedly a milestone in softening the traditional image of fans, providing a social space for those who perhaps had not been previously engaged (or had even been marginalised) in the stands.

Euro 2012 and the evolution of fandom culture

Football fans earned a particularly bad reputation, and their behaviour was broadcasted by mainstream TV news and frequently hit the front pages of major national newspapers, causing a public outcry (Woźniak 2013). The peak of the violence occurred in the late 1990s, and in 1997 the government introduced a special legal act (the *Act on Mass Event Security*) to deal with mass events. Analysis of public statistics (more in Antonowicz and Grodecki 2018) shows that with the turn of the century the number of violent incidents during football games began to decrease; however, many politicians still found football fans trying to stay above the law. And therefore, further legal and also political measures were deployed to address not only the problem of football violence but also the use of any form of pyrotechnics by ultras. To achieve those aims, radical measures were undertaken to hit football hooligans whose definition was expanded to all fans who did not follow new, increasingly draconian regulations.

One of the flagship measures was the amendment to the criminal law that introduced the fast-track criminal procedure (commonly referred to as the law on twenty-four-hour courts, March 2007) (*Act of 16 November 2006 on amendments to the Penal Code and certain other acts, Journal of Laws, 2006, no. 226, item 1648*). It purported to proceed to immediate conviction (shortly after detention) as the judicial system was generally accused of slowness in handling cases of 'sports-related violence'. However, the intentions of the legislators did not withstand the test of reality, and it ended up taking proceedings against cyclists rather than stadium hooligans (Antonowicz and Grodecki 2018, 503). The procedure failed due to the complexity of cases involving stadium crimes and petty offences. It often required the collection of witness testimonies and detailed examination of CCTV footage to identify the offenders and charge them. It turned out to be a far more complex issue to accomplish in under 24 hours. Nevertheless, football hooliganism gradually disappeared from football stadiums, mostly due to the growing effectiveness of surveillance technology, turnstiles and personalised fan cards in identifying offenders. Neither technology nor the radical political and legal measures affected the character of football fandom significantly; they just made it less legal.

A turning point in the history of Polish football fandom arrived with the announcement of Poland and Ukraine as co-hosts of the Euro 2012 tournament. It was a big surprise and also a high-profile political challenge concerning the modernisation of sports facilities but also the fandom culture. From a political perspective, the organisation of such a great event was seen as an opportunity to take a 'civilisational leap' (Kossakowski 2019) and take a grip on the traditional fandom culture. It was hoped that building modern stadium facilities with comfortable seats, catering facilities and clean toilets would shape a different type of behaviour to the old, run-down stadiums bearing the stigma of the times of anarchy. Many scholars underline the role of sports facilities in building a 'new order' – 'the civilising and taming of local, national and continental emotions can be achieved by the civilisation progress through stadium architecture and the aesthetics of urban space' (Czubaj, Drozda and Myszkorowski 2012, 13).

From the outset, it was clear that the government's agenda was not only to build modern football stadiums but also to initiate the modernisation of social and cultural practices performed passionately in the stands. It was believed that Poland could copy and paste the transformation of English football from the 1990s (see King 2002; Giulianotti 2011) where new stadiums and tough regulations triggered far-reaching changes in the fandom culture. So, the Polish government had an explicit agenda to use the draconian law to kick out all sorts of troublemakers and consequently attract new fans while offering them safe and modern sports facilities. The new legislation expanded the scope of penalisation of stadium behaviour and criminalised a wide range of minor offences, including the possession and use of pyrotechnic devices in stadiums. On top of this, clubs were authorised to impose their own stadium bans on very dubious legal grounds (Dróżdż 2014, 183). Despite some legal doubts about the scale of the penalisation of social and cultural practices carried out by football fans

(Dróżdż 2014), the position of the government was firm, that is, only tough laws can crack the traditional football culture. One could say that extreme times called for extreme measures.

The criminalisation of many social practices central to the fandom culture started an open-conflict war between football fans (at least the vast majority of them) and the government, bringing the issue of football fandom into the centre of domestic politics. Once again, the rebellious nature of football fandom let itself be known when football fans responded to government policy by mocking politicians for their failure to address real social and economic problems. In addition, public authorities failing to execute effectively restrictive stadium rules deployed more political measures by closing stadiums to fans after violent incidents. By doing so, the authorities used collective punishment for offences committed by individuals that police failed to capture and detain. So, closing stadiums became another political instrument in the conflict between the government and football fans that the state authorities used against football fans, who also 'mocked the government for taking a tough course against them and being comically submissive to UEFA' (Antonowicz, Kossakowski and Szlendak 2016, 138). The clash between the government and football fans became highly politicised as the government found that fighting against the traditional football culture could be useful in achieving short-term political goals and would improve its standing in the polls. Triggering 'moral panic' (Cohen 2011) perhaps added a few points of popularity but also worsened the already very negative reputation of football fandom in Poland. Together with the mainstream media it presented a horrific image of football fans as a mob of primitive, uneducated, notoriously violent young males who terrorised football stands, threatening families and putting them off from attending football games (Predencki 2012; Pytlakowski and Stachowiak 2007).

In fact, the hosting of Euro 2012 had far-reaching consequences for Polish football but not necessarily the way it was planned by the government and the football authorities. Undoubtedly, Polish football had undergone an infrastructural revolution. Not only it did this refer to the hosting cities where stadiums with a capacity of over 30,000 seats were built from scratch but also to numerous other locations across the country. Most of the professional football clubs have at their disposal safe and modern sports facilities (of very different capacities) with all-seated stadiums and well-developed catering and sanitary facilities. This development was meant to attract a new, more diversified audience and change the fandom culture. As mentioned earlier, it was believed that Poland could follow the English model and possibly change the social structure of football crowds (in the long term) to 'price out' traditional football fans and their cultural practices.

Contrary to what was politically planned, the shiny new modern stadiums did not spark a revolution in football fandom. Ultra fans have taken the opportunity of new infrastructure to present even more spectacular choreographies, but the content has not changed. The biggest difference refers to the increased safety in the football stands. The recent report published by the PZPN (2018) reveals that violence during football matches occurs only incidentally as far as the *Esktraklasa* is concerned. Football violence has not simply vanished, but only moved further away from football grounds into more secluded locations. Thus, it disappeared from public places but took a far more brutal, dangerous form that was also difficult for the law enforcement authorities to crack down on (for more see Antonowicz and Grodecki 2018).

The modernisation of Polish football largely liberated the stadiums from physical violence, but symbolic violence remains firm and popular. Gangs of hooligans did not vanish; they were pushed out of the stadiums and operate even more successfully outside football contexts. But it did not affect the hierarchy of power and influence in the stands where hooligans have their final say together with ultra fans who maintain their commanding role in the stands. The latter have become better organised and professionalised, and their spectacular choreographies have become breath-taking masterpieces of pop culture. Also, they happen to be a source of embarrassment to many present in the stadium as the content of those ultras' performance stands out because of its radicalism, political incorrectness and affiliation to right-wing ideology. Our observations and interviews suggest that – at least in metropolitan clubs – the ultras and the rest of football have sometimes been split by political and cultural issues. It remains unanswered what proportion of crowds supports those radical right-wing claims, but clearly homophobic, ethnocentric or often insulting choreographies do not make all those in football crowds particularly comfortable as many of them do not share such viewpoints. However, it does not affect the Polish fandom culture, which has a specific political profile as ultras are both radical and right wing. Those who do not necessarily share the views behind some of the ultras' performance distance themselves, ignore them or adapt to such a specific social and cultural environment. But, also, it is hardly possible to openly demonstrate (at least as it stands now) alternative political views.

Summing up, undoubtedly the biggest influence on the development of fan culture has been its spontaneous and rebellious roots in some links to the prison culture. They have all contributed to the hegemonic concept of masculinity and glorification of violence. Only recently has the role of external factors such as politics or economy come to the fore. Football fandom came with the help of patronising states' institutions, which organised 'fan clubs' and trips to away games. But the rebellious nature of football fandom inspired by the 'English disease' was quickly unleashed from the institutional corset and became a rebellious subculture. From the outset, football fandom was pervaded by violence, whose role systematically grew regardless of the fall of communism and the re-establishment of a democratic state. The infrastructural and moral downfall of Polish football on and off the pitch contributed to the further escalation of criminal activity that the state began to face only at the beginning of the twenty-first century. The hosting of Euro 2012 was a turning point for football fandom in Poland as it marked a major modernisation of sports facilities, which, however, did not affect the traditional fandom culture. Overall, football fandom is a classic example of a subculture dominated by young men who also enjoy a hegemonic position. Despite the gradual increase in the number of women, they remain a minority and exercise limited influence through their actions in the stands. Football fandom remains a male territory, and as such is deeply rooted in the industrial model of society and represents its hierarchy of values. Furthermore, over the last decade, despite the 'Westernisation' of Polish society that has prompted radical cultural change, the fandom culture has proved to be a telling example of conservative steadfastness and one of the last bastions of male hegemony.

Note

1 The true picture of football in the 1990s will probably never be discovered because most of the crimes committed have become time-barred. But as an indication of the scale of deprivation, it is worth noting the investigation conducted in 2004. It revealed a shocking level of organised match fixing across the country that involved hundreds of players, coaches, club managements, football associations and match officials – almost everyone involved in club football. According to the latest data, between 2000 and 2012 alone more than 638 games were set up, 467 individuals were convicted and 68 clubs fixed results or attempted to do so (Woźniak 2019).

References

Antonowicz, D. and M. Grodecki. 2018. 'Missing the goal: Policy evolution towards football-related violence in Poland (1989–2012)'. *International Review for the Sociology of Sport* 53(4): 490–511. doi: 10.1177/1012690216662011.

Antonowicz, D., R. Kossakowski and T. Szlendak. 2016. 'Flaming flares, football fanatics and political rebellion: Resistant youth cultures in late capitalism'. In *Eastern European Youth Cultures in a Global Context*, edited by M. Schwartz and H. Winkel. London: Palgrave Macmillan, 131–144.

Bäcker, R. and P. Hübner, eds. 1997. *Skryte oblicze systemu komunistycznego* [*The Hidden Face of the Communist System*]. Warszawa: Wydawnictwo DiG.

Cohen, S. 2011. *Folk Devils and Moral Panics: The Creation of the Mods and Rockers*. Abingdon: Routledge.

Connell, R. W. 1987. *Gender and Power: Society, the Person and Sexual Politics*. Stanford: Stanford University Press.

Connell, R. W. and J. W. Messerschmitt. 2005. 'Hegemonic masculinity: Rethinking the concept'. *Gender and Society* 19: 829–859.

Czubaj M., J. Drozda and J. Myszkorowski. 2012. *Postfutbol. Antropologia piłki nożnej* [*Postfootbol. Anthropology football*]. Gdańsk: Wydawnictwo Naukowe Katedra.

Doidge, M. 2015. *Football Italia. Italian Football in an Age of Globalization*. London: Bloomsbury Academic.

Dróżdż, M. 2014. 'Security of sports events in Poland: Polish act on mass events security'. *IUS NOVUM* 2: 171–186.

Dunning, E., P. Murphy and J. Williams. 1988. *The Roots of Football Hooliganism*. Abingdon: Routledge.

Free, M. and J. Hughson. 2003. 'Settling accounts with hooligans: Gender blindness in football supporter subculture research'. *Men and Masculinities* 6(2), 136–155. doi: 10.1177/1097184X03255849.

Giulianotti, R. 2011. 'Sport mega events, urban football carnivals and securitised commodification'. *Urban Studies* 48(15): 3293–3310. doi: 10.1177/0042098011422395.

Greenfeld, L. 1992. *Nationalism: Five Roads to Modernity*. Cambridge: Harvard University Press.

Grodecki, M. 2019. 'Building social capital: Polish football supporters through the lens of James Coleman's conception'. *International Review for the Sociology of Sport* 54(4): 459–478. doi: 10.1177/1012690217728728.

Hałys, J. 1986. *Polska Piłka Nożna* [*Polish Football*]. Kraków: Krajowa Agencja Wydawnicza.

Hoeber L. and S. Kerwin. 2013. 'Exploring the experiences of female sport fans: A collaborative self-ethnography'. *Sport Management Review* 16(3): 326–336. doi: 10.1016/j.smr.2012.12.002.

Kerr, J. H. 1994. *Understanding Soccer Hooliganism*. London: Open University Press.

King, A. 1997. 'The lads: Masculinity and the new consumption of football'. *Sociology* 31(2): 329–346. doi: 10.1177/0038038597031002008.

King, A. 2002. *The End of the Terraces: The Transformation of English Football*. Leicester: Leicester University Press.

Kossakowski, R. 2017a. *Od chuliganów do aktywistów. Polscy kibice i zmiana społeczna [From Hooligans to Activists. Polish Fans and Social Change]*. Kraków: Universitas.

Kossakowski, R. 2017b. 'From communist fan clubs to professional hooligans: A history of Polish fandom as a social process'. *Sociology of Sport Journal* 34(3): 281–292. doi: 10.1123/ssj.2017–0019.

Kossakowski, R. 2017c. 'Where are the hooligans? Dimensions of football fandom in Poland'. *International Review for the Sociology of Sport* 52(6): 693–711. doi: 10.1177/1012690215612458.

Kossakowski, R. 2019. 'Euro 2012, the "civilizational leap" and the "supporters united" programme: A football mega-event and the evolution of fan culture in Poland'. *Soccer & Society* 20(5): 729–743. doi: 10.1080/14660970.2019.1616266.

Kossakowski R., D. Antonowicz and H. Jakubowska. 2020. 'The reproduction of hegemonic masculinity in football fandom: An analysis of the performance of Polish ultras'. In *The Palgrave Handbook of Masculinity and Sport*, edited by R. Magrath, J. Cleland and E. Anderson. Cham: Palgrave Macmillan, 517–536.

Kossakowski, R. and T. Besta. 2018. 'Football, conservative values, and a feeling of oneness with the group: A study of Polish football fandom'. *East European Politics and Societies: and Cultures* 32(4): 866–891. doi: 10.1177/0888325418756991.

Kossakowski, R., P. Nosal and W. Woźniak. 2020. *Politics, Ideology and Football Fandom: The Transformation of Modern Poland*. Abingdon: Routledge.

Kossakowski, R., T. Szlendak and D. Antonowicz. 2018. 'Polish ultras in the post-socialist transformation'. *Sport in Society* 21(6): 854–869. doi: 10.1080/17430437.2017.1300387.

Kowalski, R. 2002. *Potomkowie Hooligana – Szalikowcy: społeczno-kulturowe źródła agresji widowisk sportowych [Descendants of Hooligan – Brothers in Scarves: Socio-cultural Sources of Aggression of Sports Events]*. Toruń: Wydawnictwo Adam Marszałek.

Kurczewska, J., ed., 1999. *Zmiana społeczna. Teorie i doświadczenia polskie [Social Change. Polish Theories and Experiences]*. Warszawa: IFiS PAN.

Marsh, P., E. Rosser and R. Harré. 1978. *The Rules of Disorder*. London: Routledge and Kegan Paul.

Morawski, W. 1998. *Zmiana instytucjonalna [Institutional Change]*. Warszawa: PWN.

Noga, R. 2016. *Żużel w PRL-u: Sport żużlowy w Polsce w latach 1948–1989 [Speedway in PRL: Speedway in Poland in the Years 1948–1989]*. Toruń: Wydawnictwo UMK.

Piotrowski, P. 1999. *Szalikowcy: o zachowaniach dewiacyjnych kibiców sportowych.* [*Brothers in Scarves: On Deviant Behaviours of Sports Supporters*]. Toruń: Wydawnictwo Adam Marszałek.

Predencki, K. 2012. 'Wizerunek kibiców i kiboli w środkach masowego przekazu' ['The image of fans and hooligans in media']. In *Polska w mediach, media w Polsce* [*Poland in Media, Media in Poland*], edited by Z. Pucek and J. Bierówka. Kraków: Krakowskie Towarzystwo Edukacyjne, 61–91.

Pytlakowski P. and J. Stachowiak. 2007. 'Piłka i pałki' ['The ball and police batons']. *Polityka* 48: 38–40.

PZPN. 2018. *Raport dotyczący organizacji i stanu bezpieczeństwa meczów piłki nożnej szczebla centralnego PZPN. Sezon 2017/18* [*A Report on the Organisation and Security Status of Football Matches at Central Level of the PZPN. Season 2017/18*] Warszawa: PZPN. Accessed 30 July 2019 www.pzpn.pl/public/2017_18_CALY_SEZON_ ORGANIZACJA_BEZPIECZENSTWO_DOIBI_PZPN.pdf

Rychard, A. and M. Fedorowicz, eds. 1993. *Społeczeństwo w transformacji* [*A Society in Transformation*]. Warszawa: IFiS PAN.

Stott, C. and G. Pearson. 2007. *Football 'Hooliganism': Policing and the War on the 'English Disease'.* London: Pennant Books.

Taylor, I. 1971. 'Football mad: A speculative sociology of football hooliganism'. In: *The Sociology of Sport: A Selection of Readings*, edited by E. Dunning. London: Frank Cass, 352–377.

Wąsowicz, J. 2006. *Biało-zielona Solidarność. O fenomenie politycznym kibiców gdańskiej Lechii 1981–1989* [*White-green Solidarity. About the political phenomenon of Lechia Gdańsk Supporters 1981–1989*]. Gdańsk: Finna.

Weber, M. 2012. 'The "objectivity" of knowledge in social science and social policy'. In: *Collected Methodological Essays*, edited by H. Bruun, S. Whimster. London: Routledge, 100–138.

Woźniak, W. 2013. 'O użyteczności koncepcji paniki moralnej jako ramy analitycznej dla badań nad zjawiskiem przemocy około futbolowej' ['On the moral panics approach as an analytical frame to study football-related violence']. In *Futbol i cała reszta: Sport w perspektywie nauk społecznych* [*Football and All the Rest: Sport from Social Sciences' Perspective*], edited by R. Kossakowski, K. Stachura, A. Strzałkowska and M. Żadkowska. Pszczółki: Wydawnictwo Orbis Exterior, 248–267.

Woźniak, W. 2019. 'Match-fixing in Polish football: Historical perspectives and socio-logical interpretations'. *The International Journal of the History of Sport* 35(2–3): 247–263. doi: 10.1080/09523367.2018.1516640.

Woźniak, W., R. Kossakowski and P. Nosal. 2019. 'A squad with no left wingers: The roots and structure of right-wing and nationalist attitudes among Polish football fans'. *Problems of Post-Communism*. Advance online publication. doi.10.1080/10758216.20 19.1673177.

Wszystko zaczęło się w Bytomiu. 2017. To My Kibice 3(186): 26–43.

Zieliński, R. 1993. *Pamiętnik kibica. Ludzie z piętnem Heysel* [*Fan's Diary. People with the Heysel Sigma*]. Wrocław: Wrocławska Drukarnia.

4 Transformation of women's status and gender relations in Poland

As has been mentioned previously, understanding the 'feminisation' of football stands should be perceived not only in the context of the changes of football fandom itself but also the socio-cultural changes in Polish society. The latter can be explained to a large extent by the 'Westernisation' of Polish society after the political turn in 1989 and the imitative nature of transformation (Jakubowska 2018). However, socio-cultural changes have also been influenced by the legacy and leftovers of socialism (Pine 2002, 98). For this reason, the analysis of gender changes in Poland and other countries in Central Eastern Europe should not uncritically adopt Western perspectives and narratives, but take into account the local context and history. Only a common analysis of global trends and local (national) phenomena can explain the current women's status and perception of gender roles and their influence on football fandom.

Women's status during the communist era

The situation of women in Poland can be seen as the result of the intersection of different influences of Polish history, the Roman Catholic Church, the socio-cultural legacy of communism and the socio-political changes after 1989 (Mikołajczak and Pietrzak 2015). The myth of the 'Mother Pole' (*Matka Polka*) that has indicated a woman's role was born in the period of partitions (1795–1914) during which sovereign Poland did not exist. This pattern of femininity presented women as heroines, capable of multiple sacrifices for the sake of the nation and focused exclusively on the family. Polish women were mainly obligated to raise children (Polish citizens and further soldiers) and take care of their households while their husbands were fighting for the country and preserving the national culture, with special care given to the mother tongue (Imbierowicz 2012). Brian Porter (2005) refers to a Polish woman under the partition in the following way:

> a strong figure, but a thoroughly domesticated one. She remained at home while her husband and sons went off to fight for Poland, but she nonetheless served the nation by educating the young in a patriotic spirit, and by sustaining home and hearth for the partisan fighters. She was characterised by a

limitless ability to endure suffering, as she watched her men sacrifice themselves to the forces of history. And when the men were gone, it fell upon the Matka Polka to keep the nation alive.

(p. 160)

The figure of the 'Mother Pole' was supported by two other symbolic figures: the Holy Mother (*Matka Boska*) and the patroness of the nation, the queen of Poland (*Mater Polonia*). All of them have reinforced the 'ethos of maternity' (Heinen and Portet 2009, 4) and have built a 'constitutive troika' of gender, faith and nation that has dominated Polish identity discourse (Gerber 2010, 33).

The Roman Catholic Church also played an important role during the communist period. It was the only legal institution that could oppose the regime and maintain the Polish national identity (Bystydzienski 2001) and the only place to develop Polish civil society. In this period more than 90% of Poles declared themselves as Catholics and religious events attracted large crowds of people, as evidenced by the pilgrimages of the Polish Pope, John-Paul II, in 1979, 1983 and 1987 and the funeral of Cardinal Stefan Wyszyński in 1981. The Polish Roman Catholic Church had also supported the independent trade union *Solidarność*, which was established in 1980. The meaning of the Church and religion in everyday Poles' lives maintained the traditional gender roles, the myth of the 'Mother Pole', that is, the important role of a woman for the family and the nation.

At the same time, the issue of women's status was included in the regime discourse and the communist state emancipated women in Poland in many ways (Grabowska 2012, 397). The authorities officially recognised women as being equal to men and 'gender equality' was included in the state propaganda. Women started to work outside of the home, and they had the opportunity to undertake full-time or part-time employment, while the state developed the systems of education, childcare and health care. Women received, for example, the right to extended maternal leave (of up to three years) and subsidised childcare, and the right to terminate their pregnancy, for reasons including difficult living conditions (Titkow 1999; Fuszara 2000). The state policy aimed to increase domestic production on the one hand, and, on the other hand, to ensure an adequate level of fertility (Gerber 2010). Therefore, it was focused on the state, not women themselves and their social status.

Women's entry into the labour market, however, did not free them of their house duties or reduce their load. The phenomenon of 'double burden' was common in the case of women – they earned money outside the home and were responsible for the vast majority of domestic labour. As a consequence, the figure of the 'Mother Pole' was maintained during the second half of the twentieth century, although its relation to the religious dimension became less important. At that time, a 'Mother Pole' could be described as a woman 'overloaded, devoting herself to her loved ones, convinced of her irreplaceable skills, a manager of family life' (Titkow, Duch-Krzystoszek and Budrowska 2004, 65). Her life could be characterised as 'a kind of multifunctionality' (Imbierowicz 2012, 141) in realising work, home and family-related duties.

The role that women played in their households has been described by Walczewska (1999) as 'home matriarchy' and the women themselves as 'gastronomic mothers' (p. 165). These terms were related to power that women had over their families, which was limited, however, to the kitchen and small decisions taken in everyday life. It was mainly women who stood in the long queues to buy food and decided, based on the acquired products, on the choice of meals. By feeding their families, they gained 'the monopoly of the kitchen power' (Imbierowicz 2012, 143), thereby reproducing the traditional gender order.

Although private lives were still organised according to the traditional gender division and roles, one could see some positive changes for women in the public sphere. They constituted almost half of the Polish workforce, more than half of the college graduates and the majority of financial sector employees. These ratios situated Poland among the higher places in the different rankings compared to other European countries (Lisowska 1998). However, in spite of some changes, the authors are unanimous that gender equality and women's emancipation under the socialist regime should be perceived as a propaganda slogan rather than a reflection of real state policy (Fuszara 1993, 2000; Grabowska 2012; Leven 2008). First, the authorities were not focused on women and their commitment to equality was low; as a consequence, they directed at women only those policies that were effective for the state. Second, the introduced policies did not challenge traditional gender roles, as evidenced by women's 'double burden'. And third, 'women-friendly' policies were imposed by the state, which had not been supported by Polish citizens (Leven 2008).

Women's status and social roles after 1989

The socio-political transformation in Poland that began in 1989 with its key changes such as the transition from a centrally planned economy to a free market and the foundation of a democratic government influenced women's status, gender construction and gender (in)equalities. Although, as mentioned, the communist state had not managed to introduce real gender equality, it provided various allowances for working mothers. After 1989, the social policy changed, and women were no longer its major beneficiaries. Financial austerity hit welfare spending and 'many programmes that were family-friendly or otherwise helpful to working women were greatly reduced or ended' (Leven 2008, 125). As noted by Pine (2002), 'the retraction of the state has either left a void in these areas, or it has replaced universal *entitlement* with new criteria, often market-driven, of individual *eligibility*' (p. 99). Moreover, the rules introduced by a privatised, market economy have privileged men, and for this reason, among others, the 'new' democracy is called 'masculinist' democracy (Pine 2002).

According to Graff (2007), the transition to democracy has also been perceived as 'remasculinisation of the national culture', which had been reportedly challenged by the communist state. At the same time, it has been supported by a powerful discourse on the return to national sovereignty and traditional values determining, among others, gender roles. Following Graff's considerations,

Gerber (2010) noted that 'resuscitating the pre-socialist gender order status quo, therefore, becomes an important "line of defence" against the intrusiveness of the accession process and a bulwark against the "(re)feminisation" of Poland' (p. 33). One of the indicators of the changes was a reconstruction of the sharp distinction between private and public space (Watson 1993), the former dominated by women and the latter being men's field. With the growing real significance of the public sphere and citizens' influence on this sphere, women's marginalisation, at least at the beginning, increased, as evidenced both by the parliamentary elections in 1989 (13% of women as compared to 20% in 1985) and the forgotten role of many female oppositionists, members of the Solidarność movement.

The parliamentarian debate on abortion that started in 1989 is perceived as the beginning of the feminist movement in Poland, allowing women to articulate their needs and establish women's organisations around them (Fuszara 2005). It is still the issue around which Polish women organise themselves. Their manifestations and other protests related to LGBT rights or artistic freedom (such as the responses to the accusations of insulting religious feelings) reveal that the debates on the influence of the Roman Catholic Church on Polish citizens' lives are still lively. Although the state and the Church are formally separate (based on the Concordat from 1993), there is no doubt that their political, historical and institutional relations are very strong, mainly when the conservative parties are in power.

In the 1990s, the first independent feminist organisations were founded, and gender studies courses, discussions and publications were introduced into the main Polish universities. Nowadays, the number of non-governmental women's organisations is estimated at 200–300 (Ngo.pl, 2019), and they differ internally, as they are focused on different issues, have diverse ideological backgrounds and are more or less related to feminism and its different kinds. However, as the main fields of interest, reproductive rights, political representation and domestic violence (Korolczuk 2014), as well as women's discrimination on the labour market, should be highlighted. In recent years, motherhood and care, as well as labour rights, have been included in the discussion on women's rights.

Polish women participate more in public life, although they still do not stand on an equal footing with men. In the current parliament (2019–2023), 28% of all members are women, which is the highest percentage in Polish history. This growth can be explained, among other things, by the quota regulation introduced during the election in 2011 and the activity of the Women's Congress organisation (Millard 2014; Śledzińska-Simon and Bodnar 2015).

When it comes to women's situation in the labour market, interesting data are provided, among others, by the Women in Work Index (2019). Poland is ranked in eighth place among 36 OECD countries; moreover, it has made the second largest improvement, after Luxembourg, in terms of the accessibility and friendliness of the labour market for women since 2000 (a rise from 11th position). The best indicators for Poland concern the gender pay gap (5% as compared to the average of 15% for OECD countries), a low unemployment rate (5%) and a high full-time employment rate (91%). On the other hand, the percentage of women in the labour market in Poland is lower than the OECD average. The latter data are confirmed by the Polish Statistical Office (2019): the report on the labour force reveals that a significantly higher activity rate characterises men (65%) than women (48%).

Moreover, female Poles have not managed to pierce 'the glass ceiling' as evidenced by the fact that they constitute only 11% of companies' board members (Women in Work Index 2019). When it comes to the companies listed on the Warsaw Stock Exchange, the data reveal that women constitute 12% of their board members, 17% of the supervisory boards, but only 6% of the presidents (Fundacja Liderek Biznesu 2016). As well as vertical segregation in the Polish labour market, horizontal segregation is also observed, as evidenced by women's dominance in health and social care (82%), education (79%), accommodation and gastronomy (70%) (GUS 2018). Women constitute the majority of the workforce in a public sector that is characterised by low salaries.

In spite of their growing professional activity, women are not relieved of household duties, which can be explained by the state cutbacks in expenditure on health services and education (Kowalska, Migalska and Warat 2014, 2), the presence of the traditional gender roles discourse and the long history of the 'Mother Pole' myth. Nowadays, the meaning of this myth has decreased; however, motherhood is still perceived as the main role of woman and her 'natural' and social vocation. The expectations towards women, which also include the embodiment of the beauty ideals, have raised the assumption of (Polish) women's resourcefulness, that is, the capacity to join the roles of a perfect mother, wife and woman (Mikołajczak and Pietrzak 2015).

As noted by Warat (2014), 'the renegotiation of women's roles in the domestic sphere was limited, and they faced the situation of a double burden of career and responsibility for the home' (p. 71). Although Poles more often declare that they live and wish to live in partner relationships (both the woman and the man work and are responsible for home duties) (Boguszewski 2017), the data concerning the division of house duties deny it. In the vast majority of households, women are responsible for washing and ironing, and in two-thirds for cooking and cleaning. Moreover, the traditional female duties remain female, while the duties perceived as 'male' are more often shared by women and men (CBOS 2018a). The state's family policy provides some institutional opportunities for men (fathers) to become more involved in family life, for example, a paid paternity leave of two weeks or parental leave that can be split between the parents. Nevertheless, while paternity leave is becoming more and more popular, parental leave is still used mainly by women (Ministerstwo Rodziny, Pracy i Polityki Społecznej 2019).

A comparative analysis of the data from previous years reveals that although men have not significantly increased their share of house duties, women have sacrificed them much less often (GFK Polonia 2013). This change should be perceived as an indicator of women's growing emancipation and involvement in beyond-home activities, such as work and leisure. Although they still feel they are responsible for the household, they use a lot of facilities (for example ready-made meals or hiring a cleaning person) to reduce time devoted to home duties.

Surveys of public opinion also reveal that social acceptance of women's professional work is growing, and the majority of Poles do not think that women's work has a bad influence on family and do not want women to leave their job even if their partner/husband earns enough to support the family at a satisfactory level (CBOS 2018b).

The perception of the family as one of the most important values has not changed in Poland over the last few decades, although its meaning, attitudes towards the family and the acceptance of alternative forms of marital life and sexuality have significantly changed (Imbierowicz 2012, 149). The acceptance of a late decision to get married, living without marriage, having fewer children and rejection of a church wedding is growing (CBOS 2019). In 2017, the fertility rate was 1,45 and it is worth mentioning that, unlike in previous years, it was nearly the same for people living in the cities and rural areas (characterised before by a bigger fertility rate). However, some differences are still observed in these two areas. In the rural areas, more weddings have a religious character, the number of divorces is smaller and the age of newly-weds is younger (GUS 2019).

The observed changes in decisions on family life may result, at least partially, from the decreasing meaning of religion. Although more than 90% of Poles still declare themselves to be believers, the data regularly provided by the Institute for Catholic Church Statistics since 1980 reveals a decrease of religious practices, including attendance at masses (Annuarium Statisticum Ecclesiae in Polonia AD 2019). The proportion of Poles who state that they live according to the Catholic Church's rules is smaller than it used to be (45% in 2018 as compared to 57% in 2000) in favour of the proportion of those who 'believe in their own way' (46% vs 40%) (CBOS 2018c). However, as mentioned, the influence of the Church is still strong, and its voice remains audible in the political discourse and has an impact on the current law and everyday life. As a consequence, although attitudes towards sexuality have changed, reproductive rights are still limited by, for example, difficult access to some forms of contraception or *in vitro* fertilisation, and as such, they focus to a large extent on feminist movements' activities (Heinen and Porter 2009).

The customary life in contemporary Poland is situated on the several continuums indicated by opposite values: liberal vs conservative, traditional vs modern, national models vs openness to other cultures, religion vs secularism (Łaciak 2015, 365). On the one hand, the liberalisation of practices and opinions concerning celebrations, family forms, sexuality and sexualisation of the body can be observed; on the other hand, this process is perceived by a part of society as the wrong influence of European or American values that threaten the Polish tradition, as illustrated by the debate on Halloween (31 October) and All Saints Day (1 November). To simplify this, one can say that Polish society is divided into two parts: (1) conservative – closely related to the Catholic Church, Polish history and traditions, supporting traditional understanding of family and gender roles; and (2) liberal – advocating a factual separation between the state and the Church that is favourable towards postmaterialist values (Inglehart 1977).

However, there is no doubt that, generally, family life has changed in contemporary Poland, as illustrated, for example, by the larger number of informal relationships, the larger number of homosexual coming-outs and the larger number of divorces. Women, besides their growing presence in the public sphere, have experienced significant changes in their moral lives. As noted by Kurczewski (1999), the emancipation of the body should be perceived as one of the aspects of transformational emancipation in Poland. Several aspects of this phenomenon can be indicated, such as the greater consent to expose and modify the body and the increased interest in sexual and erotic issues. Although these changes concern both men and women, it seems that they have a bigger influence on feminine bodies and sexuality, which has been 'awakened' and is perceived more often from the hedonistic perspective (Jakubowska 2009).

Having a better socio-economic status, achieved due to well-paid jobs and a higher level of education, many Polish women have become more independent, which has affected, among other things, their choices related to leisure time. Here, it is worth noting that although football is still perceived as a 'male' sport discipline (in regard to both players and fans), the percentage of women interested in football has increased. While the step change in 2012 was not surprising (the Euro 2012 co-hosted by Poland), the data reveal that before the World Cup in 2018, the percentage of female Poles interested in football was nearly the same as during the European Championships in 2012 (42% compared to 44%). Interestingly enough, the same data show an increase of the number of men not interested in football (29% in 2018 as compared to 17% in 2012) (CBOS 2018d). Polish women also watch other sports mega-events, such as the Olympic Games, for example before the Winter Olympic Games in 2018, 50% of respondents, both women and men, declared a desire to follow the competition (CBOS 2018e). However, similarly to the previous Olympic Games in Sochi, men declared a desire to watch all broadcasts twice as often as women, which can be explained, among other things, by women's 'double burden' and house duties, as observed in another research (Whiteside and Hardin 2011). There is no doubt that national and club (mainly football) sports attract different audiences and the national audience is much more diverse and inclusive. However, the data concerning the Polish *Ekstraklasa* also confirms a growing women's interest in the sport. As a consequence, sport, and more broadly leisure time, can be perceived as one of the fields of women's emancipation and leisure activities as the acts of resistance towards traditional gender roles (Shaw 1999a, 1999b).

Gender discourse in contemporary Poland

There is no doubt that the situation of Polish women has changed in the last 30 years. The accession of Poland to the European Union in 2004 is perceived as one of the most important factors that have influenced gender equality policy. Although some policy documents were constituted or ratified earlier (for example The Convention on the Elimination of all Forms of Discrimination against Women – 1990), as noted by Warat (2014), 'many regulations were introduced only because Poland was obliged to harmonise the national law with the directives and regulations at EU level' (p. 14). Moreover,

> since the implementation of the Act on the Implementation of Certain Provisions of the European Union on Equal Treatment, the office of the Plenipotentiary [for Equal Treatment] has become the only permanent body that cannot be removed as it is legally protected.
>
> (Warat 2014, 43)

The office was established in 2001 under pressure from the EU authorities. In the following years, it changed its name and the scope of its activities: under right-wing governments it focused on women and family issues and under left-wing governments on equal treatment. Therefore, the office's activity is 'vulnerable to political changes' (*ibidem*) and depends, to a large extent, on current government policy. In addition to the need to adapt to the EU requirements, Polish governments have developed their programmes focused on women and equal treatment, such as The National Action Plan for Equal Treatment (2013).

On the other hand, one can observe the anti-gender movement in Poland and other countries in Central Eastern Europe. According to Korolczuk (2014), they should not be interpreted in the same way as the 'backlash' observed in countries such as the US, but rather as a sign that 'the fight for gender equality is far from over' (p. 52). Although, as mentioned, the accession to the EU is perceived as a milestone in deploying gender equality policy, it has also triggered ideological discourse and actions on the part of Polish conservatives, who are very sceptical about the European Union. For example, during the parliamentary election campaign in 2019, Jarosław Kaczyński, the chairman of the ruling Prawo i Sprawiedliwość (Law and Justice) party, stated:

> We consider the family to be a social unit of fundamental importance for the continuity of generations, for the transmission of the culture of civilisation, for the sustainability of larger communities. We see the family as here, one woman, one man in a permanent relationship and their children. It is the family.[1]

During another event, he said:

> There is an assumption that is often forced upon us: if you want to live like in Europe, it has to be here, in Poland, like in Europe – two dads, two mums, etc. It doesn't have to be like this, and it won't be like this, ladies and gentlemen. We are defending the traditional family, and we are going to defend it. We will affirm it because it is the foundation of everything.[2]

Notoriously, right-wing politicians and their acolytes accuse the EU of being biased towards liberal values and norms that remain at odds with Polish tradition and its (religious) values. This discourse is supported by the hierarchs of the Polish Roman Catholic Church, as illustrated by the words of Archbishop Marek Jędraszewski:

> We had to wait a long time for it.… The red plague no longer walks on our land, but a new neo-Marxist one has appeared, wanting to control our souls, hearts and minds. Not red, but rainbow.[3]

In the same year, in his pastoral letter, Jędraszewski wrote, among other things:

> Gender ideology attempts to blur the natural differences between women and men. Moreover, through aggressive propaganda of LGBT ideology in the name of so-called 'tolerance' and 'progress', it ridicules and mocks the greatest holiness for us. At the same time, people, including believers, are being forced to promote LGBT ideology.
>
> (Jędraszewski 2019)

The meaning of the Roman Catholic Church's traditional and conservative values can be perceived as one of the biggest barriers to women's rights and gender equality in Poland. Paradoxically, the same role is attributed to neoliberalism. As noted by Kowalska, Migalska and Warat (2014), although neoliberalism seems to be gender-neutral, this policy has a lot of negative consequences for women because it is based, among other things, on freedom (instead of social justice and equality), individual choices and responsibility for one's own life and the limited role of the state in social insurance.

For a long time, the Polish feminist movement was based on neoliberalism and attracted mainly well-educated and successful women from the metropolitan cities, businesswomen, professionals or academics, that is, 'the urban Polish intelligentsia' (Grabowska 2014). However, as noted by Grabowska (2012):

> [T]he commitment to liberalism worked as a double-edged sword: while it helped to articulate feminist goals, it also alienated many feminist activists from many women, particularly working-class women, who experienced the devastating effects of neoliberal state policies that the Polish government adopted in the 1990s.
>
> (p. 396)

On the one hand, neoliberal rules favour men on the labour market, and on the other hand, the state policy is focused on women as mothers. Therefore, it is not surprising that beyond feminist organisations created by Polish intelligentsia and based on neoliberal discourse, a second branch of the feminist movement has appeared. It is based on socialism and focuses on labour rights, cooperates with the trade unions and the tenant associations and organises the Social Women's Congress.

The exceptional characteristics of Polish society due to the great influence of the Roman Catholic Church, the geopolitical location and the history resulting from it, as well as the process of 'Westernisation', mean that the fight for gender equality is still ongoing. There is no doubt, however, that in many dimensions one can talk about the emancipation of Polish women, especially well-educated female residents of large cities. Moreover, the results of the parliamentary elections of the last decade show that women more than men support left-wing parties, whose programmes are based, among other things, on secularisation, inclusiveness and identity policies. The increasing social awareness of women, their independence and empowerment (both in individual and social dimensions) influence, at least partially, the social status of men in Polish society.

Although men still constitute the vast majority of the political arena and a majority in the labour market, and their financial situation is better than that of women (Gender Equality Index 2017), the perception of masculinity has changed to some extent. The phenomenon of the 'crisis' or 'reconstruction' of masculinity, related, among other things, to the lost position as the sole breadwinner, the decreasing meaning of more traditional traits, such as the physical strength and growing meaning of the male body, observed in other countries (see, for example, Anderson 2009; Zimbardo and Coulombe 2012), has also been perceived in Poland (Melosik 2002; Wojnicka 2011; Suwada and Plantin 2014). In the context of the 'feminisation of social life' that has influenced gender order and challenged male hegemony, sport, and particularly football, can be perceived as one of the bastions of hegemonic masculinity (Messner 1988). Although, as mentioned, women's interest in football is growing, men still constitute the vast majority in the stands and, as a consequence, can impose the rules in this one of very few male worlds.

Notes

1 Kaczyński J. 2019, quoted after: PolishRadio24.pl. 7 September 2019. Accessed 29 November2019.https://polskieradio24.pl/5/1222/Artykul/2365079,Jaroslaw-Kaczynski-dla-PiS-najwazniejsze-sa-rodzina-oraz-narod.
2 Kaczyński J. 2019, quoted after: wpolityce.pl. 26 September 2019. Accessed 29 November 2019. https://wpolityce.pl/polityka/465634-kaczynski-tradycyjna-rodzina-jest-fundamentem-rozwoju.
3 Jędraszewski M. 2019, quoted after: dziennik.pl. 2 August 2019. Accessed 29 November 2019.https://wiadomosci.dziennik.pl/wydarzenia/artykuly/604141,abp-jedraszewski-msza-powstanie-warszawskie.html.

References

Anderson, E. 2009. *Inclusive Masculinity: The Changing Nature of Masculinities*. New York: Routledge.
Annuarium Statisticum Ecclesiae in Polonia AD 2019. Accessed 3 January 2020. http://iskk.pl/aktualnosci/3-aktualnosci/295-annuarium-statisticum-ecclesiae-in-polonia-2019.

Boguszewski, R. 2017. 'Modele rodziny, podział obowiązków domowych i problemy w rodzinie' ['Family models, sharing of household duties and family problems']. *Opinie i diagnozy* 37. CBOS: Warszawa.

Bystydzienski, J. 2001. 'The feminist movement in Poland: Why so slow?' *Women's Studies International Forum* 24(5): 501–511.

CBOS 2018a. *Kobiety i mężczyźni w domu* [*Women and Men in the House*]. Report 127/2018. Accessed 16 September 2019 www.cbos.pl/SPISKOM.POL/2018/K_127_18.PDF.

CBOS 2018b. *Kobiety i mężczyźni na rynku pracy* [*Women and Men in the Labour Market*]. Report 128/2018. Accessed 16 September 2019 www.cbos.pl/SPISKOM. POL/2018/K_128_18.PDF.

CBOS 2018c. *Religijność Polaków i ocena sytuacji Kościoła katolickiego* [*Religiousness of Poles and Evaluation of the Situation of the Catholic Church*]. Report 147/2018. Accessed 16 September 2019 www.cbos.pl/SPISKOM.POL/2018/K_147_18.PDF.

CBOS 2018d. *Przed mundialem w Rosji: zainteresowanie piłką nożną i ocena PZPN* [*Before the World Cup in Russia: Interest in Football and Evaluation of the Polish Football Association*]. Report 85/2018. Accessed 16 September 2019 www.cbos.pl/ SPISKOM.POL/2018/K_085_18.PDF.

CBOS 2018e. *Zainteresowanie igrzyskami w Pjongczang i ocena szans medalowych Polaków* [*Interest in the Pyongyang Olympics and the Assessment of Poles' Medal Opportunities*]. Report 20/2018. Accessed 16 September 2019 www.cbos.pl/ SPISKOM.POL/2018/K_020_18.PDF.

CBOS, 2019. *Alternatywne modele życia rodzinnego w ocenie społecznej* [*Alternative Models of Family Life in Social Opinion*]. Report 20/2018. Accessed 16 September 2019 www.cbos.pl/SPISKOM.POL/2019/K_042_19.PDF.

Fundacja L. B. 2016. *Kobiety we władzach spółek giełdowych w Polsce* [Women in the boards of listed companies in Poland]. Accessed 19 May 2018. www.fundacjaliderekbiznesu. pl/pliki/Raport_FLB_20-05_Final.pdf.

Fuszara, M. 1993. 'Abortion and the formation of the public sphere in Poland'. In *Gender Politics and Post-communism*, edited by N. Funk and M. Mueller. New York: Routledge, 241–252.

Fuszara, M. 2000. 'New gender relationships in Poland in 1990s'. In *Reproducing Gender: Politics, Publics, and Everyday Life after Socialism*, edited by S. Gal and G. Kligman. Princeton: Princeton University Press, 259–285.

Fuszara, M. 2005. 'Between feminism and the Catholic Church: The women's movement in Poland'. *Sociologický Časopis/Czech Sociological Review* 41(6): 1057–1075.

Gender Equality Index 2017. European Institute for Gender Equality, October 10. Accessed 19 May 2018. https://eige.europa.eu/publications/gender-equality-index-2017-measuring-gender-equality-european-union-2005-2015-report.

Gerber, A. 2010. 'The letter versus the spirit: Barriers to meaningful implementation of gender equality policy in Poland'. *Women's Studies International Forum* 33(1): 30–37. doi: 10.1016/j.wsif.2009.11.007.

GFK Polonia 2013. 'Prace domowe wciąż w większości wykonują' kobiety' [The majority of housework is still done by women]'. *Wirtualne media*, April 7. Accessed 19 May 2018. www.wirtualnemedia.pl/artykul/prace-domowe-wciaz-w-wiekszosci-wykonuja-kobiety.

Grabowska, M. 2012. 'Bringing the second world in: Conservative revolution(s), socialist legacies, and transnational silences in the trajectories of Polish feminism'. *Signs* 37(2): 385–411. doi: 10.1086/661728.

Grabowska, M. 2014. 'Culture war or "business as usual"? Recent instances, and the historical origins, of a "backlash" against women's and sexual rights in Poland'. In

Anti-gender Movements on the Rise? Strategising for Gender Equality in Central and Eastern Europe. Berlin: Heinrich Böll Foundation, 54–64.

Graff, A. 2007. 'The land of real men and women: Gender and EU accession in three Polish weeklies'. *Journal of International Institute* 15(1). Accessed 19 May 2018. http://hdl.handle.net/2027/spo.4750978.0015.107.

GUS 2018. *Dzień Kobiet 8 marca 2018* [*Women's Day 8 March 2018*]. Accessed 19 May 2018 https://stat.gov.pl/infografiki-widzety/infografiki/infografika-dzien-kobiet-08-03-2018-r-,25,3.html.

GUS 2019. *Informacja o sytuacji społeczno-gospodarczej kraju w 2018r* [*Socio-economic Situation of the Country*]. Warszawa: GUS.

Heinen, J and S. Porter. 2009. *Region, Politics and Gender Equality in Poland*. Berlin: Heinrich-Böll-Stiftung.

Imbierowicz, A. 2012. 'The Polish mother on the defensive? The transformation of the myth and its impact on the motherhood of Polish women'. *Journal of Education, Culture and Society* 1: 140–153.

Inglehart, R. 1977. *The Silent Revolution. Changing Values and Political Styles among Western Publics*. Princeton: Princeton University Press.

Jakubowska, H. 2009. *Socjologia ciała* [*Sociology of the Body*]. Poznań: Wydawnictwo Naukowe UAM.

Jakubowska, H. 2018. 'Poland: Underrepresentation and misrecognition of women in sport leadership'. In *Gender Diversity in European Sport Governance*, edited by A. Elling, J. Hovden and A. Knoppers. Abingdon: Routledge, 59–69.

Jędraszewski, M. 2019. '*Totus Tuus' Modlitewny maraton za Kościół i Ojczyznę* [*'Totus Tuus'. A Prayer Marathon for Church and Homeland*]. September 28. Accessed 3 January 2020. https://diecezja.pl/aktualnosci/totus-tuus-modlitewny-maraton-za-kosciol-i-ojczyzne/.

Korolczuk, E. 2014. '"The war on gender" from a transnational perspective: Lessons for feminist strategising'. In *Anti-gender Movements on the Rise? Strategising for Gender Equality in Central and Eastern Europe*. Berlin: Heinrich Böll Foundation, 43–53.

Kowalska, B., A. Migalska and M. Warat. 2014. *Who Won the Polish Transformation? Gender Dimensions of Reforms in Poland*. Working Paper no. 1.7 'Gender Equality and Quality of Life – State of Art Report'. Cracow: Jagiellonian University.

Kurczewski, J. 1999. 'Transformation as Emancipation'. *Polish Sociological Review* 126: 197–221.

Łaciak, B. 2015. 'Podsumowanie' ['Conclusion']. In *Obyczajowość polska początku XXI wieku. Przemiany, nowe trendy, zróżnicowania*, [Polish customs of the beginning of the 21st century. Changes, new trends, differentiations], edited by J. Arcimowicz, M. Bieńsko and B. Łaciak. Warszawa: ŻAK Wydawnictwo Akademickie, 365–378.

Leven, B. 2008. 'Poland's transition and new opportunities for women'. *Feminist Economics* 14(1): 123–136. doi: 10.1080/13545700701716631.

Lisowska, E. 1998. 'Women Business Proprietors in Poland'. *Women and Business* 3–4: 29–37.

Melosik, Z. 2002. *Kryzys męskości w kulturze współczesnej* [*The Crisis of Masculinity in Contemporary Culture*]. Poznań: Wolumin.

Messner, M. A. 1988. 'Sports and male domination: The female athlete as contested ideological terrain'. *Sociology of Sport Journal* 5(3): 197–211. doi: 10.1123/ssj.5.3.197.

Mikołajczak, M. and J. Pietrzak. 2015. 'A broader conceptualization of sexism: The case of Poland'. In *Psychology of Gender Through the Lens of Culture: Theories and Applications*, edited by S. Safdar and N. Kosakowska-Berezecka. New York: Springer, 169–191.

Millard, F. 2014. 'Not much happened: The impact of gender quotas in Poland'. *Communist and Post-Communist Studies* 47(1), 1–11. doi: 10.1016/j.postcomstud.2014.01.004.

Ministerstwo Rodziny, Pracy i Polityki Społecznej. 2019. *Tatusie na urlopach* [*Dads on the Leaves*]. October 25. Accessed 3 January 2020. www.gov.pl/web/rodzina/tatusiowie-na-urlopach.

Ngo.pl 2019. Portal organizacji pozarządowych. [Non-government organisations portal] Accessed 3 January 2020.

Pine, F. 2002. 'Retreat to the household? Gendered domains in postsocialist Poland'. In *Postsocialism: Ideals, Ideologies and Practices in Eurasia*, edited by C. Hann. London: Routledge, 95–113.

Polish Statistical Office. 2019. *Aktywność ekonomiczna ludności Polski IV kwartał 2018 r* [*Labour Force Survey in Poland IV Quarter 2018*]. Accessed 19 May 2018. https:// stat.gov.pl/obszary-tematyczne/rynek-pracy/pracujacy-bezrobotni-bierni-zawodowo-wg-bael/aktywnosc-ekonomiczna-ludnosci-polski-iv-kwartal-2018-roku,4,32.html#.

Porter, B. 2005. 'Hetmanka and Mother: Representing the Virgin Mary in modern Poland'. *Contemporary European History* 14: 151–170. doi: 10.1017/S0960777305 002298.

Shaw, S. 1999a. 'Conceptualizing resistance: Towards a framework for understanding leisure as political practice'. Paper presented at Ninth Canadian Congress on Leisure Research, Nova Scotia – Acadia University – Canada, 12–15 May 1999.

Shaw, S. 1999b. 'Gender and leisure'. In *Leisure Studies at the Millennium*, edited by T. L. Burton and E. L. Jackson. Stage College: Venture Publishing, 271–281.

Suwada, K. and L. Plantin. 2014. "On fatherhood, masculinities, and family policies in Poland and Sweden—a comparative study." *Polish Sociological Review* 4(188): 509–524.

Śledzińska-Simon, A. and A. Bodnar. 2015. *Between Symbolism and Incrementalism: Moving Forward with the Gender Equality Project in Poland*. EUI Working Paper LAW 2015/30.

Titkow, A. 1999. 'Poland, new gender contract in formation'. *Polish Sociological Review* 3(127): 377–395.

Titkow A., D. Duch-Krzystoszek and B. Budrowska. 2004. *Nieodpłatna praca kobiet. Mity, realia, perspektywy* [*Women's Unpaid Work. Myths, Realities, Prospects*]. Warszawa: Wydawnictwo Instytutu Filozofi i Socjologii PAN.

Walczewska S. 1999. *Damy, rycerze i feministki. Kobiecy dyskurs emancypacyjny w Polsce* [*Ladies, Knights and Feminists. Female Emancipatory Discourse in Poland*]. Kraków: eFKa.

Warat, M. 2014. *Development of Gender Equality Policies in Poland: A Review of Success and Limitations*. Working paper no. 2.2 Gender Equality Policy in Poland. Cracow: Jagiellonian University.

Watson, P. 1993. 'Eastern Europe silent revolution: Gender'. *Sociology* 27(3): 471–487.

Whiteside E. and M. Hardin. 2011. 'Women (not) watching women: Leisure time, television, and implications for televised coverage of women's sports'. *Communication, Culture and Critique* 4(2): 122–143. doi: 10.1111/j.1753–9137.2011.01098.x.

Wojnicka, K. 2011. 'Reconstructing men and masculinity à la polonaise. Men and masculinities around the world'. In *Transforming Men's Practices*, edited by E. Ruspini, J. Hearn, B. Pease and K. Pringle. New York: Palgrave Macmillan, 71–83.

Women in Work Index. 2019. Accessed 3 January 2020. www.pwc.co.uk/services/ economics-policy/insights/women-in-work-index.html.

Zimbardo, Ph. and N. Coulombe. 2012. *The Demise of Guys: Why Boys Are Struggling and What We Can Do About It*. Amazon.com Services LLC.

5 How can we explore female fandom?

This chapter will present a methodological approach to our complex and large-scale empirical investigation, which combines both quantitative and qualitative methods. By doing so, it will provide a rationale for the selection of three metropolitan clubs (Legia Warszawa, Lechia Gdańsk and Lech Poznań) as the prime focus of the studies. Furthermore, it will present in detail the purpose, scope and use of a wide range of research methods deployed when we gathered the data. The empirical findings are critical to this book; therefore, this chapter will highlight the rigorous methodological measures undertaken to provide the solid evidence that underpinned the overall analysis.

The selection of the three clubs: Legia Warsaw, Lech Poznań and Lechia Gdańsk

The Polish *Ekstraklasa* is situated on the periphery of European club football. Despite the national team being relatively highly ranked in the FIFA ranking, Polish clubs are usually eliminated from European club football competitions at very early stages and this situation has become worse in the last decade. This is the result of several independent factors, including the lack of a professional and comprehensive approach on the part of the Polish Football Association (PZPN) to youth academies, clubs' short-term thinking when investing in players and the 'muscle drain', which causes the migration of talented players to more affluent and professional leagues. This should not be a surprise given the limited economic capacity of the Polish football league (*Ekstraklasa*). The average annual revenue of football clubs is estimated to be around 9.5 million euro (Deloitte 2019). They report lower revenues than the average clubs in the second divisions of the Big Five – England, Germany, Spain, Italy and France. It ranks the *Ekstraklasa* on the periphery of European club football despite the size of the country and the popularity of football in Poland. Having said that, the founding assumption of this study is that the Polish *Ekstraklasa* is a case of a peripheral league with low budgets and a lack of success in European club competitions.

Zooming in, the *Ekstraklasa* consists of a diversity of clubs of very different social (fan base), economic and infrastructural capacity. For the sake of this study, we select three clubs as the purposive sample assuming that they represent 'the purest or most clear-cut instance of the phenomenon researchers are interested in' (Palys 2008, 697). We expected that Legia Warszawa, Lech Poznań and Lechia Gdańsk (hereafter: LLL) would stand out from the rest of the league in regard to the presence of women in the stands. The funding assumption was based on the fact that the emancipation of women is far more advanced in metropolitan cities, particularly in clubs that traditionally have a large number of fans and also modern facilities at their disposal. There is little doubt that Warszawa, Poznań and Gdańsk are among the most dynamically developing cities in Poland. Their rich and attractive labour markets attract a young creative class that contributes to the economic boom and vibrant culture of those cities. Also, politics-wise, these metropolitan cities are more exposed to Western cultural lifestyles being populated by the well-educated, open-minded, liberal middle class. Thus, in metropolitan cities, women have relatively more opportunities for professional development, may enjoy a higher social status and perform social roles traditionally occupied by males including in families (for example breadwinners). In other words, in Warszawa, Poznań and Gdańsk, there are the highest number of socially emancipated and financially independent women who could be potentially attracted by the football culture as they operate in a more inclusive environment and have key resources to overcome social barriers.

Furthermore, LLL are relatively big and wealthy football clubs. In 2017, they reported the highest revenues in the *Ekstraklasa*, that is, Legia 100.2 million PLN, Lech 57.14 million PLN and Lechia 48.34 million PLN (Deloitte 2019), standing out from the rest of the football league. In addition, they enjoy some of the biggest fan bases across the country that use the large and exceptionally modern facilities; each has a capacity of over 30,000 seats. For the purpose of the research, it is important that those stadiums have distinct sectors for ultras, families, regular fans and VIP zones (namely 'skyboxes'). Last but not least, each of the three clubs also stands out as an organisation, with its size and corporate flavour.

In other words, LLL are perfect examples of modern football clubs in Poland and as such are expected to be frontrunners of the transformation of football, attracting new fans, in particular women. So, the selection of the three football clubs is supposed to fit the model of 'extreme or deviant case sampling' (Palys 2008) to focus on football clubs in which the condition for football feminisation seems to be the most favourable. It was also assumed that the process of football feminisation would be in the most (mature) advanced stage, which would allow us to examine in depth the research phenomenon.

Although the three clubs mentioned are at the centre of our research, in the quantitative part of the analysis, we have included the answers of the fans from other Polish clubs who completed the online questionnaire. Moreover, we refer, to a small extent, to the data gathered for other research of Polish fans conducted previously by one of us – Radosław Kossakowski (data from research grant funded by Polish National Centre of Science, no. 2013/09/D/HS/6/00238).

Main research methods

The study uses 'mixed-method research', which integrates both qualitative and quantitative data within a single study (Brannen 2005). The choice to implement 'mixed-method research' is dictated by the complexity of the research problem and multidimensional character of the project. In this respect, mixed methods have strong potential and help provide a detailed exploration of women entering the football culture, which could not be achieved by either solely quantitative or qualitative research (Creswell 2013). In respect of 'mixed methods', the project adopts a 'convergent parallel' model in which the qualitative and quantitative data is collected separately and analysed independently in addressing the research questions (Halcomb and Hickman 2015, 8).

Online survey

The study was based on two core pillars: an *online survey* among fans and in-depth interviews with different actors. Surveying football fans is an extremely challenging endeavour due to the limited accessibility of the research population and also ambiguity in defining football fans. Football fans are an exemplary case of hard-to-reach groups due to their hermetic culture (Kossakowski 2017). This is shown perfectly in numerous previous studies in which surveys were used as a method of collecting empirical data (for example Kossakowski and Besta 2018). Taking into account radical constraints regarding access to personal data of fans, there was no option but to approach them directly via social media. In order to do so, a link to the survey was posted on the LLL clubs' official social media profiles (for example Facebook) and websites to ensure it would be available to a considerable number of fans.

We were fully aware of advantages and limitations regarding surveying football fans (Waddington, Dunning and Murphy 1996; Williams 1996) and also using e-surveys to access the views of football fans (Gibbons and Nuttall 2012); nonetheless, we decided to adopt it as the most effective tool. Using e-surveys to access football fans has become increasingly popular (Gibbons and Nuttall 2012), and discussions about methodological aspects of the use of online surveys received some research attention. Eysenbach and Wyatt (2002), for example, argue that the self-selection of respondents for Internet e-surveys is a form of bias. In our study, the survey could appeal more to those emotionally engaged in the club and also attract disproportionately more female fans as they could find the topic of high relevance. A younger generation predominantly uses social media and hard-core fans most frequently visit official club profiles; there-fore, these categories are probably over-represented in the sample. Also, it is undoubtedly biased against those that are digitally (social media) excluded and those that do not follow the club regularly.

Over-representation of the most loyal fans in sociological studies on football fans, in particular season ticket holders (Malcolm, Jones and Waddington 2000), has been discussed on several occasions. For example, Rex Nash (1997) notes that 'clearly regular attendees are usually systematically over-represented in such surveys, and those either outside altogether or on the periphery have less input' (p. 128). Being aware of this bias and having no intention of presenting results as representative, we celebrate a disproportionately large number of responses from ultra fans because this category of fans has the biggest impact on social and cultural norms in the stadium. They also tend to represent the most radical parts of football crowds, which – based on our earlier analysis of the grass-roots ultras' magazine *To My Kibice* (TMK) – demonstrates an exemplary case of hegemonic masculinity (Antonowicz, Jakubowska and Kossakowski 2020).

The data collection process with the use of a survey was lengthy, spanning from September 2017 to May 2018. In principle, the survey was conducted in two separate phases: (1) with fans from LLL; and (2) with other smaller clubs in Poland. However, the survey was identical for all fans. The reason behind adding fans from other (small) clubs to the survey was simple – they serve as a control group to build comparative analysis while examining the specific aspects of female fandom. The questionnaire contains 31 questions (including one open question), and data were only collected from completed questionnaires (only the open question could be left blank).

Nearly 4,300 fans completed the questionnaire (Table 5.1), including 961 female fans, who constituted 23% of the sample.

Interviews

The second core pillar of our study comprises individual semi-structured, in-depth interviews (IDIs) conducted with football fans from Legia, Lech and Lechia. Interviewing is one of the most popular methods of data collection and is aimed at exploring in-depth experiences of interviewees, particularly when topics are very sensitive. And football fandom is a sensitive issue as it often involves confession about emotional attachments, opinions about unlawful incidents and in this case also attitudes towards female fans. Providing comfortable and safe conditions is particularly important because football fans in Poland are stigmatised by mainstream society due to 'moral panic' (Cohen 2011) produced by mass media and public authorities (Antonowicz and Grodecki 2018). Also, not everyone feels equally comfortable talking about unlawful incidents in football stadiums, particularly if one was involved passively or actively. There is

Table 5.1 Number of respondents – online survey

	Supported football club	No.
1	Legia Warszawa	1,799
2	Lech Poznań	1,413
3	Lechia Gdańsk	362
4	Other clubs	730
	Total	**4,277**

little doubt that ultra zones remain under the indirect control of militant groups that like to keep fans' business in-house.

The length of each interview was scheduled for 45–60 minutes, although in practice they ranged from 25 to 90 minutes depending on interviewees' engagement in conversations, their availability and their readiness to address our questions. In general, interviewees were engaged, informative and also supportive in linking us with other potential interviewees; however, we also encountered situations where the interviews were called off for no particular reason and contacts were lost.

The recruitment of interviewees was very much based on networks that we have built while doing other research on football fandom. However, the significant difference between this project and previous investigations was the considerable number of female fans that were largely outside our networks. So, we adopted a wide range of strategies – among which the most frequently used was snowballing – to reach the specific type of fans required for the sample. The interviews were conducted in person by the authors in public places (for example coffee shops, restaurants, offices) in which interviewed fans could feel comfortable to express their views and opinions. Each of the conversations was recorded (with the permission of the interviewees) and subsequently transcribed for the sake of analysis.

The interviews were semi-structured, which means they were carried out according to the script that contained topics to be raised and questions to be asked if appropriate. Due to considerable differences between interviewees (age, social status, engagement in football culture), we gave ourselves significant flexibility to organise individual interviews in a way that would make the most natural conversation, but under control. There were three scenarios of IDIs prepared separately for (1) female fans, (2) male fans (Table 5.2) and (3) other actors within the football field. The scenarios have a common core but also contain several questions specific for each group.

The category of 'other actors' refers to people performing a wide range of important roles in Polish football, for example club managers, sponsors, club department members or employees of the Polish Football Association or *Ekstraklasa*. We selected particular individuals ($N=10$) to obtain different (than fans') perspectives on female fans and also insight or (business) knowledge to which we have very limited access. Expert interviews have long been popular in social sciences, particularly in investigating problems to which research has limited access in person. 'Conducting expert interviews can serve to shorten

Table 5.2 Structure of the sample of fans interviewed

Supported football club	Male	Female
Legia Warszawa	10	4
Lech Poznań	6	9
Lechia Gdańsk	5	11
Total	**21**	**24**

time-consuming data-gathering processes, particularly if the experts are seen as "crystallisation points" for practical insider knowledge and are interviewed as surrogates for a wider circle of players' (Bogner, Littig and Menz 2009, 2). The football world is business, and the corporate world also protects its secrets from researchers. So there is no other way to learn about clubs' approach to female fans than to obtain information from those close to them (or part of them) but also to learn how they see the process of feminisation.

Complementary research methods

To complete the data gathered from the interviews and the questionnaire, we decided to use supplementary research methods. We are convinced that the football fandom culture is a complex social phenomenon that is extremely difficult to investigate; therefore, understanding it is only possible through the use of differentiated methodology and numerous data collection techniques. For this reason, we decided to include in our project: (1) analysis of the grass-roots ultras' magazine; (2) participatory observations; (3) analyses of merchandising offers; (4) netnography of fans' forums and profiles of female groups in social media. We have collected a significant amount of data for this research, which helps us to have a better understanding of multiple aspects of the investigated process; however, as usually happens due to the limited length and clarity of reasoning, we will not be able to use all the gathered empirical data.

TMK – narratives

The research project began with a content analysis of the grass-roots ultras' magazine *To My Kibice* (TMK), the title of which can be translated as 'We are the fans'. TMK belongs to an increasingly popular type of fan magazine, which was developed from popular home-made football fanzines in the 1980s (Haynes 1995). The latter, however, were linked to particular clubs or firms, documenting their activities alone, while modern ultras' magazines (for example TMK) cover the entire country. TMK relies on contributions from fans, namely the representatives of ultra groups, which make them genuine, reliable first-hand sources of knowledge about the views and performance of ultra fans. In spite of their grass-roots character, in several countries, such as Spain (*Super Hincha*), the Netherlands (*Panenka Magazine*), Germany (*Blickfang ultra*), Italy (*Supertifo*), Turkey (*SopaliPankrat Fanzine*) and of course Poland (*TMK*), such magazines enjoy considerable popularity among football fans. TMK is also made by fans for fans, and therefore it offers first-hand narratives for which the authors (usually hidden behind nicknames) have a particularly good sense of the audience to which they also belong. In short, fans' stories are a form of narrative and 'the most typical form of social life.... People tell stories to entertain, to teach and to learn, to ask for an interpretation and to give one' (Czarniawska 2004, 650). We also state that 'narrative knowledge tells the story of human intentions and deeds, and situates them in time and space. It mixes objective and subjective aspects, relating the world as people see it, often substituting chronology for causality' (Czarniawska 2004, 651). Examining TMK helped to have better understanding of ultras fans who – based on previous studies (Kossakowski, Szlendak and Antonowicz 2018) – exercise the greatest influence upon the fandom culture by setting social norms of behaviour in the stands. Therefore, for the sake of this research project, TMK is considered to be a collection of match day diaries of Polish ultras, from which this study addresses the social roles that women performed in the ultras' culture. Although personal narratives do not necessarily offer universal truths, documentary materials may provide valuable insight, often helping to create an account of internal group hierarchies, informal norms and values.

The analysis of TMK has a supplementary character, but fans' narratives are the most accurate sources for understanding largely inaccessible communities. TMK offers genuine fans' diaries, from which we can draw the knowledge needed for analysis and avoid the interviewer effect, which can mislead an entire investigation. The analysis of TMK supplied us with a wide spectrum of narratives, proving an opportunity to understand better and critically validate data collected from other sources.

Participatory observation

An important part of collecting data is 'participatory observations', which is one of the primary sources of collecting data about, and more importantly understanding, the social and cultural norms of football fandom. Of course, football fans are the specific socio-cultural group that need to be examined within the context of the match situation. Although being a football fan cannot be limited only to match days and stadium attendance, football games are the essence of fandom. At the heart of studies lies the question about performing football fandom, namely social and cultural practices performed during the games that make this world so special. During the games, traditional social and cultural norms are negotiated (if not suspended) and a new social order emerges (Ben-Porat 2009).

Numerous previous studies underscore the importance of the exceptional atmosphere during football games (for example Wilhelm 2018) that requires participation from researchers. Football fandom transforms into a *sui generis* social phenomenon that cannot be fully understood relying solely on secondary data, TV coverage or observation from a long distance. Before participatory observations, we acquired a considerable amount of qualitative data through both IDIs and content analysis of TMK. In particular, participatory observations (Lavenda and Schultz 2012) provided us with an opportunity to contextualise and make sense of information that was previously collected.

The book's authors are quite regular match-goers with solid prior knowledge about the atmosphere in the stands. However, there is a significant difference between enjoying football games and conducting participatory observations with a specific focus on issues under investigation. Participatory observations also require methodological rigour and need to be conducted with a certain structure. Thus, before we started the process of participatory observations, the structure of observations had been established to be reported shortly after the game. We also assumed that the gender of the researcher might have an influence on the way she/he sees the course of events in the stadium, particularly if the research object is embedded in gender sensitivity. In general, to avoid researchers' influence, almost all participatory observations were conducted in teams of at least two researchers of both genders who individually reported their observations. This research design helped us to capture the course of events in the stands from (frequently) very different research perspectives. Altogether, the team carried out between 30–50 observations on different sectors of football stadiums in Gdańsk, Poznań and Warszawa.

Merchandising

The modernisation of football transformed it into a business project, and it does have far-reaching consequences. Football fans – whether they like it or not – are being increasingly seen as customers of entertainment. Thus, the proxy for clubs' sensitivity, openness and recognition of women as fans of (potentially) separate needs is merchandising offers tailored to female needs. The focus of the research was on official fan shops at the three researched clubs (Legia, Lech, Lechia), which sell their products online. It aimed to address the following simple questions: (1) whether the needs of female fans are recognised in commercial offers; (2) how important female fans are for the merchandising businesses of the clubs; (3) what profile of 'female fan' emerged from products sold by the fans' shops.

Netnography of female fans' groups

The last, but perhaps not the least important method used in the project is netnographic analysis (Kozinets 2009) of online cultures and communities formed through computer-mediated communications. Netnography is an interpretative methodological instrument that was used in our study for examining social media profiles of female fan groups. It was based on the assumption that the popular image of female fans is built and adhered to through social media. During the netnography concerning the 2016/2017 season, nine female fan groups' profiles on Facebook (six related to the particular clubs of the *Ekstraklasa* and three not related to a particular club) were analysed.

The analysis conducted in this book is based on empirical evidence collected during the project. All gathered data were interpreted with the use of an analytical framework, which was established as key aspects of female fandom. It consists of: (1) initiation into football fandom; (2) form of participation in football games; (3) socio-cultural practices; (4) artefacts with special focus on merchandising offers; (5) reasoning for following a football club and attending matches; (6) the stadium as a social space that is open to female fans; (7) perception and treatment of female fans by male fans and other actors.

The multiple research methods helped us to not only gather a wide range of evidence but also to cross-check the information acquired and finally to contextualise it. The combination of rich quantitative and qualitative data provides a solid foundation for building more general conclusions about female fandom and the impact of female fans on the football fandom culture. To the best of our knowledge, the scale of this study and the range of methodological instruments rank it among the biggest projects ever conducted about female fandom. Having said that, we must acknowledge that the research was conducted in Poland, and therefore it is analysed within a certain socio-cultural and political environment. Nevertheless, the project aspires to contribute to an ongoing discussion about the social and cultural mechanisms surrounding women entering 'men's territory' and how that entrance affects male fans as well as the internal dynamics of football fandom under the influence of women entering football stadiums.

References

Antonowicz, D. and M. Grodecki. M. 2018. 'Missing the goal: Policy evolution towards football-related violence in Poland (1989–2012)'. *International Review for the Sociology of Sport* 53(4): 490–511. doi: 10.1177/1012690216662011.

Antonowicz, D., H. Jakubowska and R. Kossakowski. 2020. 'Marginalised, patronised and instrumentalised: Polish female fans in the ultras' narratives'. *International Review for the Sociology of Sport* 55(1): 60–76. doi: 10.1177/1012690218782828.

Ben-Porat, A. 2009. 'Not just for men: Israeli women who fancy football'. *Soccer & Society* 10(6): 883–896. doi: 10.1080/14660970903240030.

Bogner, A., B. Littig and W. Menz, eds. 2009. *Interviewing Experts*. London: Palgrave Macmillan.

Brannen, J. 2005. 'Mixing methods: The entry of qualitative and quantitative approaches into the research process'. *International Journal of Social Research Methodology: Theory and Practice* 8(3): 173–184. doi: 10.1080/13645570500154642.

Cohen, S. 2011. *Folk Devils and Moral Panics: The Creation of the Mods and Rockers*. Abingdon: Routledge.

Creswell, J. 2013. *Research Design: Qualitative, Quantitative, and Mixed Methods Approaches*. Thousand Oaks: Sage Publications.

Czarniawska, B. 2004. *Narratives in Social Science Research*. Thousand Oaks: Sage.

Deloitte. 2019. *Piłkarska liga finansowa – rok 2018. Finansowe zaplecze ekstraklasy* [*Football Financial League – Year 2018. Financial Background of the League*]. Warszawa: Deloitte.

Eysenbach, G. and J. Wyatt. 2002. 'Using the Internet for surveys and health research'. *Journal of Medical Internet Research* 4(2), E13. doi: 10.2196/jmir.4.2.e13.

Gibbons, T. and D. Nuttall. 2012. 'Using e-surveys to access the views of football fans within online communities'. *Sport in Society* 15(9): 1228–1241. doi: 10.1080/17430437. 2012.690401.

Halcomb, E. and L. Hickman. 2015. 'Mixed methods research'. *Nursing Standard*, 29(32): 41–47. doi: 10.7748/ns.29.32.41.e8858.

Haynes, R. 1995. *The Football Imagination: The Rise of Football Fanzine Culture*. Aldershot: Arena.

Kossakowski, R. 2017. 'Where are the hooligans? Dimensions of football fandom in Poland'. *International Review for the Sociology of Sport* 52(6): 693–711. doi: 10.1177/1012690215612458.

Kossakowski, R. and T. Besta. 2018. 'Football, conservative values, and a feeling of oneness with the group: A study of Polish football fandom'. *East European Politics and Societies: And Cultures* 32(4): 866–891. doi: 10.1177/0888325418756991.

Kossakowski, R., T. Szlendak and D. Antonowicz. 2018. 'Polish ultras in the post-socialist transformation'. *Sport in Society* 21(6): 854–69. doi: 10.1080/17430437.2017.1300387.

Kozinets R. V. 2009. *Netnography: Doing Ethnographic Research Online.* London: Sage Publications Ltd.

Lavenda, R. and E. Schultz. 2012. *Anthropology. What Does It Mean to Be a Human?* Oxford: Oxford University Press.

Malcolm, D., I. Jones and I. Waddington. 2000. 'The people's game? Football spectatorship and demographic change'. *Soccer & Society* 1(1), 129–143. doi: 10.1080/14660970008721254.

Nash, R. 1997. 'Research note: Concept and method in researching the football crowd'. *Leisure Studies* 16(2): 127–131. doi: 10.1080/026143697375458.

Palys, T. 2008. 'Purposive sampling'. *The Sage Encyclopedia of Qualitative Research Methods*, 2, 697–698.

Waddington, I., E. Dunning and P. Murphy. 1996. 'Research note: Surveying the social composition of football crowds'. *Leisure Studies* 15: 209–214. doi: 10.1080/02614 3696375611.

Wilhelm, J. L. 2018. 'Atmosphere in the home stadium of Hertha BSC (German Bundesliga): Melodies of moods, collective bodies, and the relevance of space'. *Social & Cultural Geography*. doi: 10.1080/14649365.2018.1514646.

Williams, J. 1996. 'Surveying the social composition of football crowds: A reply to Waddington, Dunning and Murphy'. *Leisure Studies* 15(3): 215–219. doi: 10.1080/0261 43696375620.

Part III

Performing female fandom in the male reservoir

6   Women's initiation into football fandom

Men as brokers

Football fandom is a collective phenomenon and becoming a fan is a social process that is undergone through relatives and close peers. Ben-Porat (2010) notes that 'supporting a football club is a lifelong project that begins at an early age and ends with the life of the fan' (p. 277). As men dominate as fans, it is obvious that they introduce other boys and girls to this domain, providing culturally and historically well-embedded codes concerning gender identity. Men perform the role of 'significant others' and many pieces of research from different regions confirm it. For example, Kevin Dixon, in researching English female fans, mentions that 'of those participants whose fandom started in early childhood, all were introduced to the practice by influential "male" figures' (2015, 641). A similar pattern was identified by Ben-Porat (2009) in his studies on Israeli football fandom in which the role of male broker was highlighted on numerous occasions by interviewed female fans.

The figure of the father is central to socialisation into football fandom, particularly in childhood; however, other male agents – such as boyfriend/ husband, brother, male friend or other male members of the family – can also be important as gatekeepers and guides through the hermetic and masculine subculture (Ben-Porat 2009). It is interesting to note that some fans admit that their fathers treated their children equally in terms of football passion:

> Being a Besiktas fan was a family thing for both my brother and me. My father treated us equally. As the proud father of two fans, he often boasted about our devotion to the team. I never felt that I was a lesser fan because of my gender.
>
> (Erhart 2011, 84)

This appears to be a universal pattern, as in Denmark too, female respondents claim that most frequently fathers or brothers introduced them to football (Mintert and Pfister 2015). The male path of socialisation can be related to the 'in-the-blood' scheme identified by Mewett and Toffoletti (2011). They also recognise three other ways for female fans to be introduced to the sport: (1) 'learners' concerns fans 'socialising' to the sport through friends and television; (2) 'converts' describes individuals who hadn't supported any teams before and changed their attitude; and (3) 'STF', which stands for 'sexually transmitted fan', concerns female fans introduced by their partner.

All of these four types emphasise nuances in the mechanism of incorporation, but they are usually connected to male actors. However, the question of why practically only men are 'significant others' in the socialisation process concerns not only the historical background when male domination was inherent in the football culture, but also refers to decades of its development as a field of masculine hegemony and domination (see Chapters 1 and 3). Traditionally, it excluded, or at best marginalised, women on social grounds, but to be fair, those leisure activities were largely beyond women's scope due to their extensive home duties and double burden (Lewis 2009; Whiteside and Hardin 2011). But such an extremely asymmetrical division of labour and responsibilities for family affairs is becoming a thing of the past, and in Poland, too, the gradual emancipation of women offers them a variety of social opportunities, including participation in the football culture (see Chapter 4).

Overall, Poland fits well the outlined social patter in which football was men's territory to which women used to have limited access, but it has also changed recently. Nonetheless, socialisation into football normally takes place at home with the assistance of fathers, brothers or male peers, or due to partners of a mature age. This can be seen in the results of a survey conducted among football female fans. It shows that approximately 61% of respondents reported that they came to their first match accompanied by male fans. This is in line with previous studies (Ben-Porat 2009; Dixon 2015), and without any exaggeration, we can acknowledge that in Poland too football is 'men's territory' or 'men's realm' to which male relatives or friends primarily introduce female fans. To support this claim, we can underscore that only a small minority came to their first football match with their mother, sister or a female friend (Table 6.1).

It is important who performs the introductory role because they socialise 'new fans', providing them with their specific (male) understanding of football fandom. Using the organisational study approach this process can be seen as 'sense-making' (Weick, Sutcliffe and Obstfeld 2005), which is defined as 'the ongoing retrospective development of plausible images that rationalise what people are doing' (p. 409). There is little doubt that male fans serve as brokers who provide their meanings to their (male) collective experience. It gives them a considerable advantage to have a massive impact on defining sets of values prevailing in football stadiums, setting norms of appropriateness and inappropriateness as well as legitimising behavioural patterns specific to the football culture.

Nonetheless, females enter the world of football through their male peers and, based on interviews, we can identify four dominant types of circumstances under which women access the world of football or, more specifically, football fandom. The first one refers to early childhood when girls are introduced to football as daughters, sisters and sometimes even nieces by their father, brothers and uncles. Traditionally, football broadcasted by public television was watched

Table 6.1 With whom did you come to the match the first time?

Person	Female fans (N)	Female fans (%)
Boyfriend/Husband	245	20.1
Father	237	19.4
Male friend(s)	169	13.9
Female friend(s)	157	12.9
Brother	97	8.0
Kid(s)	82	6.7
Other relative(s)	79	6.5
Mother	62	5.1
Sister	50	4.1
Other people	21	1.7
Alone	20	1.6

at home as the most popular sport discipline in the country, and it was believed that it represents social value as a public good (Milne 2016, 109). Also, football was (and still is) regarded as a popular men's entertainment (IBRIS 2014; CBOS 2018). Thus, unsurprisingly the prime audience and social foundation of football fandom were males.

> I have two older brothers and a father who used to have a monopoly on TV. Whether I liked it or not, I had to watch football, and this must have had a massive influence on me. It is a masculine part of my family that sparked my interest in football.
>
> (FF1, regular)[1]

> My father was going to football games with my brother and uncle and once they offered to take me. And I went with them, and for nine years I attended Lech Poznań games.
>
> (FF2, ultras)

> When I was five or six years old, I went with my father to the old stadium for a friendly game with Śląsk Wrocław. I do not recall the exact score, I remember only that I went with my dad and I was very young.
>
> (FF3, ultras)

The data collected throughout our investigations with the use of both quantitative and qualitative methods provide solid empirical evidence that women entered football most frequently through their close male peers. The latter are usually family members or close male friends who can both be trusted and are already insiders. It is never easy to enter such a relatively hermetic and culturally distant world, particularly for young girls who do not fit the traditional image of a football fan and masculine character of football fandom. Last but not least, girls willing to enter football fandom have no choice but to step into men's territory, which is ruled by social norms unsupportive of female newcomers. And so, those girls who have wanted to express their interest in football and attend football games, thereby changing the dominant pattern, have had to count on their male relatives. There is little chance that a mother, sister or female colleague would serve as a guide into the football world.

Instead, the father or older brothers play a special role in this process as they can not only share their passion in person but also offer protection during the match if necessary. Having said that, we acknowledge that until recently, physical and cultural violence was often present in the stands, and it was irresponsible to leave children unattended. This is in line with a study on Israeli football fans by Ben-Porat (2009), who also finds that introduction by a family member or male friend facilitates physical and symbolic protection to women in the stadium. So, it is not surprising that girls who started to follow football clubs had to attend games with the company of older male fans. Unsurprisingly too, this routine often turns into family rituals that last for a couple of years or more:

> Neither my mother nor my sister was interested in sport, particularly football, and only I was very keen to go to matches with my dad.
>
> (FF4, ultras)

Although male family members perform central roles in initiation and socialisation into football fandom, some respondents also mentioned that they were introduced to the football world through close male friends. Usually, they were school mates or those living in neighbourhoods because the role of neighbourhoods was significantly different in pre-digital times and the respondents frequently referred to this:

> The first time I attended a football match with my friends was when we were in primary school. Lechia was playing in the third league.
>
> (FF5, VIP)

Initiation into football was not always intentional, and sometimes the birth of a passion for football was the outcome of an unplanned or even accidental visit to a stadium. This represents a specific case of football and fandom culture, which was seen as two separate realms. Normally, an interest in football and following football clubs precedes the passion for fandom culture. But this does not have to always be the case and it could be the fandom culture that sparks a passion for football, not the other way round. Notwithstanding the sequence of events that led to young female fans ending up as football fans, it was almost always the father, brother or male friends who first took them to a game.

The second type of circumstance under which female fans enter football refers to late teenagers or even young adults when their boyfriends or partners are undertaking the role of 'male broker' while taking them to a football stadium. Women developing a passion for football because their boyfriend or partner attends games is a direct consequence of their personal relationships. Their first visits to the stadium are carried out as a companion to a male fan, and at least initially, their passion for football is indelibly connected to their personal relationship.

> Like the majority of women, I came to the stadium with my boyfriend. When I was at the beginning of my studies, I started dating a boy who was an active fan of Legia Warszawa. At first, I was very sceptical, but he took me to the stadium.
>
> (FF6, ultras)

Introducing close ones to football is part of the process of getting to know each other and sharing each other's passion. It appears to be more than learning the rules of the game; it is about sometimes sharing extremely private, even intimate feelings of being 'in love' with the club, providing access to the collective (male) fans' rituals and their social practices. So, bringing female partners to football games can be regarded – depending on the level of engagement – as a symbol of the significance of the relationship. It is well documented that following football clubs can be a very private affair and one of the major sources of masculine identity (Winands, Grau and Zick 2019). Thus, inviting someone to participate in collective male excitement and performing fandom rituals can be regarded as something very special as people share their intimate affairs only with their close ones.

Interestingly enough, the interviewees suggested that before their first visits to a stadium, female fans felt that the stadium had always been men's territory and they (as women) had not felt particularly welcome. This shows best the cultural barrier that traditionally put many women off football stadiums, and in fact, it does not matter whether it is only a form of 'moral panic' (Cohen 2011), urban legend or self-fulfilling prophecy but it has had far-reaching consequences. Many of the female fans we interviewed claim that they would never have gone there if they had not met their boyfriends at the time. Also, if women go to football matches alone, they are frequently accused of being driven by other (than sporting) reasons (Crawford and Gosling 2004; Pfister, Lenneis and Mintert 2013). Sometimes the passion fades away with the relationship but it can also survive break-ups and – as one of the interviewees acknowledged – this necessitates changing seat in the stadium:

> The first couple of months, I was totally involved. I think I've been going for six years to Żyleta.[2] I haven't moved since last year.
>
> **Why?**
>
> Because I broke up with this guy. Now I'm dating another boyfriend. I did not want to meet or pass my ex. I am in the next sector, in the corner.
>
> (FF6, ultras)

The third type of circumstance under which women have been introduced into football again refers to their personal relations and is closely linked to their family roles. In this scenario, women become football fans at a more mature age and attend games in their social roles as mothers. This concerns the situation when kids begin to play football or simply follow their local clubs. Normally, fathers perform those roles but they cannot always take boys (or girls) to a football match, and also football matches become an opportunity for a perfect family day out. Indeed, football clubs are increasingly intensively advertising themselves as entertainment for the entire family.

Consequently, they set up special sectors in the stadium for parents with kids (family sectors), encouraging all to enter the football realm. Such dedicated sections are supposed to encourage those who might potentially feel insecure about going to the football stadium with kids, and based on the survey and interviews we can say that serious concern over safety at football grounds is clearly an important factor affecting match attendance. Mothers accompany their sons when they go to a football match and frequently become fans themselves. Modern infrastructure and the organisation of football games play a positive role in attracting new fans because previously at least some of them (particularly female fans) simply did not feel particularly comfortable in the traditional football environment with poor sports facilities. Stadiums are a key part of the clubs and a feeling of comfort and sense of security help to make spectators feel at home and encourage them to attend football games regularly.

> My son began to play football five years ago at Lechia Gdańsk, and since then I have started to attend first-team games when played at the old stadium. I did not like it. But the new stadium is very different, and I fell in love with both Lechia and the Ergo Arena.
>
> (FF7, regular)

The safety standards at football matches played in the *Ekstraklasa* have radically improved in the last two decades (Kossakowski 2017; Antonowicz and Grodecki 2018), but many respondents still recall times of anarchy at the football grounds and football-related violence. This is why one of the major concerns expressed by many female fans was safety. The long-established popular image of football matches and football fans is horrible and scary. Polish football fans have an image of primitive and aggressive vandals who, when they are in a larger group, sow terror at stadiums (and also while travelling). Also, the media frequently explore this image, triggering 'moral panic' (Cohen 2011), and even if the reality has radically changed (Kossakowski 2017), the barbarian stereotypes of football fans are present, particularly among those not attending football games.

> I knew what was happening in the stadiums from the media – in particular from TVN where I used to work at the time. My boyfriend wanted to convince me that it was a false picture, and I also wanted to prove myself that I was wrong. And I was indeed.
>
> (FF6, ultras)

For women who enter the football culture as mothers with their children, the prime concern during their first visits is fear and their male companions are supposed to provide them with security in case 'something happens'. They admit that the feeling of fear gradually disappears as women learn formal and informal rules that are obligatory in the stadium. And this is a form of informal knowledge that can hardly be acquired outside football contexts. It is a kind of learning by doing. It is worth adding that women as mothers can enter football at any age, but they fall into a similar category of 'mothers' who follow their sons' passion. They were encouraged by sons even though they had nothing to do with football.

> I had no contact with the stadiums at all, and with the football, only my sons had contact, because they played occasionally. S. [the son's name] used to go to Legia from an early age, but I didn't go to matches.
>
> (FF8, regular)

The fourth circumstance, exceptionally, is not linked to family roles but is part of a professional environment. Women can also enter football through their work peers as football has become an attractive form of entertainment. At big metropolitan clubs, attending football games has become fashionable, and the arrival of attractive rivals in European competitions or successes in domestic leagues attract numerous new fans. But it would be oversimplistic and stereotype-driven to claim that those coming with their workmates are driven by fashion (King 1997; Williams 2007). They can equally be attracted by the 'atmosphere' in the stadium and the rebellious nature of football fandom regardless of the lack of football stars and poor quality of the football.

In a working environment, football is often the subject of numerous informal conversations, naturally creating circles of football fans who tell their stories, exchange opinions and share their passion with other fans at work. On the one hand, it creates pressure to develop an interest in football, otherwise it poses a danger of becoming socially marginalised or even isolated; on the other hand, when people are passionate about something, they tend to engage those around them.

> I developed a passion for football through my friends at work because they were chatting and telling football stories during work breaks. It is they who sparked my interest and passion because I did not follow football before. Since then I have started going to football matches with them.
>
> (FF9, ultras)

And as women are fully present in almost every professional environment, they have a pretty good chance of being affected by football at work and starting to attend football matches with their workmates. Since football is still male-dominated, it is very likely that male co-workers will lead the group of friends to the stadium.

Summing up, it is acknowledged that football fandom is not only a collective phenomenon but also its norms, values and rituals are distant from modern society. They symbolise an industrial society with a sharp division between male and female social roles and, more importantly, that football is the territory of males. The study shows that there are four types of circumstances under which women attend football matches; three out of the four are closely related to family roles as daughters, girlfriends or mothers. Socialising into football fandom takes place via male brokers, mostly family members or close (male) friends who introduce them to the football culture and also provide 'cultural tickets' (Pfister, Lenneis and Mintert 2013). Some of them may never become regular fans and keep attending stadiums in their family roles, while many others can easily become fascinated by football and fully fledged fans, although they must face some harmful stereotypes and prejudice.

However, this could be changing in the future with the demasculinisation of the football culture. It should be noted that approximately 22% of female fans indicated that they were introduced into the football world by other women. This percentage can be read as one of the indicators of the changes in football itself, its increasing openness to different types of fans and the perception of stadiums as sufficiently safe spaces for women. But that doesn't change the fact that the vast majority of women still become football fans through men.

Notes

1 FF refers to female fans and regular refers to the type of the stadium's sector. To describe other parts of stadiums where female fans are sitting, we use ultras, VIP and family.
2 'Żyleta' [the Razor] is the name of the ultras stand in the stadium of Legia Warszawa. In the cases of three analysed clubs we have decided to leave in quotations Polish names of ultra sectors.

References

Antonowicz, D. and M. Grodecki. 2018. 'Missing the goal: Policy evolution towards football-related violence in Poland (1989–2012)'. *International Review for the Sociology of Sport* 53(4): 490–511. doi: 10.1177/1012690216662011.
Ben-Porat, A. 2009. 'Not just for men: Israeli women who fancy football'. *Soccer & Society* 10(6): 883–896. doi: 10.1080/14660970903240030.
Ben-Porat, A. 2010. 'Football fandom: A bounded identification'. *Soccer & Society* 11(3): 277–290. doi: 10.1080/14660971003619594.
CBOS 2018. *Przed mundialem w Rosji: zainteresowanie piłką nożną i ocena PZPN* [*Before the World Cup in Russia: Interest in Football and Evaluation of the Polish Football Association*]. Report 85/2018. Accessed 16 September 2019 www.cbos.pl/SPISKOM.POL/2018/K_085_18.PDF.
Cohen, S. 2011. *Folk Devils and Moral Panics: The Creation of the Mods and Rockers. Folk Devils and Moral Panics: The Creation of the Mods and Rockers*. Abingdon: Routledge.
Crawford, G. and V. K. Gosling. 2004. 'The myth of the "puck bunny": Female fans and men's ice hockey'. *Sociology* 38(3): 477–493. doi: 10.1177/0038038504043214.

Dixon, K. 2015. 'A woman's place recurring: Structuration, football fandom and sub-cultural subservience'. *Sport in Society* 18(6): 636–651. doi: 10.1080/17430437.2014.982541.

Erhart, I. 2011. 'Ladies of Besiktas: A dismantling of male hegemony at Inönü Stadium'. *International Review for the Sociology of Sport* 48(1): 83–98. doi: 10.1177/1012 690211427986.

IBRIS. 2014. *Badania widzów audycji sportowych [Research on the Spectators of Sports Broadcasts]*. Accessed 10 May 2015. www.slideshare.net/InstytutHomoHomini/ badanie-widzw-audycji-sportowych.

King, A. 1997. 'New directors, customers, and fans: The transformation of English football in the 1990s'. *Sociology of Sport Journal* 14(3): 224–240. doi: 10.1123/ssj.14.3.224.

Kossakowski, R. 2017. 'Where are the hooligans? Dimensions of football fandom in Poland'. *International Review for the Sociology of Sport* 52(6): 693–711. doi: 10.1177/ 1012690215612458.

Lewis, R. 2009. ' "Our lady specialists at Pikes Lane": Female spectators in early English professional football, 1880–1914'. *The International Journal of the History of Sport* 26(15): 2161–2181. doi: 10.1080/09523360903367651.

Mewett, P. and K. Toffoletti. 2011. 'Finding footy: Female fan socialization and Australian rules football'. *Sport in Society* 14(5): 670–684. doi: 10.1080/17430437.2011.575112.

Milne, M. 2016. *The Transformation of Television Sport. The Transformation of Television Sport*. London: Palgrave Macmillan UK.

Mintert, S. and G. Pfister. 2015. 'The FREE project and the feminization of football: The role of women in the European fan community'. *Soccer & Society* 16(2–3): 405–421. doi: 10.1080/14660970.2014.961383.

Pfister, G., V. Lenneis and S. Mintert. 2013. 'Female fans of men's football: A case study in Denmark'. *Soccer and Society* 15(6): 850–871. doi: 10.1080/14660970.2013. 843923.

Weick, K. E., K. M. Sutcliffe and D. Obstfeld. 2005. 'Organizing and the process of sensemaking'. *Organization Science* 16(4): 409–421. doi: 10.1287/orsc.1050.0133.

Whiteside E. and M. Hardin. 2011. 'Women (not) watching women: Leisure time, television, and implications for televised coverage of women's sports'. *Communication, Culture and Critique* 4(2): 122–143. doi: 10.1111/j.1753-9137.2011.01098.x.

Williams, J. 2007. 'Rethinking sports fandom: The case of European soccer'. *Leisure Studies* 26(2): 127–146. doi: 10.1080/02614360500503414.

Winands, M., A. Grau and A. Zick. 2019. 'Sources of identity and community among highly identified football fans in Germany: An empirical categorisation of differentiation processes'. *Soccer and Society* 20(2): 216–231. doi: 10.1080/14660970.2017. 1302934.

7 Female fans at football matches

Match attendance

As was shown in the previous chapter, the first experiences at football stadiums for female fans are initiated primarily by men – fathers, brothers, male partners or male friends. This is largely due to the cultural and social nature of football in which men wield power in defining situations (see Chapters 1 and 3). Being brokers, and holding the power to socialise into the football culture gives men a great advantage, though it does not determine the trajectory of a fan's career. The latter can be affected by a cocktail of different factors, and it is similar for both male and female fans.

Overall, the research shows that women do not stand out in terms of the frequency with which they attend football games. The results of the survey provide empirical evidence that there is a certain distribution of fans concerning match attendance. However, it needs to be underlined that distribution is similar for both genders (Table 7.1).

One of the major indicators of a fan's loyalty is the purchase of season tickets. A brief examination of the survey results indicates that approximately a quarter of fans in the sample are season ticket holders. Moreover, the distribution of women and men among season ticket holders reflects their proportion in

Table 7.1 How often do you attend football matches of your club?

	Female fans (N)	Female fans (%)	Male fans (N)	Male fans (%)
I attend every match during the season	271	31.1	1,087	28.6
I attend more than 10 matches during the season	182	20.9	908	23.9
I attend between 5–9 matches during the season	214	24.5	928	24.4
I attend less than 4 matches during the season	205	23.5	878	23.1
Total	**872**	**100**	**3,801**	**100**

the sample. It allows us to say that if women enter a football stadium, they start demonstrating similar behavioural patterns. One of the most convincing explanations is that women follow those who brought them into the stadium and socialised them into the fandom culture. But when socialisation is completed (or at least advanced) those newcomers start searching for their own place (sector), and their own companion. Female fans often admit that their passion for football came from their male brokers, but at some point, they leave their brokers and take their own fandom route. This is perfectly illustrated by one of the female fans who was introduced to football by her father, but at the time of the interview, she was attending matches independently of her father.

> Since the new stadium was built here in 2011 [the new arena in Gdańsk, built purposely for Euro 2012, is today the home stadium for Lechia Gdańsk football club – ed. authors], I have not missed any home match. I used to go with my dad, and then when I was older, I attended alone.
>
> (FF3, ultras)

The direction of development of fans' careers depends on the individuals who are introduced to football, the circumstances under which it took place, but also individual experience of the social situation of a football match. There is a multitude of factors that influence the development of a passion for football and impact the fans' identity. It could be a mixture of performance on the pitch, players (stars), tensions, glory, but also the exceptional atmosphere in the stadium. For example, one of the female fans mentioned in her interview that for her, the most important experience was the performances of ultras that she observed when she first attended:

> I don't remember much about what happened on the pitch when I was at my first match. I was fascinated by what happened in the Kocioł,[1] what was presented there. And because I saw this choreography, I decided to go to the next matches. And that's what is the most interesting thing for me at the matches, more than just the sports aspect. I am mainly interested in what is happening in the stands, how supporting is organised, conducted, how these choreographies are prepared.
>
> (FF9, ultras)

A football match is a social situation that offers a multitude of lures that attract a wide range of different fans. It has an impact on the nature of their participation in football games, determines the locations of their seats in the stadium and also influences the frequency (loyalty) of football attendance. There is no single rule about how often female fans attend their team's matches at the home stadium. Before we elaborate further, it should be noted that home matches vary considerably from away games in almost every aspect of fandom. The latter are considerably less accessible for women, more time- and money-consuming, less convenient to attend and, most importantly, far more exposed to hooligan violence. The specific nature of away games is elaborated upon in a separate section later in the chapter.

The mentioned results of the survey present evidence that gender has no impact on frequencies of attending football games, but the qualitative analysis provides us with an even deeper understanding of that social phenomenon. Many female fans presented during the interviews individual herstories of their fascination with football, sometimes giving us emotional statements that illustrate their devotion to the clubs. There is a broad spectrum of motives and circumstances that attract female fans to football fandom. In the case of female fans who are regular match-goers and attend literally every game it is – beyond any doubt – passion not fashion.

> I was maybe not at all matches, because when I worked at weekends, I didn't go to matches, but, usually, I attended every game.
>
> (FF10, ultras)

> It is the fourth consecutive season that I've been at every match.
>
> (FF1, regular)

> If the match took place in Poznań, I was at every match. There is nothing to talk about. Even when I had pneumonia, I was at the match.
>
> (FF11, regular)

Passion has no gender, and it requires a similar level of sacrifice whoever is committed to the club. Notwithstanding the ticket prices, professional duties or even severe weather conditions, female fans attend football games driven by unconditional support for, and devotion to, their clubs.

> I don't count it anymore; it's too much. I was counting when I was a child, but now it is too much. I regularly go to every match; even if I am sick, I will go anyway.
>
> (FF3, ultras)

An iconic story was provided by one Lech Poznań fan who recalls an epic game against Juventus F.C. in the Europa League in 2010/2011 when the game took place in typical winter conditions of a sharp frost and heavy snow, neither of which prevented her from supporting the team:

> I was at Juventus; it was so cold, and I still remember the pain in my feet and toes because of the cold. On the other hand, I had this desire to watch the match. Later, when the snowstorm had stopped, it was so amazing that, on the one hand, you felt such shivering and cold, but this fanaticism didn't let you leave and get warm. It was sick. I remember I was returning home by tram, and I was shivering from the cold and I tried to bring my body back to some normal temperature for three hours.... Anyway, everyone was cold; everyone was shaking. But it was worth it because the memories are amazing.
>
> (FF11, regular)

This statement presents two important massages. First, it proves that the term 'fanaticism' does not have to be reserved only for male fans, and supporting the club in such extreme conditions is proof of the 'authenticity' of being a football fan. Second, she does not glorify her commitment and she did not seem to prove herself (as a woman) to be an authentic fan. Let us draw attention to the part of her statement where she says 'everyone was cold, everyone was shaking', which suggests that facing harsh conditions is a part of football fandom and involves everyone regardless of their age, gender or political views. In this particular case, the weather affects everyone similarly.

The study shows that female fans do not constitute a separate category of fans in regard to match attendance and the reasons why they attend football matches. On the contrary, they present internal diversification concerning match attendance. While some female fans support their clubs regardless of the circumstances, others tend to be more selective and choose the most attractive matches. It could be a local derby, a match against old rivals or one against the club at the top of the table.

> It is commonly known that one always goes to Wisła Kraków or Lech Poznań as these are more emotional matches. Well, they are such eternal enemies; you always have to win against them. And besides, there is always better support at these matches. So it also matters to me, because I like going to these matches, first of all, because I like football and I like to watch it, and because it is Legia; secondly, because I can meet my friend and thirdly to watch the spectacle that is going on there. It fascinates me; I like to watch it because it is a theatre.
>
> (FF12, regular)

Female fans declared that even if their passion remains strong, forms of participation in the fandom culture change over time. Football fandom in Poland has undergone some radical changes (Kossakowski, Szlendak and Antonowicz 2018; Antonowicz and Grodecki 2018; Kossakowski 2019) and alongside these – although much less dynamic – changes in fans' behaviour in the stands. The slowness of change can be explained by the long tradition that is not only well-embedded but also cherished and cultivated as a collective heritage. But female fans emphasise that the way they participate in the fandom culture is strongly determined by personal experiences. Those female fans who have had many years of experience in the stands acknowledge that shifts in their behaviour as fans result from changes in their private life:

> I attended in the 1980s, and the 1990s too. But then there was a time, more or less since 1999, when I gave birth to children, and at the same time I worked a lot. I am also an active lawyer, and I do many other projects. I have worked and work a lot, so there was no chance not only of attending matches but also of doing any other things in my free time. So I came back

to these matches very slowly, very gradually, and now I go to every third match, more or less.

(FF13, VIP)

At first, the break in attending was related to the children, because they were born in '85 and '86. And then I had a break until 2004. I was still there at individual matches, but irregularly. But now I have a season ticket and I've been to all matches for 14 years.

(FF14, regular)

Undoubtedly, female fans are more affected than men by developments in their private life. They have to combine professional obligations and (mainly) family duties since the latter (at least in Poland) remain overwhelmingly on women's shoulders (see Chapter 4). The quoted citations show that the club is irreversibly a central part of their identity, even if life circumstances change. However, it could equally go a different way, and over time, fans' emotional attachment to the club can soften.

I regularly attended for the first five years. I had 100% attendance. Now it is less often due to work obligations and the fact that I moved my heart a little away from it. I think that this season I will be attending 30 to 40% of matches.

(FF6, ultras)

Establishing a family is a natural evolution and redefines priorities in spending free time. It is not surprising that many females need to take a step back and focus on their families. And if both partners are football fans, men still tend to go to the match while women take care of their children.

I go less often. Others laugh at me that I am 'a picnic fan' because I go when it is warm, it is not raining and for prestigious games. I lost my heart to Lechia in the sense that I have the impression that Lechia is taking my family from me. I used to look through a positive lens earlier. OK, you could go out at the weekend for a match if there were no children. You could watch something, it was something cool. But later, my priorities changed; unfortunately, my husband's ones didn't change at all.

(FF15, regular)

With a growing number of family events and other social obligations, fans have no choice but to define their priorities. Being a fan can be rewarding, but fanship also carries considerable social costs and it can sometimes be problematic to maintain good relations with those not engaged in football fandom.

There were situations when, for example, I weaselled out of some parties, or friends' birthdays. For example, Lech are playing against Legia in Poznań, so I say to myself: Well, damn!

(FF1, regular)

In short, the passion for football has no gender and female fans attend football games with a similar frequency to male fans. The study provides empirical evidence that female fans develop a great passion for their clubs; they are emotionally engaged and demonstrate a willingness to suffer a lot just to support their beloved club. There is no such thing as a 'female' approach to football fandom; there are more and less engaged fans, but it has nothing to do with gender. However, changes in private life seem to have a bigger impact on women than men, and since football is still considered to be primarily a male's sport, if both partners are fans the male tends to go to the stadium while the female stays at home with the children.

The choice of favourite sector

In modern football stadiums that are fully seated, fans can choose from numerous different locations. It is the outcome of a broader process connected to modernisation as Polish football authorities and clubs had to adapt to the regulations of UEFA before co-organising Euro 2012. For clubs, the new stadiums create opportunities to attract different kinds of supporters – the existence of ultra, VIP, regular and/or family sectors makes the supporters' choice wider. This is clearly visible in the narratives of female respondents as they often mention that they can choose their place in the stadium according to personal needs and comfort (it is not only Polish specificity – see data from the UK: Pope 2017).

Many fans have their favourite place in the stadium; they openly confess to their emotional attachment to their seats. Sometimes they choose to have a good view of the pitch, or otherwise to sit close to those with whom they like to share their emotions.

> I have my favourite place, in front of the players' entrance, because I like to look at this moment at the start of the game when they are full of hope, and so are we, no one is tired yet, or dirty, I like to look at it that way.
>
> (FF8, regular)

> [The choice] was informed, i.e. how my friend and I chose a seat, ... we chose a row to be not too close, but not too high, but to get under the roof, so it usually doesn't rain on us.... Although I would now prefer to change my seat to be a little closer to the exit because it is more convenient; on the other hand, it is more in the middle, so I can't complain.
>
> (FF12, regular)

> But to be honest, I don't have a permanent place. It depends a bit on the match. Sometimes I go back to the upper stand, to the red sector, because I have friends there who are still working at the club, so it's nice to meet them and talk.
>
> (FF16, VIP)

But female fans are in a specific situation because the choice of seats is often a consequence of being socialised into a particular part of the stadium by (most frequently) 'male brokers'. The socialisation process involves being together in physical proximity and staying in the same part of the stadium is the natural consequence of that. But in our investigation, we also encountered different situations in which bringing a newcomer female fan to the ultras zone was perceived as inappropriate and dangerous. The ultras stands have their own specific rules, which require active and continuous participation by chanting, singing, booing or simply cheering the team on the pitch. Female fans admit that this is not the best place to be socialised into the fandom culture as the lack of adequate engagement might potentially trigger a hostile reception from other ultra fans.

> Recently there were two such women in Młyn,[2] but they had to go to the family section because they opened a bag of sticks [snacks] and gave them out. It was clear that they were probably at a match for the first time. They took pictures every five minutes, which is not something you do in Młyn. They did not fit in there. Then they talked to someone, but I noticed they had come alone. Then they did a picnic, and they just had to be thrown out … well, there were a lot of women in Młyn, where they were well dressed up. But it was probably the last match of the season, and just these 'stars' came…. They didn't cheer or anything, they just stood up with their phones; it irritated me anyway. It was obvious that they should either go to the family section or the other one because they were in the wrong place.
>
> (FF10, ultras)

The ultras stands are known for their masculine character (Antonowicz, Jakubowska and Kossakowski 2020a; Hasso 2018), conformist pressure, sense of togetherness and collective soul (Antonowicz and Wrzesiński 2009), and a new female fan intruding could be inappropriate. But this statement clearly shows that norms dictated by the male part of fandom are so strongly incorporated and socialised by all fans that even female fans measure other women with such rules with no excuses. One of the respondents admitted that her brother decided not to bring her to the ultras stand as he was afraid of how she would be treated in a place generally reluctant to accept women:

> [I]t is commonly known what the attitude in Kocioł is: it is completely devoted to supporting, that these girls are not quite welcome there. What's more, my brother was on the lower tier, where the fans are even more engaged. And then I didn't know the chants; I wasn't up to date. I wasn't involved in supporting, so maybe it wasn't Kocioł for my own good and safety. So it's better for such a more neutral supporter when he/she comes for the first time on a match to be in these other stands than in Kocioł.
>
> (FF1, regular)

Several other respondents confirmed their concern about the presence of women in ultras stands. This is the most masculine part of the stadium, where masculine domination is a social norm that is hardly questioned. Standing (fans do not sit in the ultras stands) in the core of the ultras stand is a privilege and access to it can be restricted by (hooligan) rules. Such a situation – for many unacceptable – was described by one of the respondents who referred to invisible cultural barriers that women face in football fandom.

> I started going to the lower level of Kocioł [the ultras stand in Poznań has two levels: the lower for more experienced ultras and the upper for 'beginners' – ed. authors], then there was a situation where women could not be on the lower level, so I had to go upstairs, but now I've been back on the lower one for several years.

Where did this situation come from?

> A lot of women came to matches to show that they were there to take a picture and so on; it is known that their male counterparts were pissed off because they only came to take pictures and there was a ban for us.
>
> (FF2, ultras)

Another female fan of Lech Poznań mentions that there was a time when women were permanently banned from ultras stands:

> There was once a scandalous affair at the stadium, when someone from the people leading the cheering [the conductor – ed. authors] said that football is a sport for men, not for women, and there was quite a big turmoil about it. Women then also stopped coming to Kocioł, stopped coming to matches. What's worse for me is they also controlled it. I mean, it was ruled that as I am a woman, if I want to come to a match to Kocioł, I do not go downstairs, I can only go upstairs. And there was even a time that if they saw a woman downstairs, they threw her out, because football is a sport for men, they said.
>
> (FF4, ultras)

The 'ban' was so strictly imposed that even male friends of female fans didn't react to protect them:

> There was no reaction from men who were next to her like: 'Come on, leave her alone, let her stay here, why does she need to go?' Everyone confirmed: get out. There was no reaction to this.
>
> (FF4, ultras)

While ultras stands are seen as a male territory where women have to adapt to the rules made and executed by men, other parts of the stadium are more 'feminised'. Many female fans can be met in the family sector in the stadium, reflecting the traditional distinction between male and female roles in society.

Most (if not all) football stadiums provide special zones for families with children. They are generally located further away from the ultras sector so that children are not exposed to the use of offensive language. This is an important aspect for one of the female respondents:

> [B]ecause of M. [respondent's son], we go to the family section. And I'm very happy; I wouldn't go with him to Młyn. I think M. doesn't like noise. And, you know, those drums. There are also swear words. No, it's family-friendly for me, and it's full of families.
>
> (FF17, family)

Finally, the selection of the sector in the football stadium is hardly the result of random choice, so changing the sector is connected to broader changes in the identity of the fan. One female fan of Legia Warsaw started her fan's career in the ultras stand, but after a few years, she decided to leave the sector (for the regular fans who sit during a match). She explains that this is a result of maturity:

Have you grown out of Żyleta?

> It could be described as such. I have the impression that most people grow out of Żyleta at some point. I still remember the old stadium, when, after attending Żyleta for a few years there was a natural drift towards the covered stand. Something like this happened to me. I had a break of one or two years from attending matches due to private issues.… I remember one time. It was December, probably 3 degrees Celsius, snow with rain, which was falling not vertically, but horizontally. It was cruelly bad weather. And I just found that I did not want to go on Żyleta, because I would get soaked through, so I would go for a covered one. And actually, since then it has always been a covered stand, especially since there were huge student discounts. At that time, I was a student, so the difference was quite big. The place I had was also nice because actually the VIP stand was just behind me. So, for example, in winter when the heaters were turned on in the stadium, they also warmed me up, which was nice.
>
> (FF18, regular)

When choosing the sector in the stadium, some female fans naturally follow their 'male-brokers' and keep them company, which is part of the socialisation process. But it is not always possible as the access to ultras stands is limited, in particular for new female fans. Other parts of the stadium are more accessible, and some (family sectors) are indirectly dedicated to women more than others, reflecting the logic of traditional society. Luckily, the location of a seat in the stadium is not a lifelong commitment, and as fans change (become mature or radicalise in their emotional engagement in the club's affairs), they can change their seats accordingly. However, there are still (although albeit small) areas to which access is regulated and executed by male fans and there is little female fans can do about it at the moment.

The away games – the last bastion of hegemonic masculinity

In general, modern football stadiums at home games are fairly accessible to women, with perhaps the exception of ultras stands, but home games tell us only part of the story of football fandom. For many fans, away games constitute the essence of football fandom, and being an authentic fan requires experiencing the discomfort of travelling to away games. It often involves the rather unpleasant experience of law enforcement services, and rough travelling conditions, for example restrictions on toilet use. Away trips can be dangerous, but they also provide ample time for building a sense of togetherness and fostering homosocial (fraternal) bonds among fans (Hammarén and Johansson 2014; Kossakowski, Antonowicz and Jakubowska 2020). The latter is particularly important because it resonates with traditional social rules, norms and values underpinning the traditional industrial football culture. Unlike the safety standards found during home football matches with high surveillance, tough regulations and modern facilities, travelling fans often face being targeted by hooligan groups at away matches. Although the probability of such attacks is low, many myths and urban legends support the exclusion of women from away games because women are less 'useful' during such potentially physical confrontations. Additionally, lengthy travel creates opportunities for (homo)socialising and fraternising via the 'lad culture' (for example King 1997) and carnival aspects of fandom (Pearson 2012) fuelled by alcohol, bad language and antisocial behaviour. These activities are often associated with men, and women's presence might spoil this sense of fraternity (Kossakowski, Antonowicz and Jakubowska 2020).

The survey conducted for this study shows that although 'away games' remain predominantly a masculine activity, there are female fans that follow their club even when it plays away from home (Table 7.2). In this regard, we cannot make bold statements about changes in time, but a visual examination of away matches in the 1980s and 1990s allows us to make soft claims about a gradually increasing presence of women at away games.

Table 7.2 How often do you attend away game of your club?

	Female fans (N)	Female fans (%)	Male fans (N)	Male fans (%)
I attend every away game during the season	19	2.2	63	1.9
I attend more than 10 away games during the season	8	0.9	93	2.8
I attend 5–9 away games during the season	32	3.7	214	6.5
I attend less than 4 games during the season	210	24.1	1,014	30.6
I have never been on away game	603	69.2	1,545	46.6

The results of the survey – which is biased towards ultra fans – show that nearly 70% of women have never been to an away match involving their team, as compared to 'only' 46.4% of men. On the other hand, as many as 30% of female fans in our sample have some (albeit incidental) experience of going to away games, which is far more than one would expect. The naturally intriguing research question refers to reasons for not attending away games and the distribution of answers paints an interesting picture (Table 7.3).

The answers most frequently given by respondents relate to membership of ultras groups, the lack of time and money and the perception of away matches as potentially dangerous. This fits well with the conclusions coming from other studies (Antonowicz, Kossakowski and Jakubowska 2020b) that the core and most demanding activity is performed by those who belong to ultras groups because the latter are ready to make far-reaching sacrifices.

Similarly to the presence in ultras stands, male fans set the rules of participation in travelling to away games and if female fans can go to away games it is only because male fans (from the top of the hierarchy) allow them to do so. Due to the described nature of away games, it is more likely that male fans will travel to away matches. When it comes to away games, it is men who always lead the way.

> This is still an environment – I think – where men lead the way. In those more involved groups that organise travel, that are involved in active supporting, in the preparation of choreographies, there is a conviction that it is still a man's hobby, and you women can only be an addition, and without such great commitment. Yes, there are girls, women, who already have quite a lot of experience; they travel to a large number of away games, and they are taken seriously in this environment. But for a woman who would like to join these trips and does not want to join this environment at the same time, unfortunately, the task is quite difficult. Not all women may have a ticket.
>
> (FF1, regular)

Table 7.3 Why do you not attend away games of your club?

	Female fans (N)	*Female fans (%)*
I am not a member of the most ultras-groups	225	21.3
I have no time	223	21.1
Away matches can be too dangerous	153	14.5
I have no money	137	12.9
My family circumstances don't allow	137	12.9
I don't know how to get a ticket	80	7.6
I don't like the atmosphere of away matches	62	5.9

Note
* The respondents could indicate more than one answer.

Most of the rules imposed by male ultra fans are of an informal nature, but fans are aware of them. However, these rules can also be formalised and announced publicly to avoid misunderstandings. Many fan groups of clubs such as Pogoń Szczecin, Jagiellonia Białystok, Górnik Zabrze and GKS Katowice formally restrict participation in away games. Those restrictions are imposed by fans' associations traditionally run by male fans. The power those groups have is illustrated by one of the respondents (female fan) who was banned from travelling to away matches because she refused to shut down an informal fan page of the club on Facebook. It was very straightforward and explicit communication but she was found insufficiently competent to provide and share knowledge about football and the club. As she refused to follow that order (it was indeed an order), she was banned from away games.

The 'ban' from away games results from the axionormative construction of the fandom culture. It is not founded on democratic principles but rather is characterised by quite a punitive structure – controlling the behaviour of individuals through the hegemonic power of male fans. As mentioned earlier, travelling fans are often exposed to various attacks as fewer forces are deployed, and there is less surveillance than around football grounds. Therefore, clashes between fans are more likely to happen on the way to a football game than inside the stadium. The more violence occurs on the way to football games, the more likely it is that women and kids (early teenagers) will be excluded.

> I was worried because the militia [communist police – ed. authors] was waiting for us at the stations and we were led in lines. The most interesting thing happened when the train was moving, and we wondered whether we would get there or whether after 15 minutes we would have stones thrown at us. I saw such stones being hurled. And it happened a few times that we had to lie on the floor, normally on the floor of the train. We treated all of it as an adventure.
>
> (FF13, VIP)

> There were buses or trains, and there were brawls there, so I was scared. I have to tell you that I was scared. I didn't want to go.
>
> (FF17, family)

Such statements often come from female fans that are not used to violence, those who normally sit and watch games peacefully and would expect the same at away games. But this is not really the case. In many cases, travel takes many hours in extremely uncomfortable conditions, for example with limited access to a toilet (Kossakowski 2017), and one of the female fans describes what kinds of 'inconveniences' she encountered during the trip:

> And the queue for the toilet is also getting enormous. You know, I always drink a little, I take a small bottle of water, and in fact, I try not to drink different juices, cola or beer, because there is a problem with the toilet. And you have to realise that you cannot demand a stop to use the toilet.

> Five buses travel, and 'hello I'm a girl, please stop the bus, I want the toilet' and so on.
>
> (FF23, ultras)

Women who have experience of away games sometimes mention that this is a very demanding situation. Long hours of travel, tiredness, lack of sleep and the need for full mobilisation at the stadium makes the trip very exhausting:

> They bore me terribly. I get bored of this travelling to one place by train or by car. I don't like travelling so much. Maybe the match itself, in a different stadium, it's also fun to see this stadium, and the others, the opposing supporters, how they receive us. I remember when we were going to Chorzów, the journey dragged on so terribly that when I got to the stadium, to be honest, I was already tired from the trip itself.
>
> (FF4, ultras)

Also, the police sometimes contribute to the tense atmosphere during away games by imposing their rules or denying travelling access to food, drinks or even toilets for security reasons. In some cases, it is possible to avoid collective travelling with the group, and numerous female fans decide to use their own means of transport. However, we must say it this is not always possible, at least when one is not seated in the VIP zone, which is more a party venue than a stand really.

> I have to answer honestly that I travel separately, because on the one hand I know it's a bit of a mess there, let's say. I don't mind, it doesn't bother me, but it's not always my cup of tea. So if I do go, I travel separately.
>
> (FF16, VIP)

There are more common reasons why participation in away games is challenging for female fans. Other major reasons that women point out in our survey are the lack of time, the high costs of such a journey and the focus on family responsibilities. Probably in many situations, when both the man and woman are supporters of the same club, and both are willing to go to an away game, it is the woman who will stay at home and the man will follow their club. In countries like Poland, such trips to away games might take more than a day. Taking an optimistic scenario that the game is played at the weekend, for example, on Sunday, the possible consequence is to return home on Monday morning, which is almost impossible to marry with family and even professional obligations.

> It was worse with trips, because it was not always possible, and I did not always have a free day at work. And often travel to Kraków or even to Warsaw, if there was a match in the evening, and then you had to come back at night, it was not always possible for professional reasons.
>
> (FF11, regular)

We were back in Gdańsk at 8:00 am, and I got to sleep on the train at 6:00, so I had only two hours of sleep. But I drank an energy drink, had a shower at home and had a nap for one hour as my classes started at 11. I got a taxi as I wasn't able to go by bus. I was so tired and went to school. My mum said that if I want to go to an away match, I have to go to school the next day. So I did.

(FF3, ultras)

Travelling to away games remains one of the most problematic issues for female fans. Not many female fans – even the most radical ones – go regularly to away games. Most of the fans travel with male partners. The reasons we gave earlier illustrate the nature of the problems they encountered. Beside the most typical and common difficulties for all fans in travelling to away games such as the long hours and high cost of away trips, female fans have to face other, more discouraging inconveniences. The first and most obvious one is that it remains strictly a male domain (Antonowicz, Kossakowski and Szlendak 2016). Today, the number of women is growing in the stands of Polish stadiums, but away matches are still a zone of male hegemony. It is entirely up to men whether female fans can or cannot follow their clubs, because they organise the trips, establish the rules of participation on such trips and execute them. If the traditional football culture (Antonowicz, Kossakowski and Szlendak 2011) is preserved somewhere in Polish football, it is the away games, and female fans are the ultimate victims.

Notes

1 'Kocioł' [the Boiler] is the name of the ultras' stand in the stadium of Lech Poznań.
2 'Młyn' [the Mill] is the name of the ultras stand in the stadium of Lechia Gdańsk.

References

Antonowicz D. and M. Grodecki. 2018. 'Missing the goal: Policy evolution towards football-related violence in Poland (1989–2012)'. *International Review for the Sociology of Sport* 53(4): 490–511. doi.org: 10.1177/1012690216662011.

Antonowicz, D., R. Kossakowski and T. Szlendak. 2011. 'Ostatni bastion antykonsumeryzmu? Kibice industrialni w dobie komercjalizacji sportu' ['The last bastion of anti-consumerism? Industrial die-hard-fans and the commercialization of sport']. *Studia Socjologiczne* (3): 113–139.

Antonowicz, D., R. Kossakowski and T. Szlendak. 2016. 'Flaming flares, football fanatics and political rebellion: Resistant youth cultures in late capitalism'. In *Eastern European Youth Cultures in a Global Context*, edited by M. Schwartz and H. Winkel. London: Palgrave Macmillan, 131–144.

Antonowicz, D., H. Jakubowska and R. Kossakowski. 2020a. 'Marginalised, patronised and instrumentalised: Polish female fans in the ultras' narratives'. *International Review for the Sociology of Sport* 55(1): 60–76. doi: 10.1177/1012690218782828.

Antonowicz, D., R. Kossakowski and H. Jakubowska. 2020b. 'A bittersweet welcome: Attitudes of Polish ultra-fans towards female fans entering football stadiums'. Sport in Society. doi: 10.1080/17430437.2020.1737018.

Antonowicz, D. and Ł. Wrzesiński. 2009. 'Kibice jako wspólnota niewiedzialnej religii' ['Sport fans as a community of the invisible religion']. *Studia Socjologiczne* 1: 115–149.

Hammarén, N. and T. Johansson. 2014. 'Homosociality: In between power and intimacy'. *Sage Open*. doi: 10.1177/2158244013518057.

Hasso, F. S. 2018. 'Masculine love and sensuous reason: The affective and spatial politics of Egyptian ultras football fans'. *Gender, Place and Culture* 25(10): 1423–1447. doi: 10.1080/0966369X.2018.1531830.

King, A. 'The lads: Masculinity and the new consumption of football'. *Sociology* 31(2): 329–346. doi: 10.1177/0038038597031002008.

Kossakowski, R. 2017. 'Where are the hooligans? Dimensions of football fandom in Poland'. *International Review for the Sociology of Sport* 52(6): 693–711. doi: 10.1177/1012690215612458.

Kossakowski, R. 2019. 'Euro 2012, the "civilizational leap" and the "supporters united" programme: A football mega-event and the evolution of fan culture in Poland'. *Soccer & Society* 20(5): 729–743. doi: 10.1080/14660970.2019.1616266.

Kossakowski R., D. Antonowicz and H. Jakubowska. 2020. 'The reproduction of hegemonic masculinity in football fandom: An analysis of the performance of Polish ultras'. In *The Palgrave Handbook of Masculinity and Sport*, edited by R. Magrath, J. Cleland and E. Anderson. Cham: Palgrave Macmillan, 517–536.

Kossakowski, R., R. Szlendak and D. Antonowicz. 2018. 'Polish ultras in the post-socialist transformation'. *Sport in Society* 21(6): 854–869. doi: 10.1080/17430437.2017.1300387.

Pearson, G. 2012. *An Ethnography of English Football Fans: Cans, Cops and Carnivals*. Manchester: Manchester University Press.

Pope, S. 2017. *The Feminization of Sports Fandom: A Sociological Study*. London: Routledge.

8 Reasons for attending football matches

Passion and loyalty

Numerous studies show that the motivations for supporters to come to matches or sports events are very different (see, for example Gencer 2015). However, one of the most important things seems to be a feeling of identification with a club, team or player, as well as a sense of belonging with the community of other fans. The attachment to the club is expressed fully in the most crucial moments in the history of the club: the heroic matches, unexpected victories and legendary events. Sometimes, the love for a club is transformed into a deep feeling of sadness and grief – particularly when the beloved club ceases to exist, as the case of Bury FC confirms (George 2019).

One of the major sources of criticism of female fans as a new type of fan questions their authenticity, loyalty and passion. Their arrival in growing numbers is often seen as an outcome of the commodification of football and, under the label of the more general category of 'new fans', they are stigmatised by the most radical traditional fans (for example ultras) as being inauthentic and driven by 'fashion, not passion' (Redhead 1993) – as is the entire concept of modern football. These 'new fans' are ascribed various stigmatised labels in the literature, including 'flaneurs' (Giulianotti 2002), 'consumers' (Antonowicz, Kossakowski and Szlendak 2015), 'glory hunters' (Giulianotti 2005, 392) and 'armchair audience' (Meier and Leinwather 2012), among others. The advent of the so-called 'new kinds of spectator identification' (Giulianotti 2002) and, perhaps more importantly, the new (passive) football culture often triggered hostile responses from traditional fans.

To explore fans' identification with clubs, in the conducted survey, they were asked to choose the sentence that best describes their relation with the clubs (Table 8.1).

Table 8.1 presents a convincing picture that when it comes to identity, there is almost no difference between male and female fans. It is visible that gender plays no role in the fans' attitudes towards their football club. This will be presented as one of our major empirical findings because – although anticipated based on qualitative research – it has not been empirically verified on such a large sample of fans. In general, the clubs mean the same to women and men, and the same can be said about the motives that attract them to football matches.

Table 8.1 Fans' attitude to the club

	Female fans (N)	Female fans(%)	Male fans (N)	Male fans (%)
The club is all my life. My club and I are one	154	16.0	552	16.6
The club play important role in my life	425	44.2	1684	50.8
I identify myself with the club, but it does not play an important role in my life	289	30.1	942	28.4
I do not identify myself with the club, but I support it	87	9.1	129	3.9
The club is totally indifferent to me	6	0.6	10	0.3
Total	**961**	**100**	**3,317**	**100**

The loyalty to the club and atmosphere of the game similarly appeal to football fans regardless of their gender, and they are largely responsible for bringing people to the stadium. Table 8.2 also shows that for the majority of fans, football is not entertainment (like the cinema) but a much more serious experience. It seems that, in the case of the poor quality of football in the Polish *Ekstraklasa*, female fans attend football matches because they are loyal fans and they want to feel the spectacular atmosphere to which they also contribute.

As the results reveal, passion has no gender and female fans demonstrate a deep passion for, and devotion to, their clubs. Many of them treat the club as a central part of their life and pivotal source of identity, which is why for many of

Table 8.2 The main reasons to attend the matches

	Female fans (N)	Female fans (%)	Male fans (M)	Male fans (%)
Atmosphere of the football match	774	29.6	2,474	28.2
Feeling of loyalty to the club	591	22.6	2,085	23.7
Opportunity to meet friends	287	11.0	1,212	13.8
The rank of the opponent my team is playing against	290	11.1	1,004	11.4
Free time/lack of other options	258	9.9	952	10.8
The current standing of my club the league table	132	5.0	387	4.4
Good weather	162	6.2	348	4.0
Willingness to meet new people	53	2.0	108	1.2
Other reasons	69	2.6	217	2.5

Note
* The respondents could indicate more than one answer.

them attending football matches, supporting their team is critical as one of the female fans compares it to attending church every Sunday:

> And since that moment, it has been hard for me to imagine not going to the game. In our slang, we say that we are going to church. Whether it's Saturday or Sunday, we go to 'our church'.
>
> (FF16, VIP)

Football fandom is similar for both genders: it involves passion, love, hate, identity, extreme emotions and devotions; it even connotes religious faith and attachment (Antonowicz and Wrzesiński 2009). During the interviews, 'loyalty' was brought up numerous times by female fans, as they made frequent references to their strong attachment to their clubs, and their strong feelings towards the club that produce unconditional loyalty. Some female respondents went even further when they stated that the club was a critical part of their life, sometimes equally as important as the relations with their close ones:

> Legia? Yes. This is part of my life, whatever it may be. And I mean years, hundreds of matches that you have been to, hundreds more that you have seen. Lots of good and bad emotions that you remember. Many funny stories, sometimes a little sad. And while at the beginning there were matches, first of all, this fan culture in the 1990s, choreographies, it is hard to deny that footballers are a different story.
>
> (FF18, regular)

> It's a passion; it's part of life. When I set the schedule at work, I know that I have to be off because Lechia is playing. I think this is one of the most important things, I subordinate everything to matches, or I set plans for matches. I think it is such a priority for me to go to the match.
>
> (FF10, ultras)

> It is such a second love that will not leave me. When I have a bad day, I can go to the match, shout, support my club, and I know that this is my passion, my hobby. It is second place after the family. I can give my life to it, for me it is something extremely important.
>
> (FF3, ultras)

One of the female fans, when asked what her club means to her, listed the following values: 'brotherhood, emotions, honour, being, friendship for good and bad. Really, it is only these or as many as these' (FF5, VIP). Intriguingly, she mentioned 'brotherhood', that which indicates the depth of male homosociality of in football fandom and how much the extent to which club-related values are masculine at the same time. In many narratives, the love and the attachment to the club 'compensates' for a bad level of performance on the pitch and poor results of the team. The team is a part of the club, and it is important to support it in bad and in good times:

> You are for good and for bad with the club. Sometimes I go to a match with the attitude that they will lose. I already know that they will lose, OK. But I go, I always go.
>
> (FF14, regular)

> Always when someone tells me that they lost, that they are the worst, I say that everybody has their bad day sometimes and they should fight to the end, don't give up, so we shouldn't give up either, we should continue to support them.
>
> (FF3, ultras)

> Because I go there for the team. First of all, to make the team feel that I want to stand behind it with my support, I am also there for the team.
>
> (FF4, ultras)

The loyalty to the club can be manifested in various ways and celebrated through social practices that manifest the closeness to the badge and club colours in ordinary and extraordinary circumstances. Female fans shared with us during the interviews several unusual but highly interesting private stories about their intimate relations with their clubs. One of the female respondents mentioned experiences with the use of bed linen in the club's colours:

What is it like sleeping in Lech's bed linen?

Very nice, falling asleep is nice for sure because you see your badge, your stadium. It is nice.

What does this bed linen look like? Do you have more than one?

Yes, one is with the stadium, the second one is with an image of the terraces, one has a 'Lech Poznań' inscription and badge, the other is very old, has many badges and different inscriptions of 'Lech Poznań'.

How do you feel without the bed linen of Lech?

Strange.

> (FF2, ultras)

In the case of other female fans of Lech, the club's colours created a symbolic wedding entourage:

> Also, embroidered seats [the seats of a wedding car in Lech's colours – ed. authors], everything was blue and white, beautiful. And they rented this car so that I could go to the wedding. Of course, the wedding cake was in Lech colours, and so on.
>
> (FF19, ultras)

Emotional dimension

Football matches are also an opportunity to feel, and more importantly show, extreme emotions such as happiness or anger that are almost impossible to express freely in typical, everyday situations. Cultural norms dictate that emotions should be restrained at least in professional life while stadiums present the opportunity to shout out in frustration, sometimes spell out anger or uncontrolled explosions of hype, jump with joy, end up in somebody's arms freely exchanging hugs with unknown people. Also, a stadium – as a 'permission zone' (Ben-Porat 2009) – is a space where some social norms are temporarily suspended and swearing is commonly accepted. In some sense, this creates an alternative to living in a sterile, politically correct world filled with detailed procedures and strict rules of behaviour that most people obey, for example in their professional environment (Sennett 1998). This aspect is also noticeable in the narrations of female fans who treat the match time as a platform for emotional indulgence:

> Sometimes you go to shout and stomp about at the stadium, just half-jokingly and half-seriously, to let out your emotions. And for a moment, this life, all problems and so on are left behind. You enter the stadium and start thinking about something else.
>
> (FF18, regular)

> Also, it is emotional relaxation. You go to a match, leave the house, all those professional and private problems. You go and can roar, sing, and enjoy the football. Sometimes we get nervous, you know, due to the players' lack of technique, or a lost match, but it is just such relaxation for the brain, it also gives you such comfort, such rest, you just relax going to the match.
>
> (FF11, regular)

The breakaway from the daily routine and the feeling of freedom, spontaneity, but also detachment from the working environment attract female fans to football matches. Football serves as a form of carnival for both male and female fans, and also both genders seem to appreciate it.

> It was a detachment from such a typical job in a call centre. I like walking in high heels, but going to matches is breaking away from such a dress code. At the stadium, you can dress in a loose tracksuit, a loose T-shirt, and go out with friends with whom I feel really good. So it is a different world and a great moment to relax and be someone completely different, free, without such rigid frames.
>
> (FF9, ultras)

It is clearly visible that for some female fans matches are an opportunity to 'breaking the chains' of daily routine; respondents mention words like 'asylum' and 'chill-out':

> Yes, it happens, I release emotions then, and it feels good. I feel that when I am there, I can scream and no one cares, no one pays attention. This is asylum for me. After a whole week, it is a place where I can really relieve everything from the last week.
>
> (FF4, ultras)

Our data demonstrate that women express similar emotions towards their club as the men; they also similarly experience the spirit of the match atmosphere, as acknowledged in qualitative interviews:

> In some places, a lot of people do not come for the match only, they come for the atmosphere, they come just for fandom, and no matter what is happening on the pitch, it's all about shouting.
>
> (FF4, ultras)

> The atmosphere of the stadium itself. I'm not a great expert on results, no, I go rather for the pleasure of watching and this stadium's atmosphere.
>
> (FF8, regular)

> There was such an atmosphere that I still remember the shivers running through me then, and after this I started to buy a season ticket.
>
> (FF12, regular)

As mentioned before, the Polish *Ekstraklasa* is not particularly attractive to watch in terms of performance on the pitch. However, some female fans are still interested and indeed enjoy watching football live:

> I think they like football. I think it is related to the fact that you just really like football very much.
>
> (FF7, regular)

> I think there are just some women who are very interested in football as they follow games, I am talking about the European Cup, World Championships, European Championships. Some of us watch, if possible, the Copa America, because it is really interesting football. I think such a group of people exists, but I have no reliable data so can't estimate its size.
>
> (FF5, VIP)

> I wanted to see the match live because on TV it is something completely different.
>
> (FF8, regular)

As some research demonstrates, there are female fans who attend sports events not only for sporting reasons but because of the attractiveness of the sportsmen (Toffoletti and Mewett 2012; Sveinson, Hoeber and Toffoletti 2019). Some Polish female fans express similar interests, both in players:

> Piotrek Mosór [footballer of Legia Warszawa in the 1990s – ed. authors], it's hard to admit for me, especially since his son started playing in the youth team, I feel terribly old. But then all girls loved Mięciel [Marcin Mięciel, footballer of Legia Warszawa in the 1990s – ed. authors], so I had to fall in love with someone else.
>
> (FF18, regular)

… and coaches:

> [A]nd I also like to look too at the cool trainers who are elegant…. Why do I love football? Because I see such elegant guys: here is Probierz [Michał Probierz, a previous Polish player, the coach of Cracovia Kraków in the 2019/2020 season – ed. authors].
>
> (FF7, regular)

What is interesting is that female fans do not hide the fact that they find some players or coaches attractive. This seems to be in line with previous findings, for example in Denmark (von Essen 2007 quoted by Pfister, Lenneis and Mintert 2013) and Australia (Toffoletti and Mewett 2012). They spoke freely about it, not feeling that at any point it may undermine their fandom or loyalty. Perhaps the dominant logic of the discourse assumes that those feelings are somehow mutually exclusive, but the study shows that that is not the case. Appreciation of the physicality of football players does not exclude or even soften loyalty to the club and support for the team performing on the pitch.

Social dimension

The quantitative data also indicate that some female fans perceive a football match as an excellent opportunity to spend time with friends or close ones. Many female fans admit that a lot of their friends are also fans, so a match is a perfect occasion to marry both passions and socialising with friends. In particular, because football fandom is collective, it is about sharing emotions, being together and adhering to social bonds. Furthermore, a football match is more than just 90 minutes of play; it involves the journey to the stadium and back, which often takes longer than the match itself. These aspects also come from narratives as the match is becoming a family 'expedition':

> I also treat going to the stadium not only as watching a match, though of course it is that too, but I usually connect it with a family event. Because we go with two or three sons, first we go for a walk or something to eat, it

depends what time of year it is, then we support together, and then we come back together, and we usually go to dinner somewhere, then we go home.

(FF8, regular)

For them [the respondent's children – ed. authors] it is a full-on trip, we know that there will be McDonald's on the way, then there is the match, there are hot dogs, or whatever is needed. Then we go to the fan shop, so there are stickers, key rings and other stuff. And this is a whole family trip that builds bonds because you experience joy together, but you also experience failure together.

(FF11, regular)

As the main actors introducing women fans to the world of football and fandom are men (in different relations: fathers, partners, brothers, etc.), it is seen as ordinary that some women attend matches because they accompany, for example, their partners. It is common, particularly in the VIP sector:

However, there is definitely a group of people, women, who just accompany their men. They like doing it. It's not like they have to come. They like doing it. They want to share these good moments with them and I think that's very good.

(FF5, VIP)

A football match attracts numerous fans. It ultimately becomes a perfect venue for matchmaking, and since the majority of fans are (still) men, women enjoy a comparative advantage in finding a male partner. So, female fans are sometimes accused of seeking a male partner in the stands and turning it into a *vanity fair*. Those arguments are well known and also articulated by female fans who see a variety of different women attending football games and different reasons attracting them to football. This *vanity fair* is particularly evident in the VIP sector where there are many influential figures like entrepreneurs, politicians, celebrities and journalists:

The fact that they come to some places for matches to be seen, make acquaintes, take a picture and everything is styled to the maximum.

(FF5, VIP)

I think that women treat going to the stadium (as I noticed, but maybe my observation is not good) as a bit of a fashion show because they have these hats, everything is fitted, a bit of a fashion show.

(FF8, regular)

Although female fans regret such developments, at the same time, they see them as a wide cultural trend that comes from broader changes in society. One female fan explains this phenomenon as something new, as 'a sign of the time' and changes in the field of football:

And do many women go there to promote themselves?

Unfortunately more and more. Originally, I remember, it wasn't like that. Everyone was normally dressed in the club's colours and so on, but now there are girls who wear pink hats, pink jackets, they will take a selfie for Facebook, and they will filter it instantly as it did not work out well. Also, unfortunately, there are those that just want to show off.

(FF4, ultras)

The respondents interpret this new phenomenon in terms of matrimonial challenges. This means that for some – especially young women – visiting the stadium's terraces is a space for searching for a potential partner:

Often the young girls don't follow Lech, they just go hunting, I'd say.

(FF19, ultras)

Yes, I can say that there are a few girls who just go to Lechia because they must have a hooligan as a boyfriend. Or, I don't know, a boy from Lechia. There is such a thing, yes.

(FF20, ultras)

Girls who, for example, come, I don't know, to meet a boy, do you know such a phenomenon?

Yes, it is often so. They just come to show off in front of the boys. And once when I asked a girl what year Lechia was founded, she didn't know.

(FF3, ultras)

The female fans that we interviewed did not hide their criticism of the dress code of some women in the stadium. They find it disturbing and even inappropriate for such an occasion and a good reason to criticise particularly young women for turning a football match – during which they scream their throat off – into a catwalk where they can show off their brand-new and glamorous outfit to earn some attention from the male part of the audience:

And besides, if you go to a match, you go to a match, not to wear a short skirt or high heels. You should just wear sneakers, put on a loose T-shirt, and be able to roar, not be ashamed of the fact that at the moment I look daft screaming my throat off.

(FF9, ultras)

Most of the female respondents critically refer to the situation when women come to a match to seduce the male audience and catch some personal glory.

Interestingly, however, they do not notice a similar phenomenon in male fans' behaviour. The male need to grab female attention does not seem to exist even though many men in the stands take photos (some of them are definitely 'selfies') to publish on social media. This is a common trend that was observed during the participatory observation, but women somehow are more exposed to critical views because of the glamorous, often sexy outfits, while it is less striking in the case of men. Also, men are less suspected of using the stadium for seeking life partners.

The reasons mentioned for why female fans attend matches vary enormously. Women participate in football as fans because they love the club, support the team, like football in general, enjoy the stadium atmosphere and for the possibility of meeting friends, and can indulge themselves and express strong emotions that are banned in most daily practices. Ambiguous reasons for attending matches are expressed in the following statements:

> Because I like very much going to matches. First, because I like football and I like watching it. Most of all because it is Legia. Second, because I want to meet with my friend. Third, to watch the theatre that is performed there. It is fascinating for me; I like to observe it because it is a theatre that happens there.
>
> (FF12, regular)

The changing nature of football and fandom (however slow the transformations are) makes more space for women's expression of identity. The study shows that for many girls and women, football is important for the construction of their identity, and even if it still remains predominantly a male game, it is being transformed gradually into a less masculine field. Some male regulations and prevailing patterns of thinking are still dominated and strongly influenced by men , but in many cases, women are motivated just by being part of the football culture in their own authentic way.

References

Antonowicz, D., R. Kossakowski and T. Szlendak. 2015. *Aborygeni i konsumenci. O kibicowskiej wspólnocie, komercjalizacji futbolu i stadionowym apartheidzie [Aborigines and Consumers. On Fandom Community, the Commercialization of Football and Stadium's Apartheid]*. Warszawa: IFiS PAN.

Antonowicz, D. and Ł. Wrzesiński. 2009. 'Kibice jako wspólnota niewiedzialnej religii' ['Sport fans as a community of the invisible religion']. *Studia Socjologiczne* 1: 115–149.

Ben-Porat, A. 2009. 'Not just for men: Israeli women who fancy football'. *Soccer & Society* 10(6): 883–896. doi: 10.1080/14660970903240030.

von Essen, S. 2007. 'Pigerne fra Vestegnen' ['The girls from Vestegnen']. *Information*, September 11. Accessed 20 January 2020. www.information.dk/146209.

Gencer, R. T. 2015. 'Spectator motives and points of attachment: Gender differences in professional football'. *The Anthropologist* 19(1): 77–85. doi: 10.1080/09720073.2015. 11891641.

George, T. 2019. 'What happens to a town when its football club dies?' *Manchester Evening News*, October 27. Accessed 4 November 2019. www.manchestereveningnews. co.uk/news/greater-manchester-news/bury-football-club-what-happens-17154213.

Giulianotti, R. 2002. 'Supporters, followers, fans, and flaneurs: A taxonomy of spectator identities in football'. *Journal of Sport and Social Issues* 26(1): 25–46. doi: 10.1177/0193723502261003.

Giulianotti, R. 2005. 'Sport spectators and the social consequences of commodification: Critical perspectives from Scottish football'. *Journal of Sport and Social Issues* 29(4): 386–410. doi: 10.1177/0193723505280530.

Meier, H. E. and M. Leinwather. 2012. 'Women as "armchair audience"? Evidence from German national team football'. *Sociology of Sport Journal* 29(3): 365–384.

Pfister, G., V. Lenneis and S. Mintert. 2013. 'Female fans of men's football – a case study in Denmark'. *Soccer & Society* 14(6): 850–871. doi: 10.1080/14660970.2013. 843923.

Redhead, S. 1993. *The Passion and the Fashion: Football Fandom in New Europe*. Avebury: Ashgate Publishing Limited.

Sennett, R. 1998. *The Corrosion of Character: The Personal Consequences of Work in the New Capitalism*. New York: W. W. Norton & Company.

Sveinson, K., L. Hoeber and K. Toffoletti. '"If people are wearing pink stuff they're probably not real fans": Exploring women's perceptions of sport fan clothing'. *Sport Management Review* 22(5): 736–747. doi: 10.1016/j.smr.2018.12.003.

Toffoletti, K. and P. Mewett. 2012. 'Oh yes, he is hot: Female football fans and the sexual objectification of sportsmen's bodies'. In *Sport and its female fans*, edited by K. Toffoletti and P. Mewett. New York: Routledge, 99–114.

9   Participation in fandom culture

As was shown earlier in the book, female fans populate all parts of the stadium, including the ultras stand, which is heavily dominated by males. Surprisingly, in the sample of our survey, a significant number of women declared that they sit behind the goal with other ultras fans. Fans standing behind the goal are responsible for providing support either through spectacular choreography or vocal support (chanting, clapping and singing). The female fans we interviewed in this research project who purposely choose the ultras sector were fully aware that this is not a good place to watch the game. Importantly, however, some fans' practices – for example, some chants, the waving of scarves, standing and singing the club's anthem when the players come onto the pitch, clapping after a good ball or goal – connect the majority of the spectators during the game regardless of sector. Other kinds of practices fans can be involved in include activities more connected to a wider meaning of fandom culture. Some groups of supporters expand their activities beyond the match situation and are also active as non-profit organisations serving the local community, engaging in various charity activities. For fans, this is also an important part of their performance as it builds a sense of community and adheres to boundaries between fans.

To study female fandom, we examine participation in social practices (1) on match day (connected mostly to supporting the team) and (2) beyond match day (results from social engagement of fans). In discussing fans' practices, we have decided to examine separately the linguistic practices in the stadiums, assuming that because of their sexist nature, they can be problematic for female fans. The survey shows that female fans are overwhelmingly active during the match, and they provide support for their teams on the pitch. Bearing in mind that the sample is biased towards more active fans, it is worth mentioning that female fans do not stand out from the rest of the fans in our survey. It provides strong empirical evidence that gives the lie to many stereotypes and popular claims that female fans understand neither football nor the fandom culture.

Match day practices

When considering stadium practices, the quantitative data confirm that female respondents are active in most typical fandom behaviours (Table 9.1).

Table 9.1 The practices of fandom taken by female and male fans

	Female fans (N)	Female fans (%)	Male fans (N)	Male fans (%)
Common singing	771	88	2,549	87.0
Common clapping initiated by ultras sector	774	89	2,374	81.1
Common chants	729	84	2,429	82.9
Waving a scarf	674	77	2,264	77.3
Others	32	4	164	5.6

In the Polish context, most of the football songs are initiated and conducted by the ultras sector. Ultras fans support their team through the whole game regardless of the score. One very typical activity is a slogan that is repeated a few times during the game: '[T]he whole stadium is responding!' This is an encouragement for the fans from the other sectors to join the supporting actively, even for a moment. After this 'invitation', the ultras sector initiates a particular song or chant, and the rest of the stadium (in practice, only the nearest sectors to the ultras one typically respond) repeats it. Sometimes, when the result of the game is looking positive, or the players need to be supported in the final minutes of the game, the whole stadium sings. That is why it is possible that so many women can be engaged in common singing, even if they sit in different sectors. Some of the female fans from the regular sector indicate what it can look like:

> I sing in the boys' tonality, with such a voice. I want to laugh myself, as I just sing like that (laughs). Of course, I don't know all those chants so precisely, but I try to do something there. As they [ultras sector – ed. authors] roar, so the whole stadium stands up. I obviously don't sit, but I also stand up so that we generally participate actively in this whole match and we live this match.
>
> (FF7, regular)

> Not all chants, no. I sit in a sector where only a few sing. But if there is a request from Kocioł, then everyone stands up, and then you can fulfil yourself.
>
> (FF14, regular)

Given the low quality of football that has resulted in a lack of success in European club competitions, the Polish *Ekstraklasa* can be seen as an unattractive event, particularly if it is compared to other broadcasted top European football leagues (Big Five). So, it is not surprising that various fans' performances can be more attractive to fans than the actual game on the pitch. Furthermore, engagement in singing sometimes becomes more important than watching the game:

> I think that, after all, there are moments when I focus more on supporting when the match is boring, or the score is very bad. As it is hard to look at the pitch, we look around, do anything just to avoid looking at the pitch.
>
> (FF4, ultras)

> For many female fans, it is not football action that gives them the hype; it is what comes from the stands. The energy that fans can collectively produce, their prime focus is more what is going on in the stands than on the pitch. When I go to a match, when I start singing, I get into a mucky sweat, I do not know what is happening, often I do not know what the result is. I go home and I check the results. I am happy to be there, that I can be there, that I can support my team, but somehow the aspect of the result is missing.
>
> (FF2, ultras)

> My feeling is that if you are in Młyn, you are more focused on cheering. Of course, you are watching a match, a spectacle, but you give more attention to singing and so on.
>
> (FF20, ultras)

The female fans we interviewed not only highly appreciated the ultras' performances, but were also enthusiastically engaged in collective social practices in the stadium. The participatory observation that we conducted for this study showed engagement while performing fans' practices in the stands. Of course, overall, female fans demonstrate different attitudes towards fans' social practices during a game, and this is generally reflected in the sector of the stadium they choose to sit/stand in.

We shall not draw overly bold conclusions from the fact that a significant number of women declare involvement in various ultras activities. Many of them – and there is clearly a bias in the sample – attend matches in ultras stands where they are naturally involved in the whole process of presenting choreographies. Previous research on Polish ultras (Kossakowski, Szlendak and Antonowicz 2018; Antonowicz, Jakubowska and Kossakowski 2020) suggest that they are run by male fans. Ultras groups prepare a plan for performances: for example, ultras fans leave their flags on particular seats before the first whistle. The person who sits there then just has to wave the flag at the right moment:

> [I]t is known that if you have to wave flags, I'll take the flag and wave, but I'm not organising it.
>
> (FF11, regular)

One female respondent explains how hard ultras' 'craftship' can be:

> It is quite hard; you need to have a lot of time for it. These are preparations; usually, a lot of people after school do it, for example. Well, painting on such a large material and scale is not easy. They meet, sometimes, you know, they meet after school, it happens at night. Well, it's like driving around at night, coming back. I don't know, maybe there is one girl, there are definitely girls who would like to do it, right? Because they would like to see their work, and then, for example, feel such pride and say, 'oh, I painted it'. And it seems to me that this is not the place for a girl. Boys should think about this.
>
> (FF20, ultras)

Clothes, gadgets and scarves in the club colours are an inseparable attribute for most fans. The scarf is very useful because it is not only used to express love and attachment to the club. Fans wave their scarves on many occasions: after a goal has been scored and during some chants. In many cases, they hold a stretched-out scarf at the players' entrance to the pitch. During the matches of Lech Poznań, Legia Warszawa and Lechia Gdańsk it is the basic, symbolic manifestation of feelings for the club and team (observation from the fieldwork). In the case of Legia, the holding of scarves above the head (flags and other materials in the club's colours as well) is accompanied by joint singing of Czesław Niemen's song 'Dream about Warsaw'.[1] In the case of Lech and Lechia, both clubs have their original anthems fully dedicated to the club. Holding the scarf upwards resembles a religious ritual (see Antonowicz and Wrzesiński2009) – a holy symbol directed upwards in a special place that is for stadium fans (a stadium can be considered a cult place with the character of a cathedral; see Stein 1977, 36). The anthem of Lechia is as follows: 'We believe only in BKS', where BKS refers to the history of Lechia, connected with the building industry.

These are special, breath-taking and highly emotional moments for any fans of those clubs, and female fans also find them exceptional.

> Of course, the anthem with scarves, when our team is introduced as well.
>
> (FF14, regular)

> Yes, yes, waving a scarf, yes! All these elements happen (laugh). I didn't fire flares, it wasn't this section. But waving a scarf is an element I like very much.
>
> (FF16, VIP)

The results of the survey, as well as interviews and participatory observations, leave little doubt that female fans eagerly engage in collective support. They clap (in every sector) and jump (mostly in ultras stands): 'jumping, clapping', as one of our respondents summarised it perfectly, '[e]verything that is important'. (FF4, ultras).

Football language as a troublesome part of football fandom culture

A significant part of football fandom performances is the language used by fans to support their own team but also to offend the opposing team, its fans, referees, police and other persons related to football and politics that has been observed among Polish fans (for more see Antonowicz, Jakubowska and Kossakowski 2020; Jakubowska, Antonowicz and Kossakowski 2019). This language is a part of the chants that one can hear in the stadiums: group shouts initiated by the ultras fans, as well as individual reactions to the action on the pitch. As previous studies have revealed, the language in the stands is perceived on the one hand as vulgar and, on the other, as sexist (see, for example, Jones 2008; Chiweshe 2014). As a consequence, mainly in regard to the second characteristic, stadium language has been seen as problematic for female fans. At the same time, football stands can be perceived as 'permission zones' (Ben-Porat 2009) characterised by a high tolerance of obscene, offensive, uncensored and controversial chants and songs that are not heard in other social spheres.

On the basis of these studies and the concept of performative sport fandom (Osborne and Coombs 2013), Polish fans were asked about their discursive practices during matches and their opinions on the language used in stadiums. The quantitative data reveal that female fans accept the language used by fans to a smaller extent than male fans; however, 63% (as compared to 69% of men) of them agree with the statement: 'The language in the stadiums is adapted to the situation/emotions of the game and does not disturb me at all'. According to a quarter of female fans (and 19% of male fans), 'the language is characteristic of the stadium'; however, they would prefer it to be less vulgar. Around 9% of fans of both genders stated that 'the language in the stadium focuses too much on insulting the opponent instead of supporting their own team', while around 2% said that 'the level of vulgarity in the stadium is unacceptable' for them. Therefore, the language used or provoked mainly by the ultras fans is accepted by two-thirds of women in the stands, however one-third of them would prefer to hear fewer vulgar words and more positive support.

The data from the interviews allow the question to be answered as to whether female fans join other (male) fans in their verbal practices. In this aspect, their attitudes are differentiated but with one common practice – positive support of their own team. A significant proportion of the respondents stated that they prefer this form of support to negative abuse aimed towards the opposing team and their fans. As a consequence, they are more willing to sing or shout to encourage their own team and show their attachment to the team than to insult others. No involvement in abusive practices has been declared by numerous fans and can be illustrated by the following selected quotations:

> Certainly, I do not like all these so-called greetings, especially to opponents, this is simply not my way of supporting, it offends me, I do not take part in this.
>
> (FF12, regular)

I don't sing. I don't need to stand up and insult someone for 90 minutes. Well, I want to support Lechia, yes, but not … you know, there are some visiting fans there, so you know, you always have to insult them with something, because this is the way it has to be.

(FF20, ultras)

I mean, I'm not joining it, this hunting of another club.

(FF14, regular)

When it comes to songs that are supposed to support the team, I take part in them as much as possible, but when it comes to songs that are targeted at the referees or police, I don't feel the need to abuse them, so I just stand there and wait until those who feel the need to shout something like this stop doing it.

(FF4, ultras)

Non-participation in abusive language practices is not specific to fans from one type of stadium sector (it is also not specific to female fans only, as some male fans admit that this kind of language is disgusting); it can be observed among fans sitting in the ultras stands, the regular one and the places for VIPs. Moreover, involvement in these practices cannot be seen among the oldest fans, and some middle-aged fans have noticed that one can grow out of it:

It may be a process of growing out of things, but I don't like anti-support very much. Sometimes it is an element of broadly understood fan culture. But I think that if it is, it should be kept to a minimum…. I prefer the form of support directed at the team much more.

(FF18, regular)

Generally, I do not participate in any insulting chants; I think we have so many of our own cool chants that I do not do it. I have stopped. I used to yell, now I don't.

(FF19, ultras)

It should be noted, however, that the decision of the second fan is also related to a friendship with a fan of the 'enemy' football club. Another fan expressed her objection to insulting referees:

[A] referee does what he has to do, so if we shout that a referee is like this, or worse, we start yelling ugly at his family, because such situations also happen, it is a level too low for me, because this man has done nothing to us, and he has done his work and that has to be done.

(FF4, ultras)

One of the female respondents clearly states why she cannot be engaged in some chants and songs that connote extreme political content:

> I can give some examples of songs where I stand with them, and I have never sung them in my life. And I will not sing them. It is not about swearing, because this is not a problem somewhere, but as you probably know, Cracovia is a club that is considered to have Jewish roots. It disgusts me. Because I really like Cracovia for some reasons, my grandfather was a goalkeeper there, so it is a club close to my heart, even though I live in Gdańsk and support Lechia. I have never sung chants about Jews, you know, gassing people, because it doesn't make me laugh at all, because it's not something about stadiums, in my opinion. And I didn't have a problem to say it clearly. They could, of course, disagree with that. I don't know, I have never heard any strange things directed towards me.[2]
>
> (FF16, VIP)

It seems it is the action of insulting others rather than the use of vulgar language that is problematic for the majority of female fans. Only a few fans, including the two oldest, expressed their clear dissatisfaction towards the omnipresence of vulgarity in the stands. Interestingly, all of them referred to 'femininity' and the ways to perform gender:

> I refuse to swear because I don't think it's right. I don't like it and I think that it doesn't suit a woman, but guys do it really … they yell at football players, you know, it is aggression.
>
> (FF7, regular)

> [T]here may be some cursing if it doesn't work out, because they play so badly, if someone is emotional, it wouldn't bother me, but if it's just a load of such vulgarisms, then I'm not hiding that it bothers me, but maybe it's because I'm a woman, and because I don't use those words myself, maybe that is why it bothers me.
>
> (FF8, regular)

> I think one can cheer differently, and not insult someone with 'ch', 'k'[3] or even worse.... [I]f it's women who behave so vulgarly, it scares me.
>
> (FF21, VIP)

As one can see, for these fans, the performances imposed by the male ultras fans are not consistent with the performance of femininity realised in the case of these fans, as it appears according to the scripts of 'being a woman' (Ussher 1997). Also, the issue of children raised by other female fans can be partially related to this script. One of the women who attended matches with her children declared that she leaves out the swearwords from the chants and asks the children to follow suit. Another interviewed fan did not take her son to the stadium when he was (too) young because of the vulgar language.

> However, the problem is that many reasonable women will not bring their children [to the stadium – ed. authors] and we are not talking about four-year-olds, but, for example, eight-, ten- or 12-year-olds. It is certainly a situation in which some women will say no because these vulgarisms are, in fact, far too much.
>
> (FF13, VIP)

Moreover, the majority of female fans emphasised that even if they use swear-words in the stadium, they do not do so in everyday life:

> And there's also a curiosity that I've observed about myself, it's that I can get into this atmosphere so much. Generally, I'm a person who doesn't swear at all, maybe only where it's a really bad situation, just like everyone else, to be relieved, but at this stadium, you often swear together with the whole Młyn [a laugh].
>
> (FF7, regular)

> At first, I had a little problem with it; then I got used to it because I'm not a person who curses and no one has never cursed in my home.
>
> (FF12, regular)

Fans not accustomed to using vulgar language in everyday life admit, however, that they do use swearwords in the heat of the action during football matches. The action on the pitch, such as a missed shot, a foul, a referee's decision, causes emotional reactions among female fans regardless of where they sit in the stadium.

> I use uncensored words sometimes too, if the emotions take over.
>
> (FF15, regular)

> Of course, I sometimes do. It's rare, though, but there are some situations where you can't do otherwise.
>
> (FF18, regular)

> I mean, I try not to do it, but you know what it's like to be emotional. When our biggest rival comes, it happens. But generally I am a follower of this positive cheering.
>
> (FF1, regular)

Despite their unhidden enthusiasm towards collective singing and chanting, they are selective in what they sing, shout and chant.

> However, I am engaged in all the songs, roars and so on, more or less vulgar, although I try not to do this when I am with children. But if you are

in the ordinary section, without children, you can scream there again and again. It's cool.

(FF11, regular)

One female fan from Lechia observes that even people from the VIP sector, who are seemingly more 'civilised' and subdued, sometimes get carried away with the emotions and vulgar content in the stadium (however, during our participatory observations in the VIP sector, we observed that such emotions were detected only among men):

> No, vulgar ones sometimes too, if emotions take over, it amuses me that when we are in the VIP stand, my husband stands with his old friends and they scream: 'f**k off'. Also VIPs do, this is funny.

(FF15, regular)

The female fans who do not perceive the stadium language as problematic and use it during the matches are not numerous and, unsurprisingly, their seats are in the ultras stands. In this part of the stadium, the rules are imposed and executed by male ultras (or even hooligans) who hardly consider opposing views. The ultras stands are these sections of the stadium where social norms are particularly distant from what is the conventional understanding of appropriateness by mainstream society. But rules are rules, and everyone has to follow them regardless of their gender. Ultras stands are also where all chants that insult the opponents, the referee or other persons are initiated. Vulgar language is perceived as a 'natural' feature of this place:

> It's something natural in Żyleta. I have been prepared for it, and I have no problem with it. I know that some people have a problem with the way things are in stadiums. But that's what a stadium is like. In this place, one has the right, one has no problems with it.

(FF6, ultras)

Is the stadium an excuse for this type of behaviour?

A little bit like that, it's a stadium, one does not have to explain, there's no excuse, it's a stadium, and that's it.

But why is it acceptable in the stadium?

Because it's a stadium and there's no need to explain it.

(FF2, ultras)

The second of the quoted respondents also stated that she gets satisfaction from taking part in the chants that insult the opponents, while the other interviewed female fan, also from the ultras stand, emphasised the greater adrenaline, the better atmosphere and the possibility of letting all her anger out with the use of swearwords. These two fans also noted that the use of curses is common and widespread nowadays, which can also be explained by the fact that among the younger generation of female fans, their use is quite obvious and not disturbing at all.

Football stadiums are perceived by the majority of female fans as 'permission zones' (Ben-Porat 2009) in which some social norms, including language norms, are temporarily suspended. Thus, for many of them, performances related to fandom are not contradictory to everyday performances of 'traditional' femininity that exclude the use of swearwords, while for a minority of them these two identities are almost impossible to combine. Primitive and often sexist language is used to abuse other fans, players and referees by ascribing them female characteristics, as the analysis of the grass-roots ultras magazine *To My Kibice* (*We Are the Fans*) conducted by the book's authors has revealed (Jakubowska, Antonowicz and Kossakowski 2019). However, the data received from the interviews suggest that stadium language is perceived as sexist by the researchers rather than by the female fans themselves. This was also found by Mintert and Pfister (2015), who wrote that some fans accept sexism as an integral part of the fandom culture and trivialise its manifestations. Indeed, this study and our previous investigations have led us to similar and even further conclusions that football fandom is deeply rooted in abusive language and insults. They might be intentional or unintentional, they can also vary in terms of vulgarity, but there is no doubt that as it stands, rough language is a part of football culture. Most of the interviewed female fans, when asked about the sexist nature of stadium language, declared that they did not perceive this language in this way and/or that they did not pay attention to it. The following statements present the ways in which they rationalise their stands:

> I have never thought about it that way. For me, this language is not sexist, which means that perhaps I am so immune to it that it does not offend me, but at some point, I also stopped listening to these texts.
>
> (FF12, regular)

> I usually perceive it as vulgarism and I don't know, I don't dissect it into primary factors. For me, these are just vulgarisms.
>
> (FF4, ultras)

> It doesn't affect me at all, because it doesn't influence everyday life in this way.... However, I also think that rarely do women, as we once talked about this subject, because this is the specificity of fandom and there is no other way of articulating the fans' thoughts. And I think one doesn't have to look for a hidden root to it, it's just like that and we have accepted it somehow ... I treat it neutrally, I mean I don't go deeper into it, because it doesn't make sense, I go there to watch the match and relax.
>
> (FF11, regular)

These are the most frequent and most typical but not the only responses we encountered during our study. Even those who find football language sexist seem to understand its inseparable links with the fandom culture. So even though some of them found the stadium language sexist and declared feeling uneasy about it and not taking part in sexist chants, they still accept it as an element of fandom culture. It can be seen as one of the strategies for dealing with the existing, traditional frame of fandom and being accepted as 'real fans' (Jones 2008). It is a striking paradox, but a good illustration of it was given by one of the interviewed female fans.

> I don't sing. I don't like it. It bothers me. I have accepted it, but I don't like it. I can accept that this is how it looks. And that's it.
>
> (FF6, ultras)

Others would go one step further and agree that they do not feel offended by this language and it does not disturb them personally because they do not find anything chauvinistic in, for example, the phrase 'playing like a girl'. They admit that women (girls) do indeed play football less physically, dynamically and energetically. So, we can say that although female fans do not participate in all forms of linguistic performances imposed by the ultras fans, the reason for this is not related to the perception of stadium language as sexist. The awareness among female fans of sexism in the stadium is generally low, and if they do want to participate in those linguistic practices, it is motivated by an unwillingness to insult others and, less commonly, to use swearwords. Female fans rarely feel that the language of football undermines their dignity as women.

Beyond match day activities

The fans' performances during match day are only a part of the wide range of activities they get involved in. Moreover, it is not even unusual for Polish fans to engage in more civic, municipal or charity activities. This, however, requires the establishment of formal associations, which is frequently a formal requirement to be a partner for public and private stakeholders (for example to have the legal right to carry out a public collection). At the beginning of the twenty-first century, fans from many clubs set up official organisations to represent their interest in contact with other authorities. These organisations – supporters' associations – were set up mostly to deal with fans' issues, such as the organisation of trips to away matches, and improving communication and cooperation between different types of fans, including those living some distance from the club. On top of this, fans' associations professionalised the production of independent fans' gadgets (jerseys, scarves, etc.) and many of them occasionally take part in social, political and charity actions (Kossakowski 2017; Grodecki 2018). Political activism is an element specific to Eastern European football fandom and Polish fans seem to have conservative, right-wing political views (Kossakowski and Besta 2018; Woźniak, Kossakowski and Nosal 2019), and their political activism is mobilised to support patriotic and historical events. This is an important aspect of fans' activities and therefore also pivotal for the study.

Thus far, we have explored the situation of women mostly in stadiums as part of a football crowd, but being a fan can go far beyond simple participation in a football game. For example, fans of Lech Poznań commemorate the Greater Poland Uprising (1918) and collect financial means for renovating the graves of insurgents from this event. This is a spectacular grass-roots action that engages a massive number of fans regardless of their age and gender. Such activism seems to fit well with female fans who find space for their activism. Some of the female fans from Poznań are engaged in this action:

> Well, because I am a volunteer and I collect money, this is the fans' action for insurgents. And at All Saints, funds are being collected for the renovation of these insurgents' monuments, I am trying to get involved. And it depends on how I can manage it; I collected one year in Poznań, one year it was collected in Września, near my place of residence. I was also involved, and I tried to take part in it.
>
> (FF1, regular)

> When it comes to the Greater Poland Uprising, by all means, firing flares on the square. As for this, I am also interested in history, this patriotism, naturally. I like it here in Poznań that I don't have to hide my political views.
>
> (FF19, ultras)

The survey shows that civic activities are popular among female fans as a considerable number of them admit to supporting various fans' activities. Like men, nearly half of women (48%) are engaged in patriotic activities initiated by fans of their club; 67.2% take part in fans' charity actions; 57% provide money for fans' purposes (usually they are collected during the match); 29% of female fans are involved in education of younger fans; 25% are engaged in ultras activity (mostly during matches); and 7.6% have shares in designing the club's gadgets. Most of these actions don't require personal initiative, and many of them are reactive (like the transfer of funds for fans' actions). Female fans describe this kind of engagement:

> I always try to support these things somewhere, actions like money collection for tombstones, or collect plush animals for children in hospitals; there are many things … taking part in some collections there, or contributing to them, or sometimes collecting money, you just get involved.
>
> (FF11, regular)

> I participate in money collections, whether for the renovation of insurgent graves always on November 1 at cemeteries or in victory marches, which are always organised at the end of an anniversary of the uprising. Whether

they do Christmas packages for Poles in the Eastern Borderlands, or any schools or orphanages, I get involved in these actions in any way I can.

(FF4, ultras)

As there is the collection for kids I buy or add something, but I don't collect money by myself from the organisational side. But I used to go for blood donations, as it was there.

(FF2, ultras)

Fans' activism during match day and also beyond it shows that this type of activity fits female fans well. But this also poses a question about the role they can play. The interviews suggest that women's participation in fans' practices (both types) is not something unusual; however, the rules of those activities and roles given are determined by men. As Pfister, Lenneis and Mintert (2013) rightly acknowledge, 'compliance with men's rules and norms seems to be the only way to be accepted and to gain the respect of the fan community' (p. 859). No matter whether those activities are organised by formal fans' associations or through an informal ad hoc single action, they are run by male fans. There is also a sense of conformism among female fans as regards obedience of the rules. This contradicts Danish fan groups in which women are reported to be members of the governing boards of most of the official fan groups (Pfister, Lenneis and Mintert 2013, 856).

If a woman behaves in accordance with the norms that are adapted there, supports, screams off her throat, sings loudly and jumps like boys, so there is big respect.

So if someone is following the rules?

Well, yes, because all the fun lies in the fact that these rules are somewhere there. If some people do not follow the rules, then they simply have to change their place.

(FF11, regular)

Interestingly, some of the female fans seem not only to adapt to these norms but also to deeply incorporate them and treat them as a natural part of the social order.

Going into Żyleta for the first time, I knew there were rules that I wouldn't change; I'm not trying to be an activist. And I knew I had to adapt. This is a group that has been there for years. And it was somehow established that they have power. Because this is a group that has power … there is no democracy in the stadium. There's somebody who can give you a headache. This is outrageous. But it's not outrageous in the stadium. If somebody is aware of it, such things don't impress him/her. And you know you have to adapt.

(FF6, ultras)

Notes

1 Czesław Niemen, who died in 2004, was a very popular singer and composer in the Polish rock scene.
2 The quotation concerns the chants against Cracovia Kraków fans; as Cracovia's history is related to the Jewish community, some fans from opposing teams use anti-Semitic words to denigrate Cracovia and its fans.
3 The first letters mentioned by the respondent refer to the words generally regarded as extremely vulgar and abusive.

References

Antonowicz, D. and Ł. Wrzesiński. 2009. 'Kibice jako wspólnota niewiedzialnej religii' ['Sport fans as a community of the invisible religion']. *Studia Socjologiczne* 1: 115–149.

Antonowicz, D., H. Jakubowska and R. Kossakowski. 2020. 'Marginalised, patronised and instrumentalised: Polish female fans in the ultras' narratives'. *International Review for the Sociology of Sport* 55(1): 60–76. doi: 10.1177/1012690218782828.

Ben-Porat, A. 2009. 'Not just for men: Israeli women who fancy football'. *Soccer & Society* 10(6): 883–896. doi: 10.1080/14660970903240030.

Chiweshe, M. K. 2014. 'One of the boys: Female fans' responses to the masculine and phallocentric nature of football stadiums in Zimbabwe'. *Critical African Studies,* 6(2–3): 211–222. doi: 10.1080/21681392.2014.940077.

Grodecki, M. 2018. *Życie po meczu: Formy wykorzystania kapitału społecznego kibiców piłkarskich w Polsce* [*Life After Match: The Forms of Using Social Capital of Football Fans in Poland*]. Warszawa: Uniwersytet Warszawski.

Jakubowska, H., D. Antonowicz and R. Kossakowski. 2019. 'Bracia po szalu i sąsiadki zza miedzy: Narracje o męskości w środowisku kibiców piłkarskich' ['The brothers in arms and our girl neighbors: The narrative of masculinity in Polish football fandom culture']. *Studia Socjologiczne* 1(232): 95–115. doi: 10.24425/122491.

Jones, K. 2008. 'Female fandom: Identity, sexism, and men's professional football in England'. *Sociology of Sport Journal,* 25(4), 516–537. doi: 10.1123/ssj.25.4.516.

Kossakowski, R. 2017. *Od chuliganów do aktywistów? Polscy kibice i zmiana społeczna* [*From Hooligans to Activists? Polish Supporters and Social Change*]. Kraków: Universitas.

Kossakowski, R and T. Besta 2018. 'Football, conservative values, and a feeling of oneness with the group: A study of Polish football fandom'. *East European Politics and Societies* 32(4): 866–891. doi: 10.1177/0888325418756991.

Kossakowski, R., T. Szlendak and D. Antonowicz. 2018. 'Polish ultras in the post-socialist transformation'. *Sport in Society* 21(6): 854–869. doi: 10.1080/17430437.2017. 1300387.

Mintert, S. and G. Pfister. 2015. 'The FREE project and the feminization of football: The role of women in the European fan community'. *Soccer & Society* 16(2–3): 405–421, doi: 10.1080/14660970.2014.961383.

Osborne, A. C. and D. S. Coombs. 2013. 'Performative sport fandom: An approach to retheorizing sport fans'. *Sport in Society* 16(5): 672–681. doi: 10.1080/17430437. 2012.753523.

Pfister, G., V. Lenneis and S. Mintert. 2013. 'Female fans of men's football: A case study in Denmark'. *Soccer & Society* 14(6): 850–871. doi: 10.1080/14660970.2013.843923.

Stein, M. 1977. 'Cult and sport: The case of Big Red'. *Mid-American Review of Sociology* 11(2): 29–42.

Ussher, J. M. 1997. *Fantasies of Femininity: Reframing the Boundaries of Sex.* New Brunswick: Rutgers University Press.

Woźniak, W., R. Kossakowski and P. Nosal. 2019. 'A squad with no left wingers: The roots and structure of right-wing and nationalist attitudes among Polish football fans'. *Problems of Post-Communism.* Advance online publication. doi: 10.1080/10758216. 2019.1673177.

10 Female fans as customers

The transformation of football is more and more frequently perceived as a 'neoliberal concept' (Dubal 2010) that underlines the financial aspect of football. Furthermore, many professional clubs have been transformed into corporate organisations (Hamil *et al.* 2004) and commercial 'brands' through which they are converted into money-making machines by new casts of executive directors (King 1997a; Kennedy 2012). At the same time, increasingly, football fans are being perceived as customers, and many football clubs develop new strategies to deal with them, which is widely known in the corporate world as 'customer care' (Hill, Canniford and Millward 2018). This new development is more advanced in the richest European leagues (Big Five), but its logic is also echoed in the less affluent and more peripheral leagues such as the Polish *Ekstraklasa*.

The commercial approach to football is often linked to special care in regard to new fans (King 1997b; Fillis and Mackay 2014), including women. Our study assumes that investigating female fans requires the examination of different dimensions of football fandom. One of them is the commercial aspect, which is critical for the football industry, and the consumption of football also becomes increasingly essential for football fandom. This is why we examined female fans' purchasing habits and their perception of the assortment of products that football clubs have to offer.

Purchasing souvenirs

Ninety per cent of female fans that took part in the online survey declared that they wear their football club's colours during matches (as compared to 93% of male fans). These colours can be seen on the fans' scarves and T-shirts. However, it should be remembered that 40% of online female respondents were fans from ultras stands where wearing these colours seems to be compulsory. The participatory observations revealed that in the regular sectors, women wear clothes of different colours not necessarily related to the club's ones. They have the club's scarves rather than T-shirts, while in VIP sectors neither of them can be seen much among the female fans.

The data from the in-depth interviews with the female fans have provided more detailed information on the clubs' clothes, souvenirs and homeware bought by women.

Almost all of them (except for the two oldest fans) have their club's fan T-shirts and scarves, and sometimes hoodies and accessories too, for example gloves. Their selection and the number bought vary from one scarf and one T-shirt to more than 30 T-shirts and nearly 20 scarves in the case of one Lech Poznań fan: 'I've got about 30 or 40 shirts, 20 hoodies, 18 scarves. I don't even count the hats and gloves' (FF2, ultras). Usually, the respondents declared that they have one scarf or a few (three to four) of them and a few T-shirts. The latter are fans' shirts (labelled in the online stores as 'clothing' or 'fashion') rather than the club's shirts (sold as 'kits' and under the name of the main sponsor). A few fans we encountered during our research had just one club shirt, which may be due to the fact that none of the sponsors of the analysed clubs provide a female version of the kits. Some of the fans also buy fans' hoodies; however, this is less common than the products mentioned previously. One can also see that fans sitting in the ultras stand usually have more scarves, shirts and hoodies than fans from other sectors.

It is also worth mentioning that some female fans declared that they also had 'historical' ('nationalism') T-shirts. As mentioned earlier, many ultras tend to present right-wing political views (Kossakowski and Besta 2018) and show strong emotional commitment to Polish history – more precisely, some events from history, which are usually related to male heroes and the discourse on masculinity (Kossakowski, Antonowicz and Jakubowska 2020). Women, as the netnography of Polish female fans' profiles on Facebook reveals (Jakubowska, Kossakowski and Antonowicz 2018), adopt the male way to articulate their nationalism and celebrate the same events and heroes. This has also been seen in the purchase of clothing. For example, one fan from Warsaw stated: 'I buy uprising [Warsaw Uprising 1944] shirts very regularly' (FF18, regular) while a fan from Poznań bought a T-shirt dedicated to the anniversary of the Greater Poland Uprising [1918] (FF1, regular). However, the relations between nationalism and the current politics have discouraged another fan from Warsaw from buying 'patriotic' T-shirts:

> Yes, I also had patriotic ones. I will be honest with you. I stopped buying them. The political atmosphere in Poland has changed a bit, and yet this patriotic environment has stopped attracting me as much as it used to.
>
> (FF12, regular)

Female fans who underscore the patriotic aspect of football fandom are in a minority while nearly all fans, as revealed both by quantitative and qualitative data, demonstrate their fandom in the stands by wearing the club's colours on scarves and T-shirts.

Do they also wear them outside the stadium? According to the online survey, less than half of female fans do so. During the interviews, only some fans, usually from the ultras sectors, declared that they wore clothes with symbols related to their clubs in everyday life:

> I wear them. I have shirts. When it's warm. It's not just for a game, it's casual.
>
> (FF6, ultras)

I think you'd sooner meet me in Legia's hoodie or shirt in a private situation.

> (FF18, regular)

Going somewhere, I wear Lech's hoodie, not some normal one. Just like that, I open the closet and see this one and put it on.

> (FF4, ultras)

When it comes to clothes, yeah, well, I wear them every day.

> (FF3, ultras)

Other fans stated that they do not wear this kind of clothing outside the stadiums due mainly to the nature of their jobs, such as working in a bank, having a management position and/or having a work dress code. One fan has decided to wear only a small accessory, that is, a belt, to emphasise her commitment to the club's colours.

Some fans also raised the issue of wearing the club's colours outside the club's city, which can be dangerous because of the fans' (and clubs') rivalry. One Lech Poznań fan told the following story:

> Well, once when I was going to my sister's who lived in Wrocław [the city of Śląsk Wrocław football club – ed. authors] I remember that once I went to see her dressed in Lech's shirt and I had only a hoodie over it, so even though it was hot, I had to wear this buttoned-up hoodie … but it was a coincidence, I wouldn't have deliberately dared to do that.
>
> (FF4, ultras)

One fan from Legia Warszawa said that she had to buy some 'normal' T-shirts so as not to wear Legia T-shirts with Warsaw Uprising motifs at the Polish seaside.

The lower popularity of clubs' clothing outside stadiums can also be related to the offer proposed by the clubs for women:

> I've got the T-shirts, but lately, I've noticed that I wear them less. Maybe it's because I started to take more care of myself. And it's not always appropriate to go out in a man's shirt.
>
> (FF22, ultras)

Following this statement, the fan explained that these T-shirts are not in fact always male ones, but their shape is not 'feminine' and does not allow female fans to show their (traditional) femininity. However, it seems that wearing a club's colours outside the stadium depends not only on the level of identification with the club, but also on fans' dressing style and their professional situation.

The female fans were also asked if they bought the accessories offered by the clubs' stores. The results reveal that they are less popular than T-shirts and scarves; however, some fans, more often from the ultras sector, buy them. Their range varies enormously. Several women commented that small accessories, such as a pendant or a pen, in spite of their small size show commitment to the club:

> Legia accompanies me in many ways. For example, a pen engraved with the Legia's crest. It is a little thing, but it shows that you are connected to the club.
>
> (FF18, regular)

Another popular souvenir is a key leash. Usually, the female fans have one or two of them; however, one fan from the ultras sector said she had a collection of them that consisted of 36 key leashes. Several fans also indicated that they had bought their club's mugs as souvenirs. Only two fans mentioned possessing accessories that can be perceived as more 'feminine', that is, bracelets. The clubs' colours and symbols are also used by some fans in their workplaces or at school, as illustrated by club calendars, desktop wallpapers, notebooks, pencils and pencil cases. However, as mentioned by one respondent who held a management position, an expression of fandom may not always be seen positively in the workplace:

> I used to have a Lech flag here [in the work office – ed. authors], but I saw that people were surprised when they came in, so I took it off and gave it to my son because it impressed people. I had such a big one here on this board that was prepared for it anyway, but it surprised people, and I took it off, I didn't want to create a nervous atmosphere here [laughs].
>
> (FF11, regular)

Also in the fans' houses, the expression of fandom is rather modest; the fans do not hang posters, scarves and the clubs' kits on the walls or furniture, except for one fan who collects slap stickers:

> I collect slap stickers from Lechia and Śląsk [Śląsk Wrocław], and other fans' stickers, for example Stomil, so I have a whole shoebox of these stickers. The ones that are doubled I glue on the door and wardrobe in my room, they are all glued. But those that are singles are in the box, I'm collecting them now.
>
> (FF3, ultras)

Another fan also collects different souvenirs related to her club and fandom, however she does not display them:

> I have a box in which I have hidden my tickets, some stickers, slap stickers and scarves because scarves are different. There is also one scarf of my older brother who used it a long time ago. There's still an old coat crest on this scarf. So there are more historical memorabilia, and they are hidden in this box.
>
> (FF1, regular)

Club souvenirs are also popular birthday presents and many female fans that we interviewed admit that they are beneficiaries of such presents. This is interesting because it means that they are not only known for their passion for football, but their close ones appear to support it. One of the fans recalls a story from the past when she received a gift from her son on her 40th birthday that gave her great pleasure – a scarf with the inscription 'Lechistka', that is, the feminine form of a Lechia fan. As she emphasised, this special scarf, unlike the other that she already had, was 'for me, for a woman' (FF17, family). Female fans are also good customers of fan shops, which seem to have better offers for children than for female fans. Therefore, it is not a surprise that female fans not only receive the club's souvenirs as gifts but also buy them for others, mainly their children. This is in line with previous research findings that women in the stadium are expected to perform family roles. This was confirmed by the manager of the official store of Lech Poznań and her long-term observation that women buy more often for their children than for their husbands, partners or parents, and lastly for themselves.

The study gives a mixed picture of female fans as customers of the football industry as women present an extremely diverse approach to exhibiting their affection for their club. During a match, the majority of female fans have their club's branding (though not always official merchandise) but this is far less common outside the match context. Those female fans who typically support from the ultra stands seem to be much keener to use their club's products in their professional and private life. For some of them, it is important to show their commitment to the club in everyday life; sometimes they do this by wearing the club's T-shirts and hoodies, but sometimes only through small, personal belongings that can even remain invisible to others. Nevertheless, female fans are regular customers of club merchandising, even if they use it mostly in private spaces where not many people have access to it. This shows best the kind of emotional bonds that female fans have with their clubs, as decorating private space with the club's crest or colours shows the significance of the clubs in their life and also the intimate character of this relation.

Evaluation of clubs' merchandising offers

The other aspect of studying female fans as consumers of club merchandising is examining commercial offers in fan shops. This demonstrates the clubs' approach to female fans as consumers, which – as we have already discussed – is an (increasingly) important dimension of football fandom.

Knowing that the female fans buy clothes and accessories related to their clubs, they were asked about their opinions of what clubs' stores offered for women. Before their presentation, it should be mentioned that fans, both female and male, buy their club's souvenirs and clothes in two kinds of stores – the official ones, located at the stadiums (main store) and in commercial centres, and in independent grass-roots fans' shops run by fans' associations. The latter do not offer official merchandising but their own fans' brands.

All of the interviewed female fans have noticed a growing number of products, mainly T-shirts and hoodies, exclusively for female fans in both official and unofficial merchandising.

> There used to be nothing, and now there's an offer for children and women, it's great.
>
> (FF15, regular)

> There used to be no such thing. We used to wear men's shirts. Somewhere you would tie them up or put them in your pants, or you would be advised to do so. Now, for three or four years, something has been going on there, even Stowarzyszenie Lwy Północy [the Lion of the North Association] has also started to produce these women's clothes.
>
> (FF20, ultras)

> A lot has changed in the last three to four years when it comes to women's clothes.
>
> (FF6, ultras)

> The club has created a women's line when it comes to clothes; a woman can also dress well for a match, there are slim-fit T-shirts, all sizes, women's gadgets.
>
> (FF11, regular)

As mentioned earlier on numerous occasions, the number of female fans has recently increased and this has triggered a growing selection of women's products on offer. However, still, the female fans recognise the gap between the richness of the selection of products offered to men and women and the still limited offer addressed to them:

> [T]here are more things for men than for women, it is hard to find and choose something for ourselves. For example, I recently wanted to buy a T-shirt for myself, but I didn't find anything interesting.
>
> (FF3, ultras)

> It is terribly discriminating when you want to buy something, as looking at the shirts and sweatshirts in my wardrobe, most of these things I have are for men, unfortunately. Recently, a new collection of clothes appeared, so there have been more of these things, but despite everything, there is not a lot of them. It does not concern only our club things, but also fans' things. We have a fan shop in Poznań where one can buy things for fans, so the women's collection is practically non-existent there. Women's shirts or strictly female gadgets, whatever, are really rare.
>
> (FF1, regular)

Things for a woman can be found on one or one and a half pages on the store website, and for men, it is five or six. It is clear that for men it is significantly more.

(FF4, ultras)

The merchandising offers suggest that the clubs still see male fans as their prime target and female fans are less important customers than kids. The women we interviewed during our study seem to acknowledge this and substantiate it by their smaller presence in the stands. According to one Legia fan, 'there is much less for women, the proportion is maintained' (FF6, ultras). In the opinion of one fan of Lechia Gdańsk, 'the poor offer is due to a lack of demand' (FF16, VIP). According to her, even when a club has introduced new clothes with a more subtle logo and the club's colours, without big inscriptions and drawings, which could be potentially more interesting for women, such products have not achieved good sales results.

But this is only part of the story as another fan made a clear statement blaming her club for stereotypically profiling football crowds. The club, through its poor offer for women, makes it clear that it is targeting male audiences, not a female one. The data provided by Lech Poznań reveal that purchases from the women's collection comprise around 7% of all purchases of clothes. Therefore, it is smaller than the percentage of female fans in the stands, which may be due to the quite small interest of women in buying the clothes proposed by the clubs. Interestingly, fans from Warszawa and Gdańsk generally perceived the offering of the shops run by the fans' association as more considerable and attractive than that from the official club stores.

It is hard to uncover the main reasons for the significantly lower sale of female products. One of them could be women's dissatisfaction with the products offered to them; however, in this regard, their views were very mixed. Some of them described the women's clothes as 'ugly', 'unconvincing', 'awful' or 'after one fashion', while others said that the proposed clothes were 'interesting', 'fine', with a 'delicate' (i.e. smaller inscriptions and without fanatic inscriptions) or 'cool' design. They also had contradictory opinions on the emphasis on femininity by the clubs' T-shirts. For example, one fan from Poznań said:

There are feminine T-shirts, really cool, with a v-neckline and gently embroidered, really gently, with a hardly noticeable wing [a club symbol – ed. authors]. They come out with these offers, as much as possible. Some may say it is a commercial issue, well, OK, but boys can easily put on any T-shirt, in any size. We women don't; we like to feel a little feminine. Let's be those fans, but still emphasise that we are babes. And this offer comes out.

(FF19, ultras)

One fan from Warsaw praised the clothes offered by the fans' shop, not only because the T-shirt sales were donated to charity, but also because of their 'feminine' design:

> [T]hey made very cool T-shirts, feminine with such cool feminine patterns. There was a T-shirt, slim fit for a woman, and there were eyes on it and a covered part of the face in Legia's colours underneath it. And it was nice, nicely designed, feminine and it was supposed to support a girl.
>
> (FF12, regular)

While for another fan from Warsaw, this emphasis on femininity is a bad thing:

> But there's an emphasis on femininity everywhere. There cannot be a T-shirt in a woman's size with some kind of crest or something; it has to be emphasised that you are a woman. I don't like it. T-shirt with a woman etc., I don't like it. I don't need to emphasise my femininity because I'm a fan.
>
> (FF6, ultras)

This opinion, although controversial, is not an isolated one and a similar opinion was shared by other fans, such as this one from Poznań:

> The majority of clothes I have are for men. I don't like these for women. There is an inscription, Kolejorz [unofficial name of the club – ed. authors], the mount, the hearts, I don't like things like this, it is not for me. I would prefer the same T-shirts as for men but in female sizes.
>
> (FF2, ultras)

Besides those infantile symbols that are supposed to make clothing 'feminine', there is the issue of the pink colour, traditionally linked to girls and women, which was also raised in several interviews. In principle, female fans were against the use of pink in female fans' clothes, and they appreciate that 'fortunately, there's not much of that pink' (FF18, regular) and it appears mainly in the children's (girls') collection. Another fan could not understand the marketing decisions of the club:

> [I]t is not just that male patterns appear on female models, but there are completely different things, one does not know where something comes from, or that it is feminine if, for example, there is the inscription Lech Poznań on a pink T-shirt. Where does this pink come from? These are not our colours, and I don't know who in marketing thinks it is, but let him/her think about what he/she's doing because we are going in the wrong direction, completely. There is still a belief that it's a male sport, and when it is supposed to be a female sport, it has to be pink. It doesn't fit in with the club's colours, but it seems that if you are a fan, you are interested in buying something in the club's colours, not in pink.
>
> (FF1, regular)

As well as the colours that made women slightly critical of the female line of club merchandising, there was an issue concerning size. On the one hand, even the smallest male size of T-shirt is too big for them when they are short and/or very slim. As a result, they describe these T-shirts as baggy or use them as dresses rather than T-shirts. On the other hand, the female line of clothes proposed by the clubs have small sizes and are dedicated to slim, young women:

> The clothes are very small and their XL is a normal L on maximum; I wear XL and I just cannot buy anything.... For example, there are very nice dresses made of tracksuit material, very nice and I was frustrated that their cut suggested that they prefer women who are small and skinny.
>
> (FF12, regular)

> There is a collection for women, but for very small women; when you are a small, young girl it's easy, but then it gets harder.
>
> (FF14, regular)

It should be noted, however, that this problem is not limited to the clubs' offers, and throughout the fashion market the choice of small sizes is wider than the choice of clothes in bigger sizes. Thus, the clubs are reproducing the general rules of the fashion industry. However, taking into account the small offering for women proposed by the clubs, the likelihood of buying something that fits well is less than in regular shops. Although none of the respondents said that they bought clothes designed for children for themselves, this was revealed by the management of the Lech Poznań store. It concerns mainly fans wearing the smallest sizes and products that are not offered to women but only to men and children. During the interviews, a few fans raised the issue of prices, which are too high in their opinion. Nonetheless, this concerns both genders and involves all football (sport) brands.

The fans' opinions of the clubs' and fans' stores' offering for women reveal, once again, that the category of female fans is diverse. While for some of them, the performance of fandom identity is crucial and they do not want to be perceived as 'another' category of fans (a wish to have the same choice of T-shirts as men but in feminine sizes), for others, the performances of fandom and femininity seem to be equally important (a wish to buy more 'feminine' clothes). What seems to be important for the majority of them is the commitment to the clubs' colours and symbols and their objection to the reproduction of a 'pink feminine world', at least in the case of adult women. So, we can say that women found the commercial offering of their clubs unsatisfactory, sometimes infantile and limited in terms of selection. It is radically different from what is offered to male fans. There is no doubt that those shops (both official and run by fans) are focused on men, and perhaps male fans are their prime customers. Of course, women also buy clubs' souvenirs for their male partners or even sons, and in that situation they experience this asymmetric selection of products.

References

Dubal, S. 2010. 'The neoliberalization of football: Rethinking neoliberalism through the commercialization of the beautiful game'. *International Review for the Sociology of Sport* 45(2): 123–146. doi: 10.1177/1012690210362426.

Fillis, I. and C. Mackay. 2014. 'Moving beyond fan typologies: The impact of social integration on team loyalty in football'. *Journal of Marketing Management* 30(3–4): 334–363. doi: 10.1080/0267257X.2013.813575.

Hamil, S., M. Holt, J. Michie, Ch. Oughton and L. Shailer. 2004. 'The corporate governance of professional football clubs'. *Corporate Governance: The International Journal of Business in Society* 4(2): 44–51. doi: 10.1108/14720700410534967.

Hill, T., R. Canniford and P. Millward. 2018. 'Against modern football: Mobilising protest movements in social media'. *Sociology* 52(4): 688–708. doi: 10.1177/003803 8516660040.

Jakubowska, H., R. Kossakowski and D. Antonowicz. 2018. 'Visual representation of patriotism: Netnographic research on female football fans' profiles in social media'. Paper presented at EASS Conference, Bordeaux, 23–26 May.

Kennedy, P. 2012. 'The football industry and the capitalist political economy: A square peg in a round hole?' *Critique* 40(1): 73–94. doi: 10.1080/00111619.2011.640066.

King, A. 1997a. 'New directors, customers, and fans: The transformation of English football in the 1990s'. *Sociology of Sport Journal* 14(3): 224–240. doi: 10.1123/ssj.14.3.224.

King. A. 1997b. 'The lads: Masculinity and the new consumption of football'. *Sociology* 31(2): 329–346. doi: 10.1177/0038038597031002008.

Kossakowski, R and T. Besta 2018. 'Football, conservative values, and a feeling of oneness with the group: A study of Polish football fandom'. *East European Politics and Societies* 32(4): 866–891. doi: 10.1177/0888325418756991.

Kossakowski R., D. Antonowicz and H. Jakubowska. 2020. 'The reproduction of hegemonic masculinity in football fandom: An analysis of the performance of Polish ultras'. In *The Palgrave Handbook of Masculinity and Sport*, edited by R. Magrath, J. Cleland and E. Anderson. Cham: Palgrave Macmillan, 517–536.

11 Perception of a football stadium as (social) space for women

Previous research provided convincing empirical evidence that female fans have been denied the status of 'real' fans (King 1997; Pope 2017; Antonowicz, Jakubowska and Kossakowski 2020) and therefore it is worth investigating whether or not their presence is accepted in football stadiums. To do so, we asked a very fundamental question regarding whether or not football stands are appropriate places for women. Moreover, we asked female fans their opinion about female presence in different types of stands assuming that the football stadium is an internally diversified social space and that in different stands, different social norms are applied. The vast majority of female fans, unsurprisingly, strongly agree or somewhat agree that football stands are appropriate places for women (Table 11.1). Only less than 3% of the female participants in the online survey did not agree with this statement.

A comparison with male fans' answers reveals that although the vast majority of them perceive football stands as an appropriate place for women, only half of them (52% as compared to 75%) strongly agree with this statement. To a large extent, whole interviews can be treated as evidence that female fans perceive football stands as an appropriate place for them. Their participation in fandom performances, their commitment to the clubs and the frequency with which they attend the matches reveals that the football stadium is 'their' place. Generally, the research participants perceive the stadium as an appropriate place for women, as illustrated by the following citations:

> For me, definitely yes.
>
> (FF15, regular)

> The stadium is absolutely the right place for women. I don't know what's wrong with us being there, we go to the matches, cheering if we like it.
>
> (FF4, ultras)

> Today, yes. I think it is a good place for women.
>
> (FF13, VIP)

However, as already discussed, the football stadium should not be seen as a homogeneous place; therefore it was worth exploring the opinions on women's

Table 11.1 Do you believe football stands are appropriate places for women?

	Female fans (%)	Male fans (%)
Strongly agree	75.5	51.7
Somewhat agree	21.7	39.7
Somewhat disagree	2.3	7.2
Strongly disagree	0.4	1.3
Total	**100**	**100**

presence in the stands during the interviews. We specifically asked about being in the ultras stands, which are naturally populated by the most radical fans. And even in this case they show lots of enthusiasm about women's presence in the ultras stand; however, several of them highlight specific rules that are applicable in that section of the stadium. Therefore, their views are also conditional, suggesting that women will be able to go to any place in the stadium; however, they must follow the rules. This is very interesting, and it returns us to the concept of female fans as 'guests' whose presence will not interfere with existing norms and rules, the latter being imposed by male ultras fans.

> If I had a condition and wouldn't be with children, I would go to Kocioł. There is nothing dangerous there if a woman behaves following the norms that are adapted there; she cheers, shouts and sings loudly and jumps like boys, then there is great respect there. Of course, it is known that if she came in heels, they would probably kick her out of the sector right away.... If someone doesn't fit in, they just have to change their place.
>
> (FF11, regular)

It means that the rules of appropriate behaviour in the ultras stand imposed by the male majority are also accepted and adopted by some female fans who are sitting (standing) there. They seem to be completely socialised to them and treat them as their own, which is also shown by the fact that they emphasise that there is no place in the ultras stands for women who are not 'real' (authentic) fans:

Kocioł, is this a place for women in your opinion?

> I think it is a place for women, but actually for those who feel that they are going there to support the team and feel good there, and do not go there to swag themselves or to make a super, extra selfie for Facebook, or something else, because such things have also happened. That's why I think it is a place for women, but for those who feel that they want to be there and are not forced to be there.
>
> (FF4, ultras)

Do you think Młyn is a place for women?

> For some, no, for others, yes. I'd say, for those real fans, devoted fans who are always at every game, go to away matches, support this Lechia, do not

go and support only to show them up, yes, this is the place for those chosen, those who help. And for those who just want to show off, there is no place for such girls in my view.

(FF3, ultras)

Even the occasional violent incidents that involve male fans under the influence of alcohol should not be an obstacle for women because they seem not to be a problem (although one should be pragmatically aware of such incidents) and similar behaviour can be encountered nowadays everywhere:

[I]t's a bit different here because we're sitting on this straight, so you know there are more guys there. The guys sit there with beers. When they come in, they're already drunk and they drink the beers. Once I had to lean forward a little to avoid getting doused accidentally. If one is going there one has to take this into account.

(FF7, regular)

Do you think a stadium is a good place for women today?

You know, I don't feel bad as a woman going to a football match. For me, the things that happen in the stadium, it's the same things that happen in every other place. For me, it's not a problem that someone swears, because we swear the same way on the streets. Or if someone drinks beer because people drink beer in bars and on the streets too.

(FF16, VIP)

Although there is a predominant feeling that the ultras stand, like any other place in the football stands, is also a place for female fans, several interviewees took the opposite view. They argued that women do not fit there because this is a masculine place, where male fans demonstrate their hegemonic masculinity. Again it shows a deeply embedded belief that football culture has its rules and norms, which are perceived as a 'natural' or 'given' part of the social order that women (as newcomers or guests) should adapt to or leave.

Is Żyleta a place for women?

No. It looks like it's not. Women are being asked to leave the lower stands. I was in the middle, upstairs, so it was OK. I didn't have a situation where someone had a problem with my presence. But not downstairs.

Why not?

It seems to me that some people from this ultras stand take this supporting very strongly to heart. And this is the issue, showing their masculinity. One has to drink this beer on the bus, and shout. And some people have to display their masculinity. That's why women don't fit in there.

(FF6, ultras)

Other fans have also raised the role of men and masculinity – however, in different circumstances. In principle, female fans do not question the fact that there need to be some rules in the ultras stands as long as they do not exclude women. And therefore football stadiums are perceived as inappropriate for women. It is not because women do not want to be there or feel bad there, but because it is a rule imposed by male fans who have control over other fans. Because of their decisions, women are excluded from the ultras stands:

> I believe that there is no place where women should not be present, but, as I have said before, those people who are in a kind of decision-making position, who decide what is happening in Kocioł, among those more involved supporters, in their opinion these women should not be present on this lower floor or this ground floor. I think that, in spite of everything, when women are already involved, they get involved to the maximum; when they go to the match, they want to get more involved in Kocioł and they are involved much more than quite a few of the men in Kocioł. And I don't think it's fair to say to these women that this isn't the place for you, you can't come here.
>
> (FF1, regular)

Unsurprisingly, female fans are strongly convinced that a stadium is a place for women. The only concern raised was linked to the ultra stands, which seem to be controversial in that respect because of distinct rules and patterns of behaviour. The study shows that female fans find ultras stands to be an appropriate place for women if they follow social rules (as one female fan from Warsaw states: 'When I went to the ultras zone for the first time, I knew there were rules that I wouldn't change, I didn't try to be an activist, and so on. And I knew that I had to adapt' [FF6, ultras]); however, those social rules might also affect the presence of women who happened to be excluded from the ultras stands (or some part of them) by those who made and execute those rules. This is a paradox, but the interviews do not provide us with a clear-cut answer as to how women respond to the fact that they have to adapt to the rules imposed by male fans (ultras). On the one hand, they seem to agree that somebody has to make the rules, but at the same time, they do not understand why those rules are made against them. They think it is not right but there is nothing they can do about it, at least at the moment.

Although the female fans state that the stadium is a place for them, from the interviews conducted with them, it emerges that they are treated as 'guests' with great hospitality and care. However, they believe that their role as guests also imposes some limits on behaviour, including adapting to the social order and participating in social practices performed in the football stands. Female fans (as guests) are expected not to undermine or even question the social rules, norms and values that prevail in football fandom. This is because football is believed to be a men's thing, and female fans do not seem to be keen to overturn that, but they want to be part of it. In typical circumstances, invited guests – to feel themselves accepted and comfortable – do not want to change the arrangements at their hosts' house even though they might not suit them best. In other words, the role of the guest requires from women a certain level of openness, tolerance of the football culture and adaptation to the 'host's order'. Assigning to women the social role of 'guests' legitimises and reinforces the masculine character of the fandom culture.

The analysis of interviews does not reflect the revolutionary mood; on the contrary, it suggests that women adapt to the football fandom culture even though it might require hiding their female pride. Of course, not everyone enjoys the 'specific' cultural circumstances of the fandom culture, which is under-pinned by testosterone and a 'lads' culture', and where the use of abusive and sexist language tends to prevail.

> On numerous occasions, the game was outstanding, but this masculinity, vulgarity, sexism can put off many women. I had a female friend who once came to a football game and did not do it again because she did not expect what she found.
>
> (FF6, ultras)

To obtain a full understanding of how women are treated by male fans one should acknowledge that women attending football games are a complex category consisting of two ideal types, namely, 'female partner' and 'one of the lads'. Each of these categories, when triggered, is treated positively, but for very different reasons. The interviewed female fans gave very positive opinions about how other (male) fans treat them.

> I felt they were aware that I was a woman, but we are so acquainted that they allowed themselves to call me 'mate'.
>
> (FF9, ultras)

> I've been dealing with boys since the beginning of my life, so I think it influenced my relationships, that I was able to get along with them freely and I think they called me a 'mate' or a 'buddy'. Furthermore, sometimes they more frequently call me 'mate'.
>
> (FF9, ultras)

It needs to be emphasised that women are treated very differently depending on whether they attend as girlfriends, partners or wives (as guests) or they are regular fans (as mates), which is similar to Ben-Porat's concept of 'honorary males' (Ben-Porat 2009, 888). Such a sharp dichotomous approach illustrates a paradox of female fans being trapped in stereotypical models. When they become regular match-goers, they transform into 'mates' or 'one of the lads' (honorary males).

Women are perceived similarly to their male colleagues with the same respect but always with extra care. Once they become proper or authentic fans (King 2002) in the eyes of the men around them, they do not have to demonstrate their gender

(Lenneis and Pfister 2015) as they are part of a community of fans. They are not the subject of any special treatment.

> Even though we do not know each other well, and we do not know each other's names, and we recognise each other, we often talk before, during the break or after the game. Even after we have lost we cheer each other up hoping that the next time it will be better.
>
> (FF1, regular)

> After several male fans had seen us regularly at the match, we stopped attracting attention and became part of the crowd.
>
> (FF18, regular)

This model rests on the assumption that women can either perform a 'feminine' role as a girlfriend, partner or wife or a 'masculine' role as a regular fan. Paradoxically, it appears that there is nothing in between. Furthermore, in Polish, 'female fan' and 'male fan' are two separate words (*kibicka* and *kibic*) and the interviewed females who are regular match-goers associate themselves with the male form of fan (*kibic*). They want to be recognised as *kibic*. This means that fully fledged fans distance themselves from their feminine identity and want to be part of the (homosocial) fans' community.

The perception of the stadium as a space appropriate for women can be related to the issue of safety. Indeed, the survey shows that many fans link the growing population of women in stadiums to increasing safety standards in the stands (male respondents mention this aspect regularly; see the next part of the book). The female fans that we interviewed frequently acknowledged that they always feel safe and believe that, if necessary, male fans that normally sit next to them (whom they do not know well) will never let anyone abuse them.

> Apparently, they are aware that we sit nearby and they hold their horses, but also if somebody drunk pushed or pulled us or something, they would definitely step in to drag him out.
>
> (FF12, regular)

Overall, attitudes towards women are positive. The female fans had not experienced any form of sexist or expressive behaviour and had not witnessed such a situation. On numerous occasions, they repeatedly emphasised that safety is not an issue for female fans, albeit admitting that in the beginning they used to be very concerned about it.

> For sure I can say that while I have been on the ultras side nothing unpleasant or chauvinistic has happened to me.
>
> (FF7, regular)

I have never experienced a negative reaction from male fans. Moreover, even in the fan shop, where it is overcrowded and stuffy, I really notice that fans are particularly friendly to each other.

(FF11, regular)

Early studies found that women tend to be patronised by male ultras (Antonowicz, Jakubowska and Kossakowski 2020) and indeed such situations (behaviours) occur when travelling to away games. Moreover, it seems to reinforce the traditional perception of gender relations when women, as the 'weaker' gender, need to be protected and not drawn into violent events (which is possible at away matches). It seems that these types of behaviour do appear in ultras stands and in particular on public transport to away games, which are specific occurrences within the fandom culture.

And in those ultras groups that organise choreography and conduct vocal support at home and during the trips to away games, there is a strong conviction that this is a male hobby and you women can only be a nice 'addition' to it without being seriously engaged.

(FF1, regular)

This is irritating. This is irritating every day, and also here. It is ridiculous courtesy. I feel that I have to explain why I am here ... it is so natural that I am not able to engage in conversation about football as the reason I am here is that I am a girlfriend of a male fan.

(FF6, ultras)

These quotes are in line with our previous findings showing that ultras fans do not really accept the presence of women at away matches, which are spaces for (homo)socialising and fraternising via lad culture (for example King 1997) and carnival aspects of fandom (see Pearson 2012) fuelled by alcohol, rough language and antisocial behaviour. Such behaviour seems to be a natural reaction to women entering the last bastion of male hegemony and domination in the fandom culture, illustrating their helplessness. If they cannot stop them (sometimes they do), they can at least symbolically marginalise their role among travelling fans. The transformation from 'a female guest' to 'a football fan' is absolutely crucial for understanding the attitudes towards female fans. As long as female fans are seen as female guests of their male partners, they will expect to perform their 'gender' roles, which include not knowing the rules of offside or stoppage time. Their ignorance does not stigmatise them because they are not taken seriously as they are not considered to be fans. They are ordinary women that should know nothing about football. Their presence in the stadium is legitimised only by their male friends, and if they would like to gain the status of a 'real' fan, they will need to prove their knowledge: 'In a way, I had to prove that I had this knowledge and that it was just as important for me' (FF3, ultras). Typically, men are not obligated to prove they are football experts. It is believed to be natural. Ironically, a similar approach to 'female partners' could be found among female fans. Moreover, they also distance themselves from the latter, who only pretend to be football fans, giving a bad name to all women in the football stands.

> They only pretend to be football fans while they are not. They have no idea about the team or the rules of the game, and the action on the pitch does not stir their emotions.
>
> (FF18, regular)

From the interviews, it appears that football fandom is recognised by females as men's territory and social norms and values were established by men to satisfy them. Thus, it is hardly a surprise that female fans do not always feel comfortable in such an environment but at the same time admit that it is not really hostile to them (at worst it is unfriendly). They have learnt to live with it.

> When I got used to fandom culture, learnt how people behave in the stands and so on, I was more certain that nothing wrong could happen to me.
>
> (FF4, ultras)

Female fans that are deeply embedded in the fandom culture who are treated as mates express absolutely no fear over the behaviour of males. They feel safe, they never experience anything that could potentially harm them physically or psychologically.

> It is nice that they accept women. I feel safe because I know that male fans around me would always protect me if necessary. I like away games because of the atmosphere and fun.
>
> (FF3, ultras)

This does not mean that the stadium is always open to female fans. In some interviews, female fans made direct reference to the situation in which they were banned from going to away games or sitting in ultras stands (Lech Poznań). Such 'bans' can be interpreted as 'manifest resistance to authority among men who otherwise experience powerlessness because of their marginal positions in society' (Jones 2008, 518). They do not hide the fact that they do not always understand or share social rules and norms established by male fans that are biased against female fans; however, they do not intend to rebel against them. Contrary to what Ben-Porat (2009) found, the women that we interviewed neither undermined male hegemony nor challenged values, symbols and verbal practices. As guests, they might not be enthusiastic about every aspect of the hosting environment, but they do not feel like they can impose major structural change.

References

Antonowicz, D., H. Jakubowska and R. Kossakowski. 2020. 'Marginalised, patronised and instrumentalised: Polish female fans in the ultras' narratives'. *International Review for the Sociology of Sport* 55(1): 60–76. doi: 10.1177/1012690218782828.

Ben-Porat, A. 2009. 'Not just for men: Israeli women who fancy football'. *Soccer & Society* 10(6): 883–896. doi: 10.1080/14660970903240030.

Jones, K. 2008. 'Female fandom: Identity, sexism, and men's professional football in England'. *Sociology of Sport Journal* 25: 516–537. doi: 10.1123/ssj.25.4.516.

King, A. 1997. 'The lads: Masculinity and the new consumption of football'. *Sociology* 31(2): 329–346. doi: 10.1177/0038038597031002008.

King, A. 2002. *The End of the Terraces: The Transformation of English Football.* Leicester: Leicester University Press.

Lenneis, V. and G. Pfister. 2015. 'Gender constructions and negotiations of female football fans: A case study in Denmark'. *European Journal for Sport and Society* 12(2): 157–185. doi: 10.1080/16138171.2015.11687961.

Pearson, G. 2012. *An Ethnography of English Football Fans: Cans, Cops and Carnivals.* Manchester: Manchester University Press.

Pope, S. 2017. *The Feminization of Sports Fandom: A Sociological Study.* New York: Routledge.

Part IV

Female fans in the eyes of others

Male and football stakeholders' perspective

12 The response of male fans to the growing number of females in football stands

As we show in Chapter 1, most of the researches dedicated to female fans are based on an investigation of female respondents' views. This is reasonable as women's narratives are very important to obtain knowledge about the female history of fandom, the feelings women connect with football and the levels of engagement at which they are involved. Conducting interviews with female fans is an excellent way to discover their sense of identity as well. Interestingly, however, even though most citied studies agree that female fans have to operate in the hegemonic masculine environment, they do not seem to take into consideration the male point of view. So, it is impossible to evaluate the pressure male fans feel from the increasing number of women in the stands, how they perceive female fans and what social role they assign to them. By interviewing male fans, it is possible to investigate how – if at all – the presence of women influences the manifestation of particular kinds of masculinity and affects the sense of brotherhood between men.

This chapter of the book aims to fill this gap, demonstrating how male fans in Poland perceive the presence of women in the stands. Undoubtedly, the male perspective will complement the women's narratives as it is men who create the biggest part of the fandom culture and keep control over major aspects and patterns of behaviours. This perspective is presented in the following chapter, which is divided into three sections: the first analyses the reasons for the growing number of female fans that have emerged in male narratives; the second examines the roles assigned by male fans to women; and the third explores the potential influence of women on male-dominated fans' communities.

The male perception of the increasing number of female fans

In the online survey, the fans were asked about their opinion concerning women's presence in the stands. According to 74.8% of the male respondents, the number of female fans has increased in the last few years, around 22% of them stated that it has not changed, and less than 3% of male supporters stated that there have been fewer female fans in the stands in recent years. Asked about the reasons for the growing female attendance, over 18% of male fans referred to the issue of security – the stadiums are perceived as much safer and more inclusive than they used to be, and, as a consequence, they attract so-called 'new fans' (Antonowicz, Kossakowski and Szlendak 2015), including women. The second reason, related to the previous one, although indicated by 'only' 6% of male respondents, was the modern stadium's infrastructure. It offers more comfortable conditions in which to watch matches, such as covered stands, an appropriate number of toilets, and so on, but also increases individual safety due to a new arrangement of the stands and new regulations (Dróżdż 2014). Some respondents also pointed to: (1) a growing interest in football among women; (2) the fashion for football; (3) a stadium's atmosphere; and (4) wider socio-cultural changes.

The data obtained from the survey were confirmed during the interviews conducted with male fans of Lech Poznań, Legia Warszawa and Lechia Gdańsk. All of them noted that the number of women in the stands has increased in the last few years:

> Yeah, I see it in every sector. The same way I see that this spectacle has also changed, because now I see that one has to get up sometimes ten times during the match, because someone goes through, because he/she is going somewhere, I do not know if to the toilet or to get beer, popcorn or sausage.
>
> (MF1, different sectors)

> There was a time when it was probably noticed that women were starting to appear in the stadiums, that it was worth encouraging them in some way. And I think it was successful, because if you look at the attendances, now there is information in the stadium, about how many women there are among the fans, and it is a nice percentage.
>
> (MF2, ultras)

> I think it has changed but in a long perspective. When the old stadium was still there, I think that it was not entertainment for women. It was also about behaviour, there was a lot of vodkas, quite simple fun, and now I would say there is a lot of both girls and ladies.
>
> (MF3, regular)

> In the 1980s, 1990s there were few of them, less than now, especially at away matches, single ones, and now there are more of them, including at away matches. This fandom is different today, the social media, photos, certainly the number of women has increased.
>
> (MF4, regular)

Male fans are aware of the growing number of women; however, the interviews show that the stands are constantly perceived as a male bastion where women, although more numerous than in the past, are still a minority. Nevertheless, male respondents do not doubt that women have become more interested in football and the clubs are responding to this phenomenon, for example by increasing the selection of products for women in the fans' stores:

> There is a whole line of products targeted at women. I think it is great. There are different products, from cheaper to more expensive, from clothes to some accessories, and here I see absolutely no discrimination against women.
>
> (MF5, ultras)

> There are offers for women. A few years ago maybe not necessarily, because the girls had much less to choose from, but I quite often follow all these offers and women not only have a lot of discounts but also the assortment is wide, from T-shirts to headgear and accessories, there is a lot of it.
>
> (MF6, ultras)

> Offers are appearing both for women and children. For women there are hoodies, there are T-shirts in a female cut, there are some women's hats, there are things for women. There are probably fewer of them. I have never wondered what it looks like proportionally, but they are there. It's cool.
>
> (MF7, VIP)

Answering the question about the number of women in the stands, male fans focus on stadium sectors and the differentiated presence of women in them:

> There are women in Żyleta,[1] there are a lot of girls, mainly young people as I look at them, but still more women are sitting in regular sectors or family sectors.
>
> (MF5, ultras)

> Now, because there are divided stands, one can buy a very expensive ticket for VIP stands, buy one's own box, buy a ticket for the family sector; sometimes, or even often, whole families come, or husbands take their wives, and mothers often come with children.
>
> (MF8, ultras)

> I think there are some families in this new stadium, including some mothers. I would have separated such a group. It is certainly there, at one time in the 1990s I didn't see any women coming with families.
>
> (MF9, regular)

The new modern infrastructure provides a space for various experiences, and new types of fandom performance are available. This deepens the spectrum of being a fan as well as 'doing gender'. According to the respondents, choosing the stadium's sectors influences the behaviour of female fans in the stands and can also be perceived as a proxy of their fandom's engagement.

The male fans confirmed one of the most important statements from our research, saying that female fans should not be considered a homogeneous category. This also confirms one of the statements from 'performative sport fandom' theory (Osborne and Coombs 2013), namely that fans' identity should be seen through the lenses of their behaviour and experiences. Female fans are a heterogeneous group and manifest their fandom in a variety of different ways, but this does not undermine their authenticity. Experiences in ultras stands and family sectors are very different, so it is hard to measure women fans' identity by one yardstick. This was stated directly by one of the fans:

> There are very different girls and women, just as there are very different fans. There is no rule that if a woman is a fan, it is A, B, C, D, that there is a pattern. There is no such thing. Girls are very different. Some girls, like boys, are vulgar and so on, and I wouldn't want to meet them privately, because we have nothing in common. And there are also quiet women, mothers. Because often these people are in relationships already after getting married. And lawyers, doctors, clerks.
>
> (MF10, VIP)

Taking places in different sectors means that women can be engaged in a different style of supporting. In the Polish context, there is some kind of 'obligation' to be a 'staunch' fan when someone takes a place in the ultras sector (as we show in the previous parts of the book, female respondents are aware what kind of 'duties' are expected in ultras stands. They are informed about them, sometimes becoming convinced about them during the visit and – as a consequence – they have to meet the expectations or to change sector, and this 'politics' of ultras stands concerns men as well). In the opinions of all the interviewed male fans, women sitting in the ultras fans' stands are very active during matches, and support their team all the time, while others come to the stadiums mainly as accompanying persons. Commenting on the first category, the male interviewees stated, for example:

> I have often seen girls who have had more vigour than men.
>
> (MF11, ultras)

> I see women who come, often in a group, who are not partners, they consciously come here [to the stadium – ed. authors] because they want to experience something.
>
> (MF12, regular)

However, it should be noted that female fans' engagement is not exclusively characteristic of women sitting in ultras stands. The different modes of fans' identity can be performed in other sectors as well, as noted by respondents:

> I also see some families in the regular stands, and sometimes the women are more involved than the fathers. It is also a novelty compared to the 1990s.
>
> (MF9, regular)

I see that those women who go there [to the regular stands – ed. authors] permanently are just as interested as men are.

(MF13, regular)

Some women come to cheer for real and believe, love this club, and but this is probably fraction of these women.

(MF14, VIP)

The transformation of football and fandom, caused by the new modern stadium infrastructure, influences the manifestation of practices that were impossible to imagine in the times of old-fashioned stadium arrangements (to speak in simplified terms) with the terraces, the ticket office and makeshift toilets. Thanks to the designing of business lounges, skyboxes and VIP sectors, some 'new fans' can utilise a match day for different reasons than supporting the team. Male interviewees have noticed the presence of women in VIP sectors/lounges who are not at all interested in football and the events on the pitch:

But there's also the VIP sector, where I've also managed to be a couple of times, where the fashion show is. There, when we talk about women, these are the girlfriends of football players, who constitute a different category. Generally, it looks like a shopping mall.

(MF9, regular)

Those women who go to the lounge also go to certain banquets often and other such social events, to take a glass of prosecco, eat a piece of sushi and talk to interesting people, not only about sports. Some women are perhaps not business lions, but social lions, they are companions of, for example, their partners and go for the company.

(MF14, VIP)

'Networking' for whatever reason is part of the game, particularly in the new, commercialised era of football. Football matches become another space for doing business; however, some women come to the stadiums only in the role of male partners:

But usually, these girls come in the company of their (male) peers, boyfriends.

(MF5, ultras)

The most popular are probably the partners who come with their boyfriends.

(MF15, regular)

Being a fan and 'doing fandom' manifest themselves in various ways and the same concerns the different roles that fans can play during a match. Some gender roles (women as partners of their husbands, women as wives of businessmen, etc.)

seem to be moved from an outside context to the stadium. As male respondents observe, some women perform a couple of identities simultaneously: match attendee as well as a man's partner or mother. For women, being a fan doesn't mean being 'only a fan' as they are obligated to perform other roles (more than men) at the same time. Therefore, analysis of female fans' identity and performance should be undertaken not only in the frame of the match situation but in the broader meaning of power relations, gender order and duties that a particular society imposes on women (Blackstone 2003).

One male fan noted that women come to the stadium to watch their men, while another stated that women should be considered 'fuses' (MF12, regular), the ones who calm the atmosphere and take care of children (as will be shown further, in some cases, male ultras 'use' women fans as a 'fuse' against security and police). At the same time, an adult woman coming with a man to the stadium can be just 'a mate' who wants to see a match and/or fans' performances, while young girls often come with their fathers. Many male respondents associate women in the stands with their family roles, and this points to two aspects at least: first, that for some women visiting stadiums is mostly associated with family life and social relations (a match is a space for being together, the match itself is not so important); second, that it is hard for men to imagine that a woman is a fan 'herself' and that she represents the same style of fandom and level of emotional engagement as men do.

During the interviews, when asked about the reasons for the increased number of women in the stands, the male respondents pointed mainly to the new stadiums with their modern infrastructure. Thus, as has been mentioned, Polish fandom fits into the trends observed previously in Western Europe, where modern stadiums attract various categories of fans (Antonowicz, Kossakowski and Szlendak 2015; Millward 2011) to the stands. The vast majority of the male respondents attended old stadiums in the past and attend the new venues now; therefore, they have solid grounds to compare them and how the composition of the audience has changed. For example, fans of Lechia Gdańsk state:

> Comfort. It's so normal now that one will sit down, that the seats are for everyone, and not some broken benches. And now one cannot watch the game standing up. Ninety per cent of those who come to the new stadium, I suppose I can't even imagine it. And there, in fact, we often stood. Either there was nowhere to sit, or it was wet, or the chairs were broken. Or everyone just stood, because something was happening. Whether it was blasphemy or an action in the stands, one had to stand up.
>
> (MF16, family)

> I think that the new stadium certainly made it [increased the number of women – ed. authors], a different comfort to watch a match. On Traugutta Street [the location of the old stadium – ed. authors], a man would take his wife, she would come, sit on a nail that sticks out there, she wouldn't have a place to relieve herself because there was port-a-John somewhere, but

usually, everyone went under the fence, she wouldn't eat anything hot or drink, and yet if there were wind, she would say: where have you taken me? And if you had still taken a child, the child would have come back soaked and frozen, etc.

(MF1, different sectors)

One of the fans from Poznań had similar reflections:

But there is also the issue that today it is not only safer in these stadiums but also more comfortable. It does not rain on your head. There is a normal toilet, one can go there, one can also eat something, and there is no problem. This infrastructure, its level has made it more comfortable to watch the match, so a larger group of people is willing to go to the match completely socially.

(MF10, VIP)

And one fan from Warszawa commented:

Generally speaking, it's definitely an objective improvement in security. People who remember the 1990s know how it was and how it looks today, and it is a piece of cake. One can take people to the stadium one wouldn't normally take to the stadium because you wouldn't want them to get hit by a brick or stone.

(MF12, regular)

It is quite interesting to note that in talking about the differences between old and new stadiums a few respondents raised the issue of toilets (this issue was also raised in research in the UK; see Pope 2011). As rightly noted by one of them, 'a lot of people are going to say, come on, do the toilets have any influence? Well, they do, in spite of appearances, they have a big influence' (MF7, VIP). This element of infrastructure can be considered directly (appropriate toilets seem to be more important for women) but also as a symbol of new standards in the stadiums. Some fans interpret these standards in a broader sense – as a consequence of the changes in football, its commodification and mediatisation:

It's like this football is now, it was not like this before, now it is a part of pop culture, there are ads, footballers, etc.

(MF4, regular)

Football has dominated the world in sport. It is a business. It will develop because a woman is the same client as a man. She is a customer who pays for a ticket.

(MF17, regular)

Although there are very few direct references to the phenomena that have changed football, the statements about the new, comfortable stadiums, modern infrastructure and improved safety at sports venues can also be read from this perspective.

The new venues provide not only improved comfort to watch the matches but also influence, as the respondents stated, the atmosphere and fandom culture. In the past, a stadium 'was a less friendly place for women, it was less friendly in general, in the sense that the conditions were just primitive, including in terms of the behaviour' (MF3, regular), while nowadays 'a stadium is a theatre, it has changed the habits, its culture and the fans' (MF1, different sectors). These transformations can be related to both the modernisation of stadiums and Polish society in general and the civilising process of fandom as well. The former refers to changes in football infrastructure forced by football authorities, for example UEFA (Włoch 2013), but also the government's attempts to build an image of Poland as a modern country. After the decision to host Euro 2012, Polish authorities began a multidimensional process of overhauling sports infrastructure and football culture (Antonowicz and Grodecki 2018; Kossakowski 2019). But it was also a time of changes in the national sensitivity of Poles as it was several years after the transformation of the system in 1989, and access to the EU, when Poland aspired to be a modern, Western country like other members of the EU. This also had an impact on expectations concerning football culture – along with modern infrastructure and very restrictive laws, the 'civilising process' (Elias 1997) of the fandom culture was initiated (Kossakowski 2017a, 2017b). The modern stadiums are a huge part of broader social changes that – together – led to the attraction of a larger number of women.

The importance of safety and security, as well as new regulations concerning them, was raised by many male respondents. As they stated, a greater diversity of fans and a larger number of women were made possible by making stadiums safer places:

> I have the impression it's safer than it used to be.
>
> (MF14, VIP)

> This stadium has begun to be presented as a safe place, because in fact, in the 1990s there were brawls at the stadium; later at the stadium it was safer, there were no brawls at all.
>
> (MF18, ultras)

> The separation between these, let's say, fanatical and calm sectors is also technically so large that it is known that there are certain places of comfort and safety at the stadium, where nothing will happen. Today it is practically not happening anymore. As a result, such enclaves have appeared at the stadium where it is known that there is a peaceful place, where one can come with a small child or a baby.
>
> (MF10, VIP)

The last but not frequently raised reason for the stadium feminisation identified by male fans is the larger socio-cultural change concerning mainly women's status in Polish society. In general, male fans tend to focus their attention narrowly on football-related issues rather than elaborate on blue sky ideas and broader social changes. However, some of them stated:

> I think it is probably also a little bit due to such a social maturity and equal treatment of women in social life in general.
>
> (MF5, ultras)

> In my opinion, the feminisation of stadiums is linked to general perspectives, change or lack of change in the status of women in society. And changes in patterns. There are probably more women than there used to be. This is generally linked to the end of the industrial society and the fact that we all work in the service sector. We often have de facto unregulated working hours, or we end up at very unusual times. And in this mosaic of social structure, women are also inevitably more likely to be in the stadiums.
>
> (MF19, different sectors)

It is striking that when male fans interpret reasons why women attend football matches, they mostly take into consideration transformations of stadium infrastructure and changes in the essence of contemporary football, but they very rarely point to aspects connected to women's identities and social status. Men perceive the fact that female fans do not constitute a homogeneous group and women adapt to different patterns of behaviours in various sections of the stadium. However, when the majority of male respondents think about social circumstances attracting women to the stadiums, they most frequently associate them with their family responsibilities such as caring for their children or keeping partners/husbands company in their male entertainment. Also, men do not hide the fact that they see some women seeking male partners in the stands, which is an obvious choice as the pool of candidates is rich. Only a few male respondents give any attention to broader social changes that let women take part in different leisure activities in a more open and emancipated way. Nevertheless, even for men who have been brought up in the new, democratic times of modern Poland, the emancipation of women has weak links with their fan identity. As a result, male fans still assign 'non-emancipated roles' (i.e. 'family roles') to women in the structure of fandom. As we show in the following paragraphs, women are not considered 'real' fans, but rather instrumentalised and patronised and, as a consequence, their role in the fandom culture is drastically marginalised (Antonowicz, Jakubowska and Kossakowski 2020).

Female fans and their roles assigned by men

Treating women mainly as 'new' fans, attracted by modern, comfortable stadium infrastructure, also has another consequence. The 'new' fans are welcomed – to some extent – but not in terms of being regular fans who can influence social norms in the stands. Men still maintain their hegemonic position in the stadium and define the situation in the stands (men play leadership roles in sport in general; see Burton and Leberman 2017). And having the power to define rules and roles means exercising influence on behaviours, attitudes and values in a match situation. Men reproduce a particular set of practices and these also involve a gender dimension. Controlling gender order and practices in fandom culture can be seen as an aspect of another (beyond the labour market, state and family) dimension or structure of reproducing gender order (Connell 1985, 1987). In the structure of fandom, this aspect is clearly visible; fans intensively reproduce and sustain gender relations (men from a powerful position and women from a position of being subordinated; for more about the structure of the fandom culture in Poland, see Kossakowski 2013). Being a fan is associated with certain values and a sense of identity that are characteristic of fandom culture. Therefore, it is reasonable to state that the field of football fandom is another form of social structure where men can reproduce their superior position. This mechanism reinforces external hegemonic masculinity (Demetriou 2001) as by assigning (from a dominant perspective and – typically – beyond women's heads) inferior roles to women, men strengthen their hegemony and dominance over women.

In a situation where men have a dominant position in a wider social environment, it is hard to speculate that they would assign equal or meaningful roles to women. It is not just that men aim to celebrate their power over women, but it serves as a sense-making instrument that helps to adapt male fans to rapidly and irreversibly changing social circumstances that influence the homosocial culture of football fandom. This is why assigning social roles says more about true male attitudes towards female fans than the numerous public declarations they made to be politically correct.

Many male respondents commented on the presence of women in stadiums with respect. However, during the interviews, we had the impression that the statements of the interviewees were 'politically correct' (although single voices criticised the appearances of women coming to the stadiums). Therefore, in this section, quotations from the interviews are supplemented by a content analysis of the match reports written by male ultras fans in the fan magazine *To My Kibice* [*We Are the Fans*]. Since the researchers did not evoke them, they seem to be a reliable illustration of what roles are assigned to women by at least some fans. The triangulation of methods and sources (Flick 2017) in this case is not an attempt to objectify the research process, but is to ensure (as far as possible) that results (as fully as possible) are reported in full scope and depth.

As we have shown in the previous sections, men speak freely about women at football stadiums. In their narratives, regardless of the type of fans and the place in the stadium they occupy, social roles given to women are most frequently linked directly to their family statuses: 'I'll tell you how you go out with your beer buddies and your wife, my wife, or any wife, girlfriend, it's not really the same anymore' (MF5, ultras). The analysis of interviews demonstrates that male fans most often refer to women in the stands as 'wives', 'girlfriends' or 'partners' who are being taken to the game by their male partners. Women are attributed supportive roles, which only fosters a sense of masculinity among football fans. Female fans considered as 'girlfriends' or 'wives' are easily accepted because – by definition – as partners/wives, they are not 'real' or authentic fans. In other words, they are not seen as fans, but those who only keep them company and this pattern is commonly identified through many interviews.

> No woman in our group is simply a woman. They are simply partners of those who brought them into the stadium.
>
> (MF12, regular)

The emerging image of women coming to football matches is mainly (although not exclusively) in the company of men. Less frequently but coherently male fans refer to an image of a woman who comes alone to football matches as someone most likely looking for a male partner. Women in stadiums are frequently pictured by both male and female fans as either 'bimbos' or 'tomboys' (as we demonstrate in the third part of the book, most women are also critical of other women who see a football match as a 'matrimonial' event or a space for 'auto-promotion' and taking 'selfies'). While the first type appears to be a kind of (stereo)typical judgement, the latter one intrigues analytically. One fan sees their appearance in the stands as aiming to compensate for women's physical deficits, overcome physical unattractiveness and increase social popularity among men.

> It is cruel what I am going to say, but this is what I think: there are an awful lot of unattractive women in the stadium, which means that they are something like … it is terribly rude what I'm going to say, sexist perhaps even to some extent, but in my opinion, there is an unreasonably large number of unattractive women who visit football games, in my opinion, as if they want to compensate for other shortcomings, right? Because they are just such 'tomboys', in the sense that they are not attractive to guys because of their appearance, for their beauty, yes. But, you know, a tomboy comes here to drink here, shout and swear. It's that kind of fan at the stadium I see a lot at every game.
>
> (MF12, regular)

Another male fan, remembering the historical events, mentioned some women who behaved not so much as men did but rather women of loose morals:

> I mean, they were somewhere around, I was 17 years old then. I don't know loose women but in general … I would not be interested in making an appointment with them for coffee, so to speak. And there they were different. However, when it comes to today, there is a bit of this pathology, but it seems to me that at this new stadium, say families and mothers appeared. I would separate a second group. I'm sure that in the 1990s I did not see women who had families at all.
>
> (MF9, regular)

This 'tomboy' image plays an interesting role. It stems from interviews that this is a girl who tolerates all aspects of fan culture, even the most vulgar (even sexist) ones. Furthermore, she participates in all forms of support, including the most radical forms of manifestation of the homosocial nature of fans' community. This also applies to ritual forms of expression such as the collective jumping while holding each other's shoulders, a ritual fan practice that is not expected to be followed by female fans, but some of the girls do not hesitate to join in.

> Women also find themselves in these aggressive places, and if they are with their partners, they also feel safe. Besides, some really tough women can also answer or hit someone.
>
> (MF14, VIP)

> I go back to the concept of a tomboy. She accepts that there are, you know, vulgar jokes about cocksuckers and so on, and the more she can joke about it, the cooler she is, so the more she can legitimise her participation in this group.
>
> (MF12, regular)

The statement from the last quotation is symptomatic. It clearly demonstrates that a woman, to be accepted into the structure of fandom, has to behave 'properly', and in most cases this means behaving like a man. It results in the establishment of a particular gender identity, described by Stacey Pope (2017) as 'masculine femininity'. It describes women behaving in a style traditionally assigned to men: being rude, aggressive, rejecting all signs of weakness and stereotypical femininity. But, as we show in our analysis, the opposite identity, called 'feminine femininity' (Pope 2017), when a woman plays roles conventionally assigned to women, that is, being delicate, sensitive and having a well-cared-for physical appearance, is also recognised by male respondents. It turns out that male fans discern women in stadiums practically only in such a clearly defined dichotomy: either as 'masculine' or 'feminine' (being a wife or girlfriend is included in the latter).

In some sense, in the structure of the fandom culture, the traditional gender relations and roles are maintained and continuously performed. Most women are perceived through the dominant prescription of 'emphasised femininity' (Connell 1987), which contains such features as being rather submissive to a male partner, being the caretaker of her family and children, being a person who should not be involved in staunch fandom activities.

Male fans appreciate such dimensions, and they respect women as their partners and so on, but it is clear that maintaining the image of 'emphasised femininity' as a major role hinders women from gaining the fully recognised status of authentic fans. This type of femininity, described by Schippers (2007) as 'hegemonic femininity', 'consists of the characteristics defined as womanly that establish and legitimate a hierarchical and complementary relationship to hegemonic masculinity and that, by doing so, guarantee the dominant position of men and the subordination of women' (p. 94). The research findings clearly show that the dichotomy between men and women is holding tight, and there is no space for anything in between these two extreme concepts. There is no space for less traditional concepts of either masculinity (for example an inclusive one, Anderson 2005, 2008, 2009) or femininity (McRobbie 2009; Gill and Scharff 2011; Budgeon 2013).

Despite pressures, some women break structural borders by internalising, as 'tomboys', some 'male' features. Such a strategy has far-reaching consequences because it requires compromising their 'feminine' character. Therefore, women entering stadiums have to face 'false' alternatives. They either want to keep their traits and take the risk of not being accepted as 'real' fans, or they choose a 'masculine' role. Using Goffman's (1959) terms, they take the risk of performing a role that is a kind of masquerade. This kind of identity 'deadlock' seems to correlate with performative fandom theory perfectly. Female fans' performances are assessed by 'guards of authenticity' (male fans); women perform different forms of femininity but men recognise mostly two extreme versions of them: 'feminine' more often, 'masculine' less often. Similarly to men (who should only perform 'hegemonic' fandom, at least in the ultras sector), the space for other kinds of femininity is strictly limited.

Performances of femininity are also limited because of the idea of fraternity. A brotherhood joins the ultras fans and their experience of a sense of togetherness. Polish fans often define themselves as 'brothers in scarves', and this slogan refers to the whole community, no matter if there are some women in a group. However, it is based on the male nature of the ultras community and illustrated in their choreographies only by male figures (Kossakowski, Antonowicz and Jakubowska 2020). Although these expressions of brotherhood are almost invisible in the regular stands, one can see that their match experience is shared by male fans mainly with other men. As mentioned in the previous part, our observations have confirmed that male fans naturally turn to other male fans, even if women are sitting closer, to engage them in conversation about football. While fans exchange their opinions, mutually reinforcing their expert status, female spectators watch and perform the role of a passive audience in discussions between 'real' fans, who are also (or perceive themselves as) experts. Therefore, even though male fans say they treat women as regular fans when it comes to match day (and around match day) practices, they tend to ignore them as partners in experts' conversation. There is no doubt – as we show earlier in the book – that women have to overcome harmful stereotypes and prove themselves as fans, and part of this process is to convince men that they have football-related knowledge.

Moreover, female fans need to compromise their feminine dimension to be recognised as mates (for example Coddington 1997). Some of them want to play male roles and not be associated with female fans or girlfriends. Instead, they see themselves in the roles of male fans because being a fan requires embracing masculinity to a large extent. In some cases, male respondents tend to appreciate women's efforts to perform more masculine roles, highlighting their 'fanatical' (therefore authentic) identity:

> If you ask about such female fanatics, of course, some girls go to away matches, and are involved in the association.
>
> (MF8, ultras)

Overall, the status of women fans is much more difficult to enhance due to obstacles stemming from the structure of fandom culture. Some respondents treated the role of the 'mate' as a symbol of peer recognition of being a 'real' football fan. This recognition is something natural for men but is connected to some paradoxes for women as the attribution of the role of 'mate' is a form of inclusion in a homosocial community of football fans. Close relations with male fans, recognition in their eyes and being included in the fans' community are inevitably connected with the role of a 'mate' (colleague) and do not blend with female social roles. Being fully fledged as a 'real' fan attributes to women a new status, which is almost automatically given to men but hard to attain for women. But being a mate and enjoying the status of a real fan has its consequences, as those women lose parts of their feminine dimension because they are no longer seen as women.

The examination of empirical material collected for this study shows that the process of assigning social roles to women is determined by the position of the interviewed supporters in the social structure. In their perception of women, they strongly express how women are perceived in their social strata. In other words, they perceive supporters from a structural point of view. On the other hand, as we mentioned previously in this section, interviews with male respondents provide some elements of 'political correctness'. So it is important to cross-check data from different sources that are biased by the presence of researchers. The additional data derive from the content analysis of match reports written by ultras fans.

It should be emphasised that the most coherent view on women is expressed by the ultras fans, who appear to be a relatively homogeneous group. This issue was identified and widely discussed in our earlier study (Antonowicz, Jakubowska and Kossakowski 2020). We found that ultras see women in instrumental roles either as 'exotic' ornaments or as means to fit their purposes. Those roles may vary significantly depending on the circumstances, but what they have in common is that they instrumentalise women. Furthermore, they reduce women to secondary roles, whose presence, although respected, is complementary and strengthens the sense of masculinity. One can even say that women perform auxiliary roles – girls, partners, mothers and maidens – towards the men present in the stadium, allowing them to feel a little bit more masculine, and in that respect ultras' narratives fully correspond with data from interviews. Some reports mention that even engaged and respected female fans in ultras groups perform 'female' duties such as preparing food and looking after children in the family sector.

The cult of physical strength, violence and the generally aggressive nature of ultras attribute to women the role of potential victims, people incapable of self-defence, and at the same time incapable of acting as 'real' supporters. This stems indirectly from the specific character of ultras' fandom driven by historically grounded, working-class values that were biased against women again. It is worth noting that the ultras produced the most coherent narrative about social roles attributed to women based on a sharp distinction between female and male social roles. It is endorsed by the power of collective action which enforces group conformism and axionormative unity (for an analysis of the fandom community as Durkheim's mechanical solidarity, see Kossakowski 2013).

However, the analysis of ultras' reports also reveals other interesting aspects. Apart from the mentioned assigning of traditional roles to women (girls, mothers, caretakers etc.), what may downplay women's role is their perception of themselves as 'weaker' persons, who require protection and are unfit to be real fans (who are supposed to fight). The reports shed light on how male fans react when women fans try to engage in the core (i.e. masculine) ultras activity. When ultras' match reports state the number of fans, female fans (as well as younger fans) are not included, and their number is given separately. This distinction is the best indication that in the world of ultras, they simply do not count as regular fans.

During clashes between fans and police or security guards, women fans are painted as the victims of thoughtless violence on the part of the security services. They play the roles of innocent victims that show best the scale of aggression of security towards 'weaker' members of the public, but also – as a consequence – it makes women unfit to be members of ultras groups. It also results from the gender dichotomy as the lack of women's involvement in fights stems from the 'chivalrous' attitude of many male fans. Men feel that they have to protect women at any cost. It is dishonest to fight against women and/or let women fight. As one report notes, '[w]e have rules not to involve girls and spectators' (Antonowicz, Jakubowska and Kossakowski 2020, 69). An even stronger 'hegemonic' attitude is revealed when male ultras comment on the odd behaviour exhibited by women fans: '[W]ithout our knowledge, one of the female fans … approached the sector of visitors and attempted to steal their flag' (Antonowicz, Jakubowska and Kossakowski 2020, 72). The author of this report underlines the unusual character of a female fan's action. Typically, stealing a rival's flag is a massive challenge and symbol of superiority, and even just an attempt to take it is appreciated and regarded as brave – particularly in contemporary times when CCTV systems and security services significantly hinder such 'conquests'. But similar action undertaken by women is treated as an undue risk that is most often taken without the 'authorisation' of the top hooligans who normally have to give the 'go-ahead' for such actions.

The fact that men are the dominant actors in fandom culture and have the power to assign roles to women does not necessarily mean that women in the stands are treated in an uncivilised way. On the contrary, most women are treated with huge respect and extraordinary kindness, and male fans are very often willing to demonstrate their 'chivalrous' manners. Some themes of 'chivalry' (for example knights with swords, shields with the club's logo) are important parts of the masculine identity and ultras often relate to it in their choreographies (Kossakowski, Antonowicz and Jakubowska 2020). This could be regarded as nostalgic restoration of some idealistically considered older times when the duties of manhood referred to fighting in compliance with the principles of honour. In such 'older' times, knights conquered the enemy's land and protected the 'weaker ones', namely women, children and older people. Nowadays, such topics should be seen as 'invented tradition' (Hobsbawm and Ranger 2012), and ultras around the world are producers of similar discourses when it boils down to their tradition or ideology (Doidge, Kossakowski and Mintert 2020). Although the 'chivalry' demonstrated by Polish fans can be considered an idealised concept (or simply an attempt to give nobility to criminal acts such as fights), our respondents made numerous references underscoring that the 'chivalrous' approach to women is a relatively common attitude:

> [I]f a woman is not such a typical member of a group, then it is rather conventional chivalry, and we protect and defend her and impress her. It is rather in a positive sense, and such conventional chivalry is waking up.
>
> (MF20, regular)

> But also the fans are overly gallant there because they have had a few beers and here we are letting ladies go through first.... They try to be knightly, it is a little pretentious, but there is something in it.
>
> (MF9, regular)

Of course, having said that, the question arises as to whether such attitudes are typical of Polish society standing out with its conservative attitudes or football fans in the match situation are the exceptions in such an attitude:

> It is even independent of football, generally, women are not supposed to be beaten, well, that's what normal people do, well, supporters are normal people. These are myths created by some environments that fandom is a pathological environment, and I don't know, there are some incredible things happening.
>
> (MF8, ultras)

Such chivalrous attitudes towards women can be perceived in a positive light, but on the other hand, they are also the consequence of assigning to women the status of 'others', that is, non-regular fans who need to be approached with extra care and require special treatment.

> I was even a witness to giving up the place to girls. And at the stadium my wife was also given a place.

Do men behave differently towards women than they do to other supporters?

Well, definitely. Generally at the stadium … I will tell you so, I have never seen a conductor [leading the supporting – ed. authors] throwing a shoe at a girl because she is not singing. I don't know if it results from the fact that they are all singing, or from the fact that, in general, a conductor has some value, and he throws at men, curses at them and screams at them to go out.

(MF5, ultras)

So yes, Miss Ola. It happened a few times that some guy in a row below just asked her: Miss Ola, can I smoke a cigarette here? And Miss Ola let him smoke. So yes, it is just stadium courtesy.

(MF3, regular)

Chivalry is not a contemporary phenomenon, and it has created the desired attitude of manhood from ages. Historically, chivalry was associated with physical strength and endurance, as referred to in many old songs, poems and books (Mesley 2019). A chivalrous man exemplified such positive features as braveness, steadfastness, honour, courage, sacrifice, friendship and determination, and all these characteristics designate the 'moral' trajectory for the masculine part of football fandom. As the analysis of ultras' performances demonstrates (Kossakowski, Szlendak and Antonowicz 2018), Polish fans tend to present and glorify war heroes particularly from the period of World War II and especially those fighting against the communist regime (1945–1953). Matthew M. Mesley points out that in the case of chivalry, '[m]orality and the performance of good deeds were equally important' (Mesley 2019, 153). Medieval chivalrous crusaders protected children and women, as mentioned in previous paragraphs. Analogously, football fights involving women and children are dishonourable and unacceptable in the football subculture. Violating this rule is the ultimate reason for massive outrage, disrespect and stigma in the fans' community. In many ways, fans' hegemonic masculinity draws inspiration from historical symbols – the chivalry motifs are frequently evoked in ultras' choreographies, which display mighty knights on horses that hold swords, banners and shields in the club's colours.

However, as Mesley states, honour is 'much like chivalry, a slippery concept' (2019, 154). Being chivalrous and morally ascendant can often be idealised or romanticised and, as our investigation demonstrates, there is not a single chivalry code of conduct between male fans. Some of them treat female counterparts instrumentally, definitely not in a chivalrous way:

I remember it happened on our trip to Olsztyn and I. [a woman's name] got there and she was taken by them all the way. I do not know on what basis it was, I just went through the train and saw that there were lascivious acts, but it was, let's say, not my atmosphere to the end.

(MF9, regular)

As regards this percentage of 'Barbie' girls, let's call them that, it is minimal. I think that they were not allowed in, and there was a selection in this respect. I also personally know a couple of girls who tried to get through, but they were usually chicks who came with older guys from the group and these guys were able to smuggle them. But these were not repeated situations, guys took them to show off to other colleagues, but these are individual situations, really.

(MF11, ultras)

Some male fans sexualise women. An extreme example of the objectification of women was given by the 'Sharks', the hooligans of Wisła Kraków (Jadczak 2019). They treated girls primarily as sexual objects, as evidenced by the hooligans' behaviours and vulgar language (the girls were called, for example, 'the sluts', as the disclosed content of text messages has revealed).

The 'double' standards towards women also appear in the context of symbolic humiliation of male opponents from the rival's team. As the analysis of ultras' performances demonstrates (Kossakowski, Antonowicz and Jakubowska 2020), it is common to abuse fans from opposite clubs by 'attributing' to them female components and traits. Fans from rival clubs humiliate each other with labels such as 'whore', 'bitch', 'cocksuckers', 'faggot' and so on. As one male fan emphasises, 'feminisation' of rivals serves to belittle them:

Women are generally considered the weaker sex, much more gentle, more sensitive, in contrast to menhood. And it works like that. That they [the fans of a rival team – ed. authors] are unmanly, that they are sensitive, crying and so one, and we are 100% testosterone.

(MF10, VIP)

Chivalry as a basis for assigning inferior roles to women stems from old, traditional features of manhood. It interlocks with the concept of 'hegemonic masculinity' of football fans, which also embraces some moral obligations derived from such an attitude. However, as our research presents, it should be considered a 'selective chivalry', meaning that 'men protect women who conform to traditional gender stereotypes, but not women who violate their assigned gender roles' (Gill, Kagan and Marouf 2015, 5). This selective approach was referred to in several interviews as male respondents acknowledged that some women (partners, wives, mothers) deserve a gentleman's adherence fully, and others, for example 'tomboys', are approached differently.

Micro-changes and macro-steadfastness of (male) fandom culture

As previously mentioned, football terraces are considered a definitely male space. Data collected from the content analysis of the Polish fan magazine *To My Kibice* clearly shows that themes related to masculinity are the most important aspects of choreographies prepared by ultras (Kossakowski, Antonowicz and Jakubowska 2020). Their performances refer to fighting, brotherhood, strong and muscled men's bodies, historical male heroes, and the illegal and underground character of fandom. The opponents are sometimes presented as submissive individuals in the act of brutal sex and 'feminised'. Masculine aspects of those displays are strongly connected to the hegemonic nature of masculinity. Furthermore, any other forms of masculinity (for example homosexual) and femininity are treated as something weaker, inferior and disrespected. Hegemonic masculinity plays an overriding role in terms of gender in Polish football stands. This results in the situation in which women's influence on fan's behaviours seems hard to imagine.

Beyond any question, football fandom is a man's world, dominated by traditional masculine values and the area of 'rituals' adhering to brotherhood and homosocial boundaries:

> They [women – ed. authors] had to accept that they were treated like men. And unfortunately, they had to be equal to men. So all these, so to speak, male rituals that were on these trips. There was beer, there were cigarettes, swearing, bawdy jokes were made. If a man wanted to be a bit gallant towards women, it wasn't there for sure. But it wasn't some kind of anti-woman attitude. But it was 99.9% of the lads who were led by these primal instincts. We go on a trip; I fight, we will be representing our tribe here and so on. So it's a little bit … It's like in a war. Well, on the front.
>
> (MF10, VIP)

As we showed earlier, the statement 'they have to accept that they are treated like men' is strongly related to the male hegemonic nature of fandom. Women are treated in the context of traditional femininity; another alternative is to perform 'masculine' traits. From a gender perspective, the fandom culture can seem like a bastion of a traditional form of masculinity, but it has to be emphasised that this is the result of a long, historical process (as we show in Chapter 3 on the history of Polish fandom; see also Kossakowski 2017a). And changes in social spheres progress slowly. Traditionally, fandom groups have mainly contained men, as one fan recollects:

> Somewhere, this subculture was growing from this male. I remember my grandfather supported Warszawianka [one of the Warsaw clubs – ed. authors], but my grandmother didn't even listen to matches on the radio. It was only men who came. It has been growing from male rules since the nineteenth century and this is a man's world.
>
> (MF13, regular)

We do not recall this quotation to investigate the history of fandom in detail. It rather serves as background for further analysis of whether, and to what extent, the increasing number of appearances of women can have an impact on the behaviour of particular male fans and, in general, on the fandom culture.

Having investigated the roots of hegemonic masculinity in the structure of fandom, it is unsurprising that some male fans comment that it is women who should adapt themselves to male rules rather than vice versa:

> They [women – ed. authors] are aggressive, and one could observe they are provocative or aggressive, and they format themselves in men's style, because we are always striving for a male model, there will never be femininity in the stadium.
>
> **How would you describe 'femininity'?**
>
> I mean femininity in the classic sense, gentleness, sensitivity and a sweet smile. I simplify, of course, and now it is not like that, the world does not look like this, but there is always a woman in a group of fans who will try to be like guys … there is no female component here. If there is a woman – it is always in a 'male' form.
>
> (MF20, regular)

Again, this view is in line with our observations on the gender dichotomy based on male hegemony. Football fandom is embedded in social norms that see the authentic fan as able to confront opponents, aggressive (physically or verbally) and provocative, and failing to comply with those requirements denies fans status. To scrutinise this phenomenon in terms of homosociality (Hammarén and Johansson 2014), the fandom culture is formally accessible to women, but the truth is that only women who perform a 'masculine' role are good enough to be part of the 'homosocial' community.

Traditionally embedded masculine traits function mostly in the most hard-core parts of stadiums – primarily on ultras stands. Male leaders have managed the latter since their beginning. However, women have more opportunities to be physically present as modern stadiums offer them sectors for less engaged fans, for example families and VIPs. The latter are very often places that entrepreneurs and company owners can use for networking, socialising and developing business opportunities. In the VIP sectors or lounges, there are female leaders – businesswomen, politicians and celebrities – with high social and economic capital who try to impose their own rules of the 'game':

> In this man's world of business boxes, there are more and more independent women, for example independent in business. So they are also presidents and board members; they come and do business and set some limits. There are more and more such women, but this is a tendency that I see also in the business world, and then it translates into the stadium. Because the stadium is a place to do business, and if they want to gain something from a man who is just easy-going because the result is good, he drinks alcohol, so these women use it.
>
> (MF14, VIP)

It doesn't mean that VIP sectors are characterised by gender inclusiveness as some traces of 'hegemonic masculinity' are detected in such areas. Our observations suggest that VIP lounges are often *vanity fairs* populated with attractive women who use their access to VIP sectors to socialise with affluent and popular males. Although it is not acceptable to behave in the same way in this place as in the ultras stands (i.e. being aggressive), women have to confront other, more subtle, social barriers, for example those specific to a business world.

The relation between men and women in the context of football gains an extraordinary significance when it comes to men using football as an escape from the daily routine and work stress. In such a situation, even life partners, for example wives, have to acknowledge the superiority of football passion:

> The supporters' wives are screwed up, I have to admit. Because it's a bit like with my wife, that if a woman tries.... And she is dealing with such a fanatic then if she tries to get in the way of his passion, it usually ends badly. Because often this is the only escape from his job. Either stress in the corporation or frustration because they play poorly. So this guy goes to this match, and he is someone there. And if there is no understanding of this, that it is such a safety valve and it is a real passion. I saw lead to very serious crises and break-ups. Therefore, these supporters' wives also have to learn to live with these husbands. If they start accepting things, these guys are then happy. However, there were times when I saw such marriages falling apart, marriages literally falling apart.
>
> (MF10, VIP)

This statement interestingly illustrates that the football and fandom field is masculine multidimensionally. As we demonstrated before, historically men were founders of fandom cultures, and they set rules and norms and defined a sense of appropriateness. And women were outside this process, so naturally their voice was unheard and unconsidered. This resulted in 'hegemonic masculinity' being a major driver shaping men's attitudes towards women. These are the roots of traditional football culture (King 2002), but culture is a dynamic concept, and the emergence of modern football (Dunning, Murphy and Williams 1988) gave it a different shape by adding new commercial aspects. Having acknowledged this and also adding dynamic changes in modern societies that (at least in Europe) have eliminated any tolerance of physical violence we shall state boldly that there are still 'permission zones' (Ben-Porat 2009) where men can do and say more. Therefore, even men who are not interested in the aggressive, staunch mode of football fandom must adapt to the traditional fandom culture when entering the gates of the stadium and this is a part of a wider concept of the escape from the family/partnership context.

It doesn't mean that they cultivate a deeply embedded misogynistic nature, but rather that from time to time they need to spend leisure time in a 'homo-social' environment where they can drink alcohol and talk about football with other male 'mates'. Bearing in mind the strongly male character of the match day experience, is it possible that the growing number of female fans has any impact on men's behaviour and homosociality?

Male fans see the stadium and match event as their own space, the space of 'masculine leisure'. The strong feeling of homosociality is enhanced by historically embedded hegemonic masculinity. But on the other hand, the growing number of women in the stadium is also widely acknowledged by men. Therefore, it is reasonable to investigate whether male respondents perceive any changes behind the growing number of women. Is any kind of impact traceable? Has the match atmosphere been changed (even slightly) due to women's presence? Male fans were faced with these questions, and some of them felt that such an impact doesn't exist:

> No, that is absolute bullshit. No. Someone from outside wrote that. There was the belief that if a man comes with a woman he will behave differently. Absolutely not. It is a total aberration.
>
> (MF10, VIP)

> In my opinion, it has no impact. Women are treated like guys, like mates. It doesn't matter if it is a woman or a man. If they emphasise their femininity, they are automatically put aside.
>
> (MF11, ultras)

This clearly indicates the 'status quo' of the homosocial character of the stands. Women, even if present, are 'invisible' or treated as 'mates'. Their presence does not cause any 'softening' or civilising of male attitudes and behaviours. The old culture is deeply embedded, and it appears to be resistant to change. However, it should also be said that some fans referred to specific situations when the presence of women has influenced the rules of men's conduct:

> I think that there are more women and more couples at matches, you can make a kiss camera at the stadium.

Kiss camera?

> Yes, we will show hearts. But I think it is encouraging if there is a situation that there will be more and more women. I think it is positive. If there is a woman, then later it will be easier to take their child, she may catch the bug for football, maybe it will be easier if she was involved in the upbringing through sport, football or other disciplines. Because maybe she would think that her son would make his debut at the club one day.
>
> (MF1, different sectors)

> It changes because if I take a woman to a match, I have to look after her. I have to, unfortunately, yes. I go out earlier; I don't stay with the boys for a whisky after the match. I'd rather drink wine. I'd also rather keep her interested and not get bored with the match. However, my behaviour is completely

different: between watching the match and then my behaviour before and after the match is completely different.

(MF14, VIP)

Taking the entire study into account, we can say that these quotations represent rather isolated cases that should be treated as 'exceptions' rather than the rule. Moreover, when it comes to structural and cultural imperatives, the 'softening' attitude of some fans is met with the sharp reaction of leaders who set the rules of football fandom and also execute them brutally. In Poznań, the excessive dispersion of men's attention (caused by women) has resulted in a firm reaction from ultras leaders. The stadium is not a place for dating and 'romantic' fairy tales but only for supporting the team on the pitch:

> In a sense, at some point, this type of situation appeared, and there were so many of them that they led to such distraction of these guys that they were all thinking somewhere not in the direction they should be in the stadiums. You are at the stadium; you are here to support, not to hug, hold her hand. You will leave this stadium, do whatever you want, but not at the stadium. And it has clearly been demonstrated here that we don't do such things at the stadium if you want to be a part of the ultras sector.
>
> (MF2, ultras)

Such a bold reaction is symptomatic as it indicates a strong control component – no inaccurate behaviour can be accepted. Fans in the stands must be uniform in their motivation and performance. In this respect, the fandom's hegemonic masculinity resembles a military environment, where there is no democracy, and charismatic leaders issue ordinances, and others must comply – it is either 'their way or the highway'. It is a perfect exemplification of an external (towards women) and internal (towards men) hegemonic environment.

Thanks to the broader scope of our research, we managed to interview fans from different sections of the stadium, representing different ways of thinking. It is interesting that even though some 'hegemonic' imperatives define fandom culture, several male fans assume that the growing number of women is signalling a wind of change. This particularly concerns men who are more open-minded and have a sense of understanding women's needs and sensibility. They believe that the growing number of females provides solid evidence of the 'civilising process' of the masculine form of football fandom:

> [O]h, it's a little bit that men generally are mellowing with women, even in situations outside the stadium … there is often a tense situation that someone swears on the street and the girl pulls him away, and he calms down. Well, it's how women act with men. Well, in general, these women are in a better state than these men … so they are more rational and think a little, so to speak, they are such a catalyst for certain actions. I think they work soothingly, you could say.
>
> (MF5, ultras)

I think that if something is important on the pitch, some foul, or the referee whistles for offside, where our player went for a good position, then this guy no longer screams with everyone: 'Fuck PZPN', because he also sees that he has a partner next to him, I don't think he wants to embarass her so much here.

(MF6, ultras)

I think that a woman is a good customer. I mean, in the sense that it reduces the aggression level, in the same way as there are policewomen, that it causes the situation to calm down a little, generally. This level of aggression, which is sometimes uncontrollable at the stadium.

(MF3, regular)

As we demonstrated in Chapter 1, the significance of women's presence at stadiums is often connected to the broader processes of modernisation and commercialisation of football. Some respondents recognise the influence of female fans – even if it concerns individual men, mostly the women's partners. But in male fans' narratives there are also assertions that the changes in conduct are a result of a broader social and cultural process – both in society and football:

When I started to attend more consciously, there was such a transformation of this environment that there were fewer and fewer hooligans looking for a brawl, and more and more people who came there to support the club. I think it just results from the development of our society, that somewhere in the 1990s after communist times, it was still a time when society rebelled, and it was visible, it was reflected in the stands, at the stadium. Then, when I came to this stadium, I think it was at a time when we were developing as a country, we as a society also improved our material situation. The ticket prices went up, and it could have caused the worse side of the fans to have moved away, maybe somewhere out there, maybe somewhere grown-up. Maybe they already had some children, families, and they just stopped being interested. But I also think that football around Poland started to be cool then because fans have worked hard to make this league look better and better.

(MF2, ultras)

The study shows that football fans are fully aware of the ongoing transformations of society and football that produce a growing number of women in stadiums. There is a mix of evidence about the impact they have on fans' communities. On the macro scale, the syndromes of changes have not yet been identified and Polish football culture seems to be change-resistant; however, on a micro level the traditional masculine character of football fandom seems to crack. There is evidence – though it is hard to say how representative it is – that women can have an impact on men and their presence (locally) undermines the traditional pattern of gender roles in the football stands. However, the dominant narratives demonstrating that the stadium remains the 'bastion' of masculinity are holding on tightly, and the process of women's admission to the leading roles in the community of football fans is progressing slowly. The aggressive nature of football fandom is still detected in the core of this environment. Without a doubt, the appearance of women has not changed the essence of male homosociality in the stands. However, incremental changes are appearing, and women are slowly but gradually gaining their place, but it is not right to assume that gender practices, relations and performances in the fandom area are on the verge of revolution.

Note

1 'Żyleta' [the Razor] is the name of the ultras stand in the stadium of Legia Warszawa.

References

Anderson, E. 2005. 'Orthodox and inclusive masculinity: Competing masculinities among heterosexual men in a feminized terrain'. *Sociological Perspectives 48*: 337–355. doi: 10.1525/sop.2005.48.3.337.

Anderson, E. 2008. '"Being masculine is not about who you sleep with …": Heterosexual athletes contesting masculinity and the one-time rule of homosexuality'. *Sex Roles* 58: 104–115. doi: 10.1007/s11199-007-9337-7.

Anderson, E. 2009. *Inclusive Masculinity: The Changing Nature of Masculinities*. London: Routledge.

Antonowicz, D. and M. Grodecki. 2018. 'Missing the goal: Policy evolution towards football-related violence in Poland (1989–2012)'. *International Review for the Sociology of Sport* 53 (4): 490–511. doi: 10.1177/1012690216662011.

Antonowicz, D., H. Jakubowska and R. Kossakowski. 2020. 'Marginalised, patronised and instrumentalised: Polish female fans in the ultras' narratives'. *International Review for the Sociology of Sport* 55(1): 60–76. doi: 10.1177/1012690218782828.

Antonowicz, D., R. Kossakowski and T. Szlendak. 2015. *Aborygeni i konsumenci: o kibicowskiej wspólnocie, komercjalizacji futbolu i stadionowym apartheidzie. [Aborigines and Consumers: On Fandom Community, the Commercialization of Football and Stadium's Apartheid]*. Warszawa: Wydawnictwo IFiS PAN.

Ben-Porat, A. 2009. 'Not just for men: Israeli women who fancy football'. *Soccer & Society* 10(6): 883–896. doi: 10.1080/14660970903240030.

Blackstone, A. 2003. 'Gender roles and society'. In *An Encyclopedia of Children, Families, Communities, and Environments*, edited by R. Miller, R. Lerner and B. Schiamberg, 335–338. Santa Barbara, CA: ABC-CLIO.

Budgeon, S. 2013. 'The dynamics of gender hegemony: Femininities, masculinities and social change'. *Sociology* 48(2): 317–334. doi: 10.1177/0038038513490358.

Burton, L. and S. Leberman. 2017. *Women in Sport Leadership: Research and Practice for Change*. Abingdon: Routledge.

Coddington, A. 1997. *One of the Lads: Women Who Follow Football*. London: Harper Collins.

Connell, R. W. 1985. 'Theorising gender'. *Sociology* 19 (2): 260–272. doi: 10.1177/003 8038585019002008.

Connell, R. W. 1987. *Gender and Power: Society, the Person and Sexual Politics*. Stanford: Stanford University Press.

Demetriou, D. Z. 2001. 'Connell's concept of hegemonic masculinity: A critique'. *Theory and Society* 30(3): 337–361.

Doidge, M., R. Kossakowski and S. Mintert. 2020. *Ultras: European Football Fandom in the Twenty-first Century*. Manchester: Manchester University Press.

Drożdż, M. 2014. 'Security of sports events in Poland: Polish act on mass events security'. *Ius Novum* 2: 171–186.

Dunning E., P. Murphy and J. Williams. 1988. *The Roots of Football Hooliganism: An Historical and Sociological Study*. London: Routledge & Keegan Paul.

Elias, N. 1997. *The Civilizing Process: The History of Manners and State Formation and Civilization*. London: Blackwell.

Flick, U. 2017. 'Mantras and myths: The disenchantment of mixed-methods research and revisiting triangulation as a perspective'. *Qualitative Inquiry* 23(1): 46–57. doi: 10.1177/1077800416655827.

Gill, R. and C. Scharff, eds. 2011. *New Femininities: Postfeminism, Neoliberalism and Subjectivity*. Basingstoke: Palgrave Macmillan.

Gill, R., M. Kagan and F. Marouf. 2015. 'Chivalry, masculinity, and the importance of maleness to judicial decision making'. *UNLV William S. Boyd School of Law Legal Studies Research Paper*. doi: 10.2139/ssrn.2616502.

Goffman. E. 1959. *The Presentation of Self in Everyday Life*. Garden City: Doubleday.

Hammarén, N. and T. Johansson. 2014. 'Homosociality: In between power and intimacy'. *Sage Open.* doi: 10.1177/2158244013518057.

Hobsbawm, E. and T. Ranger 2012. *The Invention of Tradition*. Cambridge: Cambridge University Press.

Jadczak, S. 2019. *Wisła w ogniu. Jak bandyci ukradli Wisłę Kraków [Wisła on Fire. How the Bandits Stole Wisław Kraków]*. Kraków: Wydawnictwo Otwarte.

King, A. 2002. *The End of the Terraces: The Transformation of English Football*. Leicester: Leicester University Press.

Kossakowski, R. 2013. 'Solidarność mechaniczna zrekapitulowana: o przydatności teorii Emila Durkheima w opisie kibiców piłkarskich' ['Mechanical solidarity revisited: The use of Emil Durheim's theory in analysis of football fans']. In J. Kosiewicz, T. Michaluk and K. Pezdek (eds). *Nauki społeczne wobec sportu i kultury fizycznej* [Social Sciences in Addressing Issues of Sport and Physical Culture]. Wrocław: Wydawnictwo Akademii Wychowania Fizycznego, 101–114.

Kossakowski, R. 2017a. 'From communist fan clubs to professional hooligans: A history of Polish fandom as a social process'. *Sociology of Sport Journal* 34(3), 281–292.

Kossakowski, R. 2017b. *Od chuliganów do aktywistów? Polscy kibice i zmiana społeczna. [From Hooligans to Activists? Polish Supporters and Social Change]*. Kraków: Universitas.

Kossakowski, R. 2019. 'Euro 2012, the "civilizational leap" and the "supporters United" programme: a football mega-event and the evolution of fan culture in Poland'. *Soccer & Society* 20(5): 729–743. doi: 10.1080/14660970.2019.1616266.

Kossakowski, R., D. Antonowicz and H. Jakubowska. 2020. 'The reproduction of hegemonic masculinity in football fandom: An analysis of the performance of Polish ultras'. In *The Palgrave Handbook of Masculinity and Sport*, edited by R. Magrath, J. Cleland and E. Anderson. Dordrecht: Springer, 517–536.

Kossakowski, R., T. Szlendak and D. Antonowicz. 2018. 'Polish ultras in the post-socialist transformation'. *Sport in Society* 21(6): 854–869. doi: 10.1080/17430437.2017.1300387.

McRobbie, A. 2009. *The Aftermath of Feminism: Gender, Culture and Social Change*. London: Sage.

Mesley, M. 2019. 'Chivalry, masculinity, and sexuality'. In *The Cambridge Companion to the Literature of the Crusades*, edited by A. Bale. Cambridge: Cambridge University Press, 146–164.

Millward, P. 2011. *The Global League. Transnational Networks, Social Movements and Sport in the New Media Age*. Basingstoke: Palgrave Macmillan.

Osborne, A. C. and D. S. Coombs. 2013. 'Performative sport fandom: An approach to retheorizing sport fans'. *Sport in Society* 16(5): 672–681. doi: 10.1080/17430437.2012.753523.

Pope, S. 2011. '"Like pulling down Durham Cathedral and building a brothel": Women as "new consumer" fans?' *International Review for the Sociology of Sport* 46(4): 471–487. doi: 10.1177/1012690210384652.

Pope, S. 2017. *The Feminization of Sports Fandom: A Sociological Study*. London: Routledge.

Schippers, M. 2007. 'Recovering the feminine other: Masculinity, femininity, and gender hegemony'. *Theory and Society* 36(1): 85–102. doi: 10.1007/s11186-007-9022-4.

Włoch, R. 2013. 'UEFA as a new agent of global governance: A case study of relations between UEFA and the Polish government against the background of the UEFA EURO 2012'. *Journal of Sport and Social Issues* 37(3): 297–311. doi: 10.1177/019372 3512467192.

13 Female fans in the view of other football stakeholders

The visible presence of women as fans is a relatively new phenomenon, not only for fans but also for clubs' managements and football authorities. As we have shown, supporters perceive women primarily through the lenses of particular social roles that require specific types of behaviours and adaptation to the values prevailing in the fandom culture. For clubs' managers, women can be seen in a broader but still instrumental perspective, for example as an opportunity to increase attendance at stadiums and help to transform football matches into family entertainment. It is, therefore, crucial to investigate how they perceive the roles and importance of women and how they react to their growing presence. Therefore, the analysis in this chapter will be based on individual in-depth interviews with football authorities and the management of football clubs, as well as the examination of merchandise offered in official club shops. Based on the gathered data, the chapter will show whether or not the mentioned stakeholders perceive women as a separate category of fans with distinct needs, views and expectations, and, if so, suggest some measures to address them.

Recognition of the growing number of women

All interviewed stakeholders, who represented different professions and relations to sports clubs, have admitted that the number of female fans in the stadiums has increased. This is very much a fact, even though it is hard to capture the exact figures.

> Surely it is getting better and better, there are more and more women in the stadium. I am not able to provide the statistics, of course, but they do not constitute the majority, it is still, as you know very well, the domain of men, but it is not the case that only men come to the stadium.
>
> (FS1[1])

> I notice that there are many more women in the stands, this quantitative increase is certainly noticeable.
>
> (FS2)

[I]t seems to me that there are more and more of them. It seems to me that this growth is noticeable mainly in non-ultras sectors.

(FS3)

According to these respondents, the biggest number of women can be seen in the family sectors, then in the regular stands, while the smallest number is seen in the ultras stands. The participatory observations in many stadiums across the *Ekstraklasa* conducted by members of our research team are also in line with this. Unsurprisingly, the ultras sectors are the most masculine ones, heavily dominated by male fans who also keep central positions. But even there, a growing number of women has been identified, as it has been in another specific section of the stadium – the VIP stands. However, we can say without hesitation that a growing number of female fans is distributed disproportionally across the stadium. These observations are well captured in one marketing specialist's statement:

As I see it, when it comes to family stands, there are usually many of them [women – ed. authors], because there are families with children, when it comes to ordinary stands, where they come with friends, boys, husbands, there are also a lot of them, and relatively, what is interesting, there is a lot of them in the VIP area.

(FS4)

The latter observation has also been confirmed by one of staff of the hospitality unit of one of the analysed clubs:

There are more and more women among them: business owners, people invited by business owners, wives, partners, daughters.

(FS5)

The data provided by the analysed clubs reveal that female fans buy about a fifth of the tickets and season tickets. In the case of Legia Warszawa, the number is estimated at 21%. At Lech Poznań, in the seasons from 2017 to 2019, women bought 9%–11% of all carnets and in the 2018–2019 season 17% of tickets on average. At the same club, their participation in the *Lechici* programme dedicated to the fans amounted to 18%.

The main reasons that have influenced the increase in the number of female fans identified by the representatives of football stakeholders are the new modern stadiums, greater safety in the stadiums and the organisation of Euro 2012. It should be noted that these factors are interrelated and mutually reinforced. Numerous stadiums have recently undergone modernisation or have been built from scratch, offering new levels of quality and comfort for fans. The new sports facilities are far from what Polish fans experienced ten years ago and as rightly noted 'fit the twenty-first century' (FS6). So it should not be surprising that other interviewees have also emphasised the role of infrastructure in attracting women to stadiums:

> [T]he issue of these infrastructure changes has certainly played a role here.
>
> (FS1)

> [B]ecause we have new venues and these stands are cool, cosy and nice, the women are appearing more, but perhaps this is not the result of cultural change in the fans' environment, but rather changes in the infrastructure and comfort of watching a match.
>
> (FS3)

> [W]omen, however, are largely aesthetic, this coming to the stadium, which is elegant, which is pretty, which has a nice environment, certainly for the part it that matters and attracts them.
>
> (FS4)

As one of the symbols of these changes, the interlocutors have indicated the stadiums' toilets:

> [E]ven such a simple thing, it shows the leap we have made, that there are more toilets to use, they are not a port-a-John, as it was in the old stadium.
>
> (FS1)

> [E]ach architectural design of the stadium takes into account the needs of women … when designing, for example toilets, certain assumptions are made as to the percentage of men and women in the events that take place there.
>
> (FS3)

Among the other important elements of the stadiums' infrastructure, the respondents indicate a medical office, a place for changing babies and food courts. These statements are quite similar compared to the voices of male fans who put, however, a bigger emphasis on safety. Furthermore, Euro 2012 should be perceived as a milestone in changing the fandom culture but also an event that showed football itself and its fans in a different way:

> 2012 we can treat not as a caesura, but as a kind of collective experience in which some women suddenly saw that football is sexy. There was no such event before, until then we had no new stadiums almost, and then suddenly it was a big event where all those who were not interested in football sat and watched matches in the fan zones, saw that football is sexy, that there are new stadiums, that there are cool people who cheer.
>
> (FS4)

The stadiums, the Euro effect, the Polish national team, it is not without significance that this fashion for football was also a driving force. We also had individuals, Lewandowski and a few others, who showed up in the international arena, but also that these new venues in big cities attracted fans who simply wanted to see them.

(FS7)

Euro 2012 was very important in terms of gender issues. During the preparations for the championship and during the tournament itself, there were many critical voices coming from the feminist environment, claiming that Euro 2012 was only designed for men and women were brought along as sexual objects (Jakubowska 2012). The conducted study, however, shows the opposite: numerous respondents, as well as desk research, provide empirical evidence that Euro 2012 was a real game-changer and made a positive impact in terms of women's inclusion in the fandom culture. Moreover, the clubs' initiatives and activities were mentioned as reasons contributing to the increase in the number of women in the stands. If clubs carry out such initiatives and activities, their efforts are focused on the most lucrative parts of the stadium, that is, the VIP sector. Hospitality employees, primarily women, declared that they 'educate' companies and try to convince them that a football stadium is an attractive place for business, net-working and team-building meetings. Only one respondent (similarly to the interviews with male fans) indicated larger socio-cultural changes as a factor in the stadiums' feminisation:

Women are beginning to have a different role in the world. Referring to the occupational position, and the maintenance of the house and financial status and family positions…. I think that it should be not perceived only through the prism of football itself, but that the world has changed a little bit. And it translates. I think there is a strong correlation here.

(FS6)

Infrastructure appears to be a natural explanation, as the quality of sports perfor-mance in the Polish *Ekstraklasa* is hard to recognise as a so-called 'pull factor'. However, it seems to be difficult to understand why managers do not note the socio-cultural changes that increasingly allow women to participate in various domains of social life, including sport and leisure. The respondents confirm that, on the one hand, the atmosphere in the new modern stadiums, including their enhanced safety, is perceived as one of the main explanations of the growing number of women. On the other hand, their increasing participation is seen as a factor that changes this atmosphere. Women, as a new type of fan group, are recognised as generally introducing more cultural and civilised behavioural patterns into the stadi-ums that are particularly warmly anticipated by commercial football partners:

[O]ne should take care of a female fan because she means that we have more young people at the venues, families also come, which softens the atmosphere and it becomes definitely more interesting because every sponsor would like to have as little aggression as possible at the venue, as little as possible of those fan behaviours that can scare off the fans.

(FS8)

According to some interviewees, male fans behave in a different way when women accompany them:

When men come with women, they behave differently. They are more reserved, more official.

(FS5)

I think it is a little bit more cultivated, in the presence of women, men who are not ultras or rude behave a little bit differently, a little bit calmer.

(FS2)

[L]et's not hide from it, women who are in the stands soften customs to a large extent.

(FS4)

However, other interviewees suggest – confirming our earlier findings – that being still a small minority in the stadiums, women cannot simply change the prevailing atmosphere and cultural patterns. One of them noted that a football stadium is a specific place where the emotions are experienced extraordinarily, and causal norms of appropriate behaviours are temporarily suspended. There is no doubt that women's influence varies from one sector to another:

I would divide them again because, unfortunately, we have female ultras fans; they are not much different from men, because they drink beer, use vulgarisms and are probably even aggressive at times, while normal women, women coming to venues, are most often just a 'safety fuse', the ones who soften customs.

(FS8)

Interestingly, this group of respondents confirm voices from male fans stating that female fans do not change the fandom culture, albeit they can influence the behaviour of an individual male fan and control his manners while being nearby. The interviewed stakeholders do not perceive female fans as a homogeneous group, and this also goes hand in hand with earlier male fans' narratives. They distinguish different categories of female fans based on their motivation to come to a stadium, their behaviour and their chosen sector in a stadium. For example, one respondent from Legia Warszawa divided female fans into two categories:

The first is the people who come to ordinary sectors, to ordinary stands, and the second is the group of women, to be precise mothers, mothers who come to family sectors, together with their children or husbands.

(FS9)

Another respondent, representing a sponsor, stated:

> [Women] sitting in the sectors specially dedicated to families or in sectors where there are so-called 'picnics',[2] there are certainly far fewer of them in these typical fan [ultras – ed. authors] stands.
>
> (FS8)

According to the interviewees, some women are very involved in supporting, are 'great fans' (FS8), and show their emotions in the stands. Their level depends, among other things, on the stands they choose:

> [I]t's mostly a more normal cheering, watching is calmer, but some women go to Żyleta[3] and go there because there is a cool atmosphere, one can shout there, be a little bit crazy.
>
> (FS9)

> [In ultras stands] these ladies behave the same way as men, which means they obey the commands of the person who leads the cheering. As far as other sectors are concerned, I notice some differences, however, that there is less spontaneity, because these other sectors react rather to field events, when goals are scored. For women it is rather difficult, I find it harder to imagine that they react strictly to field events, maybe outside the goal, because this is something so obvious.
>
> (FS2)

As noted by the representative of the Polish National Football Association (PZPN), the most engaged female ultras fans sing all the fans' chants, while a few of them even use physical violence towards the female fans from other clubs. The different attitudes are demonstrated by some women sitting in VIP lounges for whom 'a match is of secondary importance' (FS5) and who only accompany their partners.

> [W]omen often come there because they are, sorry for the word, the decoration of their men, so often men make sure that the woman appears there. They want to show off a little bit with those women who look better there or 'are made up' [through cosmetic treatments and surgeries].
>
> (FS8)

Female fans as a target group of customers

The conducted interviews revealed that in spite of recognising different categories of female fans, women are perceived by the clubs' stakeholders mainly as mothers, part of a family. This was stated directly by one of the commercial partners:

> [S]he [a female fan – ed. authors] is a part of a certain team that comes to the sports event, that is, family, so, of course, she is very important to encourage children who mainly appear with their mothers.
>
> (FS8)

Interestingly, asked about the clubs' offers for female fans, some interviewees immediately started to speak about the offers for the families, as illustrated by the following quotations:

> In my opinion, in those clubs where these family sectors exist, it works very well.
>
> (FS8)

> The main emphasis here is placed on these family sectors, on the fact that as many families as possible come to the stadium, children, but also women because men are in the majority in our stadium.
>
> (FS9)

The focus on the families and a mother's role has been explained in different ways by the respondents. First, children are perceived as the future of football fandom; therefore, a lot of activities are directed at them. Second, children are treated as the best 'clients' because they want to eat and drink something during the matches as well as get some clothes or gadgets from the fans' stores. Moreover, parents are more generous when it comes to children and tend to meet their requests, at least to some extent. Third, as mentioned by one of the respondents, children can attract those women (mothers) who are not interested or have not been interested in football so far. And finally, the development of family sectors, including the presence of professional animators who take care of children, can allow women to focus on football and follow the action on the pitch.

> I would not want to be misunderstood that I am using some stereotype, that a husband is watching a match and a wife is with a child somewhere, but this is one of the reasons why it is certainly easier for us to present matches as entertainment for the whole family and it certainly sells itself. So, of course, from the moment one enters the stadium we provide new opportunities, and what follows is that we have seen a growth in the number of female fans, or families with children in general.
>
> (FS1)

> That's a bonus. Such added value when these women can also feel that they are coming to the match. So they come as a family. Women do not have to take care of the children so much because somebody is taking care of them. And then, at that point, women can also devote themselves to the games. And they cheer very loudly and are very happy.
>
> (FS6)

When it comes to the offers targeted directly at women, based on the data received during the research, three kinds of offers can be distinguished. The first one, implemented by all the analysed clubs, is related to particular days, such as the International Women's Day (8th March) or, more rarely, Saint Valentine's

Day (14th February). On Women's Day, female fans can get free match tickets or buy them for a token fee. Also, they receive flowers from the clubs' representatives or can attend the meetings with the players. These club activities, taking place in the stadiums or the city centres, are in line with the celebration of this day in Poland, where men buy flowers and chocolates for women while shops offer women numerous discounts.

The second offer, proposed by Lech Poznań, is also related to Women's Day, however it has a quite different nature and is dedicated to selected women, who are not even always football fans. 'The female side of Lech Poznań' is depicted by the event organised by the hospitality department of the club on the match day in March. The event takes place in the Premium Business Lounge and is directed towards women from different companies from the city and surrounding region. During the event, the invited women can see the match but also take advantage of many offers prepared by business partners, which include, for example, beauty treatments, massages, flower arranging and fashion shows. As the employees of the hospitality and ticketing departments explain, the event has a business aim, that is, the club wants to make people aware of the existence of such facilities at the stadium and present the stadium's lounges as a place that can be used for business meetings, training courses or integration meetings.

The third offer is very specific because it was terminated at the request of women. With the opening of the new stadiums of Legia Warszawa and Lech Poznań, both clubs introduced reduced prices for their female fans to mark a 'new beginning' and encourage a larger number of women to attend football games. However, after a few seasons, they abandoned the special rates for female fans on the firm request of female fans themselves, who could no longer accept their exceptional (abnormal) status in the stadium.

> We had a meeting with the fans, and it turned out that, of course, girls and women appreciate the fact that there are special tickets, but they think it is a kind of discrimination that they are treated better. They feel like fans; it is not this way of thinking that is the reason they come to the stadium as a woman and want to have better; they want to be a normal fan and want it to be normal.
>
> (FS9)

> [T]he girls told us: 'OK, we have this discount ticket, but actually, why?' They were a little surprised. We withdrew it, and there was no bitterness or anything here on the part of the women to tell us that, no, this discount made us stay here because it was cheaper. No, they said OK, there aren't many places where women are honoured in this way.
>
> (FS7)

Currently, the clubs offer discount tickets for children and for a person attending family sectors when a family buys a few tickets. At Lech Poznań, female fans can buy a ticket with a 20% discount, but only when they come to the stadium with at least one child. This pricing policy confirms that women are recognised by the clubs and are attractive to them, mainly as mothers and family members. It is also worth mentioning that a 20% discount is not applicable in the case of men/fathers, which could be seen as discriminatory but could also recall traditional thinking about gender roles. Perhaps male fans are also considered to be 'real' fans who do not deserve extra encouragement to attend football games. Overall, the bonus for families and not for women themselves is also supported by one of the interviewed sponsors:

> I am in favour of rewarding families, maybe not rewarding a woman herself, but if it is a larger group, that is, a family comes, and it could be a multi-generational family, it is a group of people, it is definitely yes, they should be rewarded in this way, that is, the more of you there are, the lower the cost of your stay at the facility is.
>
> (FS8)

In general, clubs have no policy towards female fans, and they do not recognise them either as a business or as a social opportunity. The lack of a developed policy targeted at female fans can be explained by the fact that they are not perceived as a major or important target group. The interviewees related to clubs' marketing pointed at men over the age of 35 or moderately wealthy people aged 35–55 as their main clients. This is a similar strategy to that used in the English Premier League where moderately wealthy middle-class people have become a target group replacing representatives of the working-class and young people who can't afford to buy a ticket (Giulianotti 2011). One of the respondents also mentioned Millennials as an interesting generation purchasing a new line of products and services, including mobile applications. Moreover, these remarks suggest that families are also an important target group, especially children, as future club fans.

Of course, the official viewpoint of clubs and their partners (commercial and social) is that all fans are (should be) equally important for the clubs and the most important aim is to increase the number of fans attending the matches. This is particularly difficult considering the poor quality of the Polish *Ekstraklasa* and the growing number of European leagues being broadcast by an increasing number of thematic football channels.

> I would be interested in the fact that the attendance at every stadium, not only at our stadium, should be as high as possible, and whether it be women, men or mixed, this is a secondary matter. Everything depends on the preferences of individual people, whether they like sport, whether they like football, whether they feel good here, whether they feel safe or not.
>
> (FS9)

> As a club, we stopped, I'd say from the perspective of the last five or six years, thinking this way: now let's do something for a group of students,

and then let's do something for a group of seniors, some special occasion. And let's do it for women, and let's do it for someone else, and so on.

(FS7)

It is, as I said, football for all, which means that we are not trying to reach out to women strictly through these campaigns, but rather to the widest possible audience, that is, to children, the elderly, people with some kind of disability and women as if they were just one of these groups, and not the main objective of these activities.

(FS2)

Therefore, the majority of respondents, the people responsible for the ticket sales and marketing, do not perceive a necessity to organise special actions directed at female fans, which also concern women working for the clubs – 'there should not necessarily be more action targeted at women. A fan is a fan' (FS5). Only one interviewee, who had international fandom experience, agreed that women should be treated by football clubs and authorities as attractive supporters. They have already been identified as such by Western football clubs:

Women are very attractive supporters for managers; first, they are purchasing power, which is half of the world. If we already have men convinced, we already have these customers, no matter what typology of men we have, we reach everyone, but we still have to reach women, the other half, who also have great purchasing power, and who, moreover, often decide on certain aspects of going out at home, so it affects children, for whom, instead of buying blocks, they may buy a ball.

(FS4)

Although women are not recognised as an important target group to a large extent, their growing number has influenced and widened the merchandising offering proposed by the official fan stores. A wider choice of the clubs' clothes and gadgets is important because it gives women the opportunity to 'manifest their affiliation [to the club – ed. authors] by displaying symbols such as badges, buttons, stickers or jerseys' (Ruehl 2010, 17).

The female selection in the shops has expanded over the years, which was acknowledged by the respondents:

As I said, we created some new T-shirts for women. We have a special collection for women.

(FS6)

For a long time, we have had special products for women as well. Once it was much less, some single gadgets, single products, now we can propose more to the female part of the fans.

(FS9)

The selection is broad and it is up to the individual woman to decide whether this clothing, these elements or these accessories are a more feminine style, and appeal to their taste, but yes, there is a wide range of offers. They are also available in their entirety on the website of the online store.

(FS7)

Despite this rather positive change for women, there are still deficits that women identified in the interviews (see Chapter 10). They might be seen as ordinary complaints about mechanising offers, but as we collected them all together, they presented a coherent and appealing picture of women being second-class customers. In short, they should either fit into males' selection or use traditional (sexist) supertight clothes. The merchandising offer interlocks with social roles assigned to women in the stands. Among the complaints was the lack of women's football jerseys, which was justified by the fact that the team is male, women buy less in the fans' stores, which reflects the fans' structure, and also women buy more often for their children (for which the offer is bigger than for women) and husbands/ partners than for themselves. The research participants' observations were confirmed by the data concerning Lech Poznań added by the management of the club's store. In 2010, when the first catalogue of Lech Poznań's merchandise was created, inside one could find two T-shirts and two hoodies for women. Since that time, the offering for women has systematically grown, for example in the 2013–2014 season, female fans could choose between eight T-shirts, four hoodies and one jacket. In the last analysed season (2018–2019), the female collection constituted 20% of all offers and consisted of ten T-shirts, six hoodies, one shirt, one jacket, two leggings and one dress. Additionally, women could buy some jewellery (earrings, bracelets and chains). The growing female collection can also be observed in the store's catalogue: while in its first edition it was presented on only two pages, now there are significantly more pages.

During the 2018–2019 season, the female collection of Lech Poznań represented 7% of clothes sales; moreover, one could see the big differences between the sales of the most popular female and male T-shirts, for example in 2015, the shop sold 1,908 'Mistrz Polski' (Champion of Poland) female T-shirts and 13,669 'Mistrz Polski' male T-shirts. This T-shirt was the most popular among both female and male fans, while the other most popular female T-shirts were bought by 1,400 women ('I love Lech') and over 860 women ('Tarcza biała' [White shield]). It should be noted, however, that female fans sometimes decide to buy male T-shirts in appreciation of their wider choice and more interesting design, in the opinions of some. They also buy male and children kits, which are not available in a female version.

The interviewees from Lech Poznań also emphasised that women working for the clubs decide on the final choice of female clothes' design. They play the same role for one of the sportswear sponsors from another club:

In my case, as far as X [the enterprise's name] is concerned, that decision-maker is certainly a man, because it is a more technical product. Women in my case, and in the case of our products, often decide only at the final moment when it comes to the choice of the design itself, that is, if we have two similar devices, often the woman is important in the decision because one is nicer and she often decides with her eyes, in fact.

(FS8)

An analysis of online stories conducted in August 2018 has provided more information about their offering for women. The store websites of Lech Poznań, Legia Warszawa and Lechia Gdańsk consist of a few website tags, usually one dedicated to the brand that provides the kits, another called 'fashion' or 'life-style', one dedicated to the clubs' souvenirs (accessories) and one dedicated to special collections, related to, for example, the club's anniversary or sports success. Adidas, New Balance and Macron, which are responsible for the clubs' kits, provide clothes only for men and male juniors, therefore if a woman wants to buy a match T-shirt, she must buy a men's or children's size. In the case of casual clothes, clubs use three or four categories: men, women, children and babies. A comparative analysis of the offers is possible mainly between Lech Poznań and Legia Warszawa (Table 13.1) because the categories proposed by Lechia Gdańsk are much less clear, as will be discussed later.

One can see a big imbalance between the number of products offered to male and female fans; moreover, children (their parents) have a wider choice than women. On the one hand, the proportions are respected, taking into account the fact that women do not comprise more than a quarter of football match attend-ances. The bigger offering for children can also be quite easily explained by the popularity of football among children, mainly young boys who play a part in the clubs' football schools and the fact that parents are more willing to buy gifts for the children than for themselves. However, on the other hand, women have very limited choices, mainly in the case of products such as jackets and trousers. It should also be added that both the aforementioned clubs had a dress among their

Table 13.1 The official merchandising offer in Legia Warszawa and Lech Poznań store

The products	Legia Warszawa			Lech Poznań		
	Men	Women	Children	Men	Women	Children
Hoodies	20	4	8	30	10	17
T-shirts	30	9	14	33	11	21
Jackets	10	1	2	10	1	1
Pants	4	2	1	8	2	8
Accessories	30	9	8	10	0	0
Polo shirts	–	–	–	7	0	0
Tracksuits	–	–	–	2	0	0
Total	**94**	**25**	**33**	**100**	**24**	**47**

Note
Additionally, both clubs proposed a few products for babies.

offers, the only product dedicated solely to a feminine audience; however, it was only one dress at each club. Other specific products include female swimsuits offered by Legia Warszawa and a bracelet offered by Lech Poznań.

Women not only have a limited choice of clothes, compared to men, but usually they also have a different choice. In the case of Legia Warszawa, only two of the same T-shirts were proposed both for men and women. In other cases, female products were different from male products. The female clothes more often had light colours, discreet inscriptions and five of them hearts, while the male clothes were more often in dark colours and had bigger inscriptions with the name of the club or the date of its foundation. In the case of Lech Poznań, both T-shirts and hoodies were differentiated in colours and with a variety of small and big inscriptions. However, only one hoodie had the full name of the club on it, and none of them had the club's crest (in the case of male hoodies – half of them had a crest). Moreover, similarly to Legia Warszawa, women had a distinct choice from men except for one T-shirt, which called the fans the 12th player. The products offered by the stores labelled as souvenirs, gifts or accessories were not divided into male and female categories, except for the bracelet mentioned and two cosmetics for male fans of Lech Poznań.

The offering of Lechia Gdańsk's store is also labelled by categories, such as men, women, boys, girls, children, babies and all; however, the allocation of products to different categories is unclear and not separable. At the time of the analysis, the most commonly used category, 'men', consisted of products dedicated to men but also children. Moreover, the accessories offered by the club were described as 'for men' (74 products) and 'for everyone' (3 products), and the same was true about souvenirs for the home and the office. First, it was difficult to guess what the criteria were for distinguishing between male and 'neutral' products; second, none of the products had a specific male character, such as a trimmer (a product sold by Lech Poznań). A scarf, used by many female fans, as the data reveal, was also labelled as a male product. Moreover, although the tag 'girls' appeared on the store website, its content was empty. As regards the choice of clothes, the club proposed 38 products for men and four for women – three T-shirts and one hoodie, only one of which was in the club's colours, although the others had the name of the club on them. Similarly to the clubs from Poznań and Warszawa, the offering for children was bigger than the one for women.

The analysis of the clubs' stores' offering for women and interviews with other stakeholders demonstrate that the presence of women is becoming something obvious in Polish football. Stakeholders – in a similar way to supporters – recognise the set of particular factors that have influenced the increasing number of women at the stadiums. The most important factor in the eyes of respondents is the new, modern stadium infrastructure – the result of preparations for Euro 2012. Respondents also see that women appear in specific social roles – as mothers or partners; they also confirm the statements of male supporters that women have not influenced changes in the culture of supporting. Some stakeholders perceive a marketing opportunity in the increasing number of women because they can help to transform the stands into a more friendly place (in connection with bringing children to the stadium). The interviewees treat women as the 'new fans', who – in some cases – deserve special treatment (lower ticket prices or souvenirs on the occasion of Women's Day). Women are not treated as traditional fans, but they are becoming an important category – consumer fans. This can also be seen in the club stores' offering. The offering for women is smaller than that addressed to men. Compared to the number of women in the stands, however, this offering seems to be relatively rich.

Notes

1 FS – football and clubs' stakeholders.
2 'Picnic', Pol. *Piknik*, is a colloquial expression describing a consumer fan who attends football games just for fun and entertainment and is not 'fanatical'. Ultras fans in Poland use this expression to divide the fandom culture into 'authentic' fans and 'picnics'.
3 'Żyleta' [the Razor] is the name of the ultras stand in the stadium of Legia Warszawa.

References

Giulianotti R. 2011. 'Sport mega events, urban football carnivals and securitised commodification: The case of the English Premier League'. *Urban Studies* 48(15): 3293–3310. doi: 10.1177/0042098011422395.
Jakubowska, H. 2012. 'Kobiety i "kobiecość" w dyskursie o Euro 2012' ['Women and "femininity" in the Euro 2012's discourse']. *Czas Kultury* 1: 34–46.
Ruehl, M. 2010. 'Fan identity and identification drivers: Stoking the flames of the phoenix'. Master diss. Victoria University of Wellington.

Conclusion

This extensive research project, based on the mixed methods that we have conducted, has allowed us to draw several conclusions about female football fandom. Some of them have already appeared in the content of particular chapters, but here they will be collected and highlighted. One should emphasise that our study concerns Polish fans, therefore some findings may be specific to this country or region of Europe, while others, we suppose, may have a more general nature. In both cases, we are convinced that the received data enrich the existing state of knowledge for at least two reasons. First, the vast majority of research conducted so far have concerned Western fans and fandom culture; second, to the best of our knowledge, their findings were not based on quantitative research carried out on such a large sample. The mix of qualitative and quantitative approaches, and the use of different methods and data for analysis have allowed us to create a more in-depth and nuanced image of the process of women entering football fandom.

One of our main findings is that female and male fans do not differ at the identification level. Both the online survey and interviews revealed that a lot of women are passionate about football; they are loyal to their club and its crest and colours. The club plays an important role in their lives, influencing their everyday plans and routine (even such specific things as the selection of bed linen) as well as special events, such as weddings. Moreover, their attitudes towards the club (for example home match attendance, their reasons for being there, their feelings towards the club) are similar to male attitudes, which is particularly visible among the ultras fans, who constituted a significant proportion of the online survey's participants. However, the narratives of the female fans from other sectors of stadiums also provided solid evidence of their passion, sacrifice and engagement. There is no doubt that the club's loyalty means a lot to female fans; therefore it is hard to defend false, unjust stereotyping claiming that women (contrary to men) are not 'authentic' or 'real' fans (King 2002) and their interest in football stems from 'fashion, not passion' (Redhead 1993).

The second main finding reveals that female fans should not be treated as a homogeneous category. On the contrary, female fandom (like male fandom) is differentially performed (Osborne and Coombs 2013) on multiple levels: match attendances, practices during the matches, the purchasing of club souvenirs and so on. The selection of their place in the stadium entails a level of involvement in the fandom culture and fan practices. The chosen sector defines, more than gender, the ways in which fans support their clubs. Additionally, age also seems to be a critical factor in the way football fandom is performed. Differences between generations are visible in the stands; they have also been recalled in fans' narratives. For example, older fans explained changing place in the stadium by 'growing up' from the ultras stands and/or raising a family; they have also identified the dress code in the professional environment as limiting opportunities to exhibit their club loyalty. During the study we encountered numerous female fans who had not missed any home matches for years, had some experience of away matches and who engaged in cheering throughout matches in ultras stands. On the other hand, some fans attended only some matches, sat in regular sectors and just enjoyed watching the game. Some of the respondents talked about their huge collection of club souvenirs, while others had only one scarf, received as a gift. Overall, there is mixed evidence regarding the code of conduct during football matches. Some of the female fans were firmly against swearing in the stadium but others admitted that sometimes they swore in response to what was happening on the pitch. Yet others actively participated in the vulgar insulting of the opposing team and their fans. This only adds more weight to our conclusions about the rich diversity of female fandom. Therefore, there is no doubt that women perform fandom in many ways (which has been noted not only by us but also by the respondents, both women and men, themselves) and it is not possible to create a consistent definition of female fandom.

Third, the heterogeneity of female fandom also concerns the ways of performing (Butler 1990) or doing (West and Zimmerman 1987; Ussher 1997) gender. The majority of female fans perform (or begin their fans' life in) traditional family roles of mothers and wives/partners – they come to the stadiums with their children or accompany male fans. This does not mean that they are not interested in the game (although in some cases they are not), but that they come to the stadium because of their feminine, family roles and stay focused on these roles during the match. Some women decide to play a script of 'being a girl' (Ussher 1997) in the stands, that is, they demonstrate their femininity and emphasise their physical attractiveness to attract the attention of male fans. However, it should be noted that this kind of performance is not accepted in the ultras stands by either men or other women. The performance of 'emphasised femininity' (Connell 1987) can also be observed in VIP lounges, which should not be surprising given that affluent and well-connected male figures dominate them. At the other end of the continuum, one can meet female fans, usually very young women, described by one of the fans as 'tomboys' (or 'cool girls' using his words). They do not demonstrate femininity; on the contrary, their performance of fandom is constituted by all the behaviours of ultras fandom, including drinking, swearing, jumping and other practices perceived as unfeminine. By 'being cool' and denying traditional femininity, those fans, as one might suppose, (try to) legitimise their belonging to (male) ultras fans. While this type of female fans does not seem to be popular, there is a significant number of female fans who perform the role of 'mates', being 'one of the lads' (King 1997) or 'honorary males' (Ben-Porat 2009). They are fans who regularly attend the matches, take part in a lot of fans' activities and are perceived similarly to their male colleagues. They neither exhibit nor deny their femininity, their gender remains invisible to a large extent; one could also say that they do not perform their gender (Lenneis and Pfister 2015). However, it does not mean that football stands, mainly ultras stands, have become gender-neutral; they still have a homosocial male nature – women become 'mates' by adapting male rules and male behaviours.

The next finding is that football fandom is firmly a masculine realm. It is organised, controlled and run by male fans and it serves their hegemonic purposes. Women's 'enculturation' into the fans' world is carried out by men – relatives or peers – and men also impose the rules in the stands and maintain fans' hierarchy. New stadiums with modern infrastructure have increased the perception of fans as consumers, and have led to a bigger presence of women in the stands, but they have not guaranteed that women are treated on an equal footing with male fans. Women are not allowed to play central or main roles in the stands; on the contrary, they are designated supportive roles that allow men to legitimise their presence in the stands (Antonowicz, Jakubowska and Kossakowski 2020). Although there is no doubt that there are significant differences between the ultras sector and the rest of the stadium in fandom performances, when it comes to women's perception, these differences are barely visible. The majority of male fans, regardless of the sector, assign the same role to women, although fans from the regular and VIP sectors do it more subtly. Some discrediting practices of female fans illustrate this. For example, male fans tend to exclude women from discussions about what happens on the pitch; women are recipients of male commentaries, witnesses of male conversations but the vast majority of them do not participate in them. They are not treated as football experts, 'real' fans with sufficient knowledge to comment on the match. Such social practices are even more visible in the ultras stands where women have a more peripheral position. In general, the more militant character a group of ultras has, in terms of their narratives about being able to fight for the club and defend its symbols, such as flags, and also militant factors influencing the inner group hierarchy, the less likely it is that they will engage female fans in different roles than sexual objects or a weaker gender that needs to be protected in a chivalrous way.

Another important finding allows us to state that the gender hierarchy and order imposed by men is also maintained by female fans. As mentioned, female fans adapt to the rules and social practices in the stands; they do not propose their own ways of supporting and rarely form their own, female-only, groups. Even if they do not agree with all the informal regulations imposed by men, they perceive them as a 'natural' part of the football fandom culture. Interestingly enough, the vast majority of them do not perceive stadium language as sexist, although our research of ultras fans' choreographies revealed that this language is both sexist and homophobic (Jakubowska, Antonowicz and Kossakowski 2019). Women want to be recognised as 'real' fans. This can be illustrated by their resistance to the feminine form of the word 'fan' distinguished in Polish and to special ticket rates for women. The latter practice seems to be perceived by female fans as treating them as 'others' and downplaying their status to that of children, a category of fans that requires special treatment and protection.

In general, the situation of female fans stems from a cocktail of factors starting with the conservative values underpinning Polish society. However, women entering a football stadium are confronted with a heavily institutionalised environment that offers them two sets of internally coherent expectations as to the roles they perform in the stand. They can either demonstrate their gender by performing 'feminine' roles (girlfriends, wives, mothers) or by becoming 'tomboys' and adopting typical masculine behaviours. Regardless of which roles they choose, football culture is doomed to reproduce traditional gender order in the stands by adapting to male rules. As previous research revealed, this is one of the strategies for dealing with an existing, traditional frame of fandom (Jones 2008; Pope 2017); for many of the interviewed fans, it seemed to be the only possible way to be legitimised as 'authentic' fans. In between these two extremes there is still little space for women to develop their own style of fandom and overcome the 'script' that framed them into traditional social roles (that's why there are only a few separate, official female-only groups in Poland).

Typically, women from Poland and other countries are not allowed to play important and leading roles in fans' structure. Although generally women are not active actors in supporters' associations, the progressive change is visible. For example, in Sweden, women have their representatives on supporters' boards in the cases of Malmö FF (two out of eight board members) and Hammarby IF (three out of ten board members). In 2016, the first woman was elected as president of the Swedish Football Supporters Union (Radmann and Hedenborg 2018, 246). A significant number of women are represented in the Supporters' Trust of English Football Clubs (Dunn 2017). A woman – Daniela Wurbs – was CEO of the biggest fans' organisation in Europe, namely the Football Supporters Europe, from 2009 to 2016. It seems that women have easier access to democratic football organisations as they are not based on the male domination that is observed in the case of Polish clubs. Moreover, one can refer to the generally low participation of Polish women on the boards of sports (Jakubowska 2018) and other organisations (Women in Work Index 2019), with fans' associations being perceived as an example of a wider social phenomenon.

Polish society is relatively conservative in comparison to other countries in the EU, but numerous top positions are held by women both in politics and the corporate world. Neither women being prime ministers nor CEOs in Poland seem to be anything exceptional, although the gender representation in the top positions remains unbalanced. Having said that, we should underline that football fandom is heavily masculine and women have no access to leadership positions, so it is fair to say that Polish football fandom represents ultra-conservative attitudes to gender issues and embodies hegemonic masculinity.

Another important conclusion from our study refers to the perception of female fans by clubs and football authorities. There is no doubt that a larger number of women in the stands can have significant financial consequences for the clubs as women can impact the revenues coming from various sources. Bigger attendances could easily be transferred into stronger interest from sponsors as more supporters are able to watch advertisements around the pitch. And women's visits can convince the sponsors that have not been interested in investing in football thus far – for example, producers of goods for women. Our research reveals that Polish clubs' authorities have noticed a growing number of female fans, as evidenced by the increasing offering for women in the clubs' stores. However, the interviews disclosed that women are perceived mainly in the family context, as mothers who come to the stadiums with their children (the future fans of the clubs), buying not only tickets for a match but also souvenirs for their children, snacks and meals. For the clubs, the financial benefits are therefore not seen through the prism of women themselves, but that of families. Thus, clubs reproduce traditional thinking about women, perceiving them mostly in the role of mother. The reproduction of traditional femininity is also visible in the stores' offers for female fans (more subtle designs, lighter colours, fitted shapes of T-shirts, etc.) and the events organised on the occasion of Women's Day (beauty services, fashion shows, flowers attached to tickets, etc.). Therefore, although the local and national football authorities recognise the growing presence of female fans, they reinforce the existing gender order in the stands.

The 'feminisation' of Polish stadiums should be understood as an increasing number of women in the stands and in the number of women passionate about football. However, it cannot be perceived as 'feminisation' or 'gender neutralisation' of the rules of football culture. We cannot consider it in terms of a radical change of habits and social consciousness in the fandom area. Without doubt, the Polish football fandom culture remains a bastion of traditionally established and performed gender roles. Women's emancipation, and their increasing status in Polish society, makes the football stands an enclave of 'hegemonic masculinity', a place dominated by men, and traditional thinking about male and female roles. Although this statement refers mainly to ultras stands, our research has revealed that more subtle forms of reproduction of male domination are practised by fans sitting in different sectors and by the authorities. The opportunity to investigate the male perspective on female fans' appearance allows broader conclusions to be drawn as our research clearly shows that male fans still see the stadium and football culture as a space for experiencing a rough, masculine and politically incorrect way of behaving that is becoming – step by step – 'inappropriate' in other social domains. Even men who treat their wives or female partners in an emancipatory way very often perceive the occasion of a match as an outlet of emotions not necessarily accepted in 'sterile' work environments. Comparing the male and female perspectives makes our conclusions stronger and more reliable as some findings are supported – independently – by narratives from men and women. We perceive this as a methodological asset of the whole project as the opinions of representatives of one gender could provide only one side of the situation. The 'two sides of a coin' aspect is something new in comparison to existing research.

As a result, we find not only that men set the rules and force others to act according to them, but also that women themselves reproduce the existing gender order and do not propose their own way of supporting. Fandom is performed in very individualised ways, depending on the sector, age, professional work, family situation and so on. Female fans very rarely organise themselves to express their fandom freely, as has been observed in other countries (Llopis-Goig 2007; Lenneis and Pfister 2015), or propose (make) any changes in the stands. The reasons for this and their subordination to male rules are worth emphasising and require further study.

The presence and significance of women in contemporary football is obvious, and their role is growing encouragingly. However, it is hard to state that we are experiencing a 'gender quake' in football in terms of a breath-taking power shift from men to women (the number of women among fans in most European countries still rarely exceeds 25–30%). The role of women will probably become more significant in the coming decades, but even today they can be perceived as one of the biggest assets of the football field. Our research clearly demonstrates that the quantitative factor can only be meaningful when it is supported by qualitative change – the change in the cultural dimensions of the fandom culture. In this respect, there is still a long way to go.

However, it is possible to list very concrete and attractive social benefits for football connected to the presence of women in the stadiums. First, women can bring different actors to attend matches. The growing number of women can make a new path of socialisation possible, redefining its form through its, albeit slow, demasculinisation. Contemporary female fans engaged in football and strongly emotionally attached to their clubs would be the alternative 'significant others'. Second, many women can provide different, less homophobic and more open fandom (even though some women fans reproduce the masculine order in the stands). This can influence the general atmosphere in the stadiums, as well as the attitude of male fans and football authorities. The latter (UEFA, FIFA, etc.) place a strong emphasis on the idea of equality and anti-discriminatory projects, and more diverse football stands seem to support such an attitude. Women represent many, very different kinds of fandom identity and all of them should find their space in the football field. However, only the future will show whether deep changes can be implemented by female fans in the football field.

References

Antonowicz, D., H. Jakubowska and R. Kossakowski. 2020. 'Marginalised, patronised and instrumentalised: Polish female fans in the ultras' narratives'. *International Review for the Sociology of Sport* 55(1): 60–76. doi: 10.1177/1012690218782828.

Ben-Porat, A. 2009. 'Not just for men: Israeli women who fancy football'. *Soccer & Society* 10(6): 883–896. doi: 10.1080/14660970903240030.

Butler, J. 1990. *Gender Trouble*. New York: Routledge.

Connell, R. W. 1987. *Gender and Power: Society, the Person and Sexual Politics*. Stanford: Stanford University Press.

Dunn, C. 2017. 'The impact of the supporters' trust movement on women's feelings and practices of their football fandom'. *Soccer & Society* 18(4): 462–475. doi: 10.1080/14660970.2014.980729.

Jakubowska, H. 2018. 'Poland: Underrepresentation and misrecognition of women in sport leadership'. In *Gender Diversity in European Sport Governance*, edited by A. Elling, J. Hovden and A. Knoppers. Abingdon: Routledge, 59–69.

Jakubowska, H., D. Antonowicz and R. Kossakowski. 2019. 'Bracia po szalu i sąsiadki zza miedzy. Narracje o męskości w środowisku kibiców piłkarskich' ['The brothers in arms and our girl neighbors: The narrative of masculinity in Polish football fandom culture']. *Studia Socjologiczne* 1(232): 95–115. doi: 10.24425/122491.

Jones, K. 2008. 'Female fandom: Identity, sexism, and men's professional football in England'. *Sociology of Sport Journal* 25(4), 516–537. doi: 10.1123/ssj.25.4.516.

King. A. 1997. 'The lads: Masculinity and the new consumption of football'. *Sociology* 31(2): 329–346. doi: 10.1177/0038038597031002008.

King, A. 2002. *The End of the Terraces: The Transformation of English Football*. Leicester: Leicester University Press.

Lenneis, V. and G. Pfister. 2015. 'Gender constructions and negotiations of female football fans. A case study in Denmark'. *European Journal for Sport and Society* 12(2): 157–185. doi: 10.1080/16138171.2015.11687961.

Llopis-Goig, R. 2007. 'Female football supporters' communities in Spain: A focus on women's peñas'. In *Women, Football and Europe: Histories, Equity and Experiences*, edited by J. Magee, J. Caudwell, K. Liston and S. Scraton. Oxford: Meyer and Meyer Sport, 175–189.

Osborne, A. C. and D. S. Coombs. 2013. 'Performative sport fandom: An approach to retheorizing sport fans'. *Sport in Society* 16(5): 672–681. doi: 10.1080/17430437.2012.753523.

Pope, S. 2017. *The Feminization of Sports Fandom: A Sociological Study*. New York: Routledge.

Radmann, A. and S. Hedenborg. 2018. 'Women's football supporter culture in Sweden'. In *Female Football Players and Fans: Intruding into a Man's World*, edited by G. Pfister and S. Pope. London: Palgrave Macmillan, 241–258.

Redhead, S. 1993. *The Passion and the Fashion: Football Fandom in New Europe*. Avebury: Ashgate Publishing Limited.

Ussher, J. M. 1997. *Fantasies of Femininity: Reframing the Boundaries of Sex*. New Brunswick: Rutgers University Press.

West, C. and D. H. Zimmerman. 1987. *Gender and Society* 1(2): 125–151. doi: 10.1177/0891243287001002002.

Women in Work Index. 2019. Accessed 3 January 2020. www.pwc.co.uk/services/economics-policy/insights/women-in-work-index.html.

Index

abortion, Polish debate 58
abusive language 42, 121, 125, 145
alcohol 99, 143, 147, 172
Anderson, E. 31
Angels of Fenerbahçe 14
anthems 119
anti-gender movements 62
Antonowicz, D. 44, 46, 48
armchair audience 105
atmosphere of the stadium: away games
    148; influence of women's presence
    158, 183–184; influence on behaviour
    123; male 'qualities' 15; as motivation
    for match attendance 87, 106, 110;
    new venues 160, 183; Polish economic
    transformation and 44
attachment to club: and acceptance of poor
    performance 107–108; connotations
    with religious faith 107; expression
    through clothing 119; as motivation for
    match attendance 105
attractiveness of sportsmen, as motivation
    for match attendance 111
Australia 111
authentic fandom: determinant
    characteristics 14, 20, 93, 99, 172, 197;
    experiencing discomfort and 99;
    gendered perception 14, 16, 21,
    145–146, 163, 197; inconsistency of
    femininity with 17, 164; social and
    culturally constructed expectations 19
away games: and access to toilets
    101–102; atmosphere of the stadium
    148; comparison with home matches
    91–92; female fans' attendance 99–103;
    as last bastion of hegemonic masculinity
    99–103; potential exposure to violence
    at 91–92, 101, 147; restrictions on
    female attendance 101, 148

bad language 99; *see also* language;
    swearing/swearwords
bankrupt football clubs, Polish fans'
    provision of help for 48
banning of women, from match attendance
    101, 148
Barcelona, FC 12
Bayer Leverkusen 12
bed linen, in club colours 108, 194
behaviour, norms of in 'permission zones'
    2, 17, 109, 120, 125
behaviour in stadiums, women's influence
    183–184
Ben-Porat, A. 81, 84, 145, 148
Beşiktaş, women-only fan group 13–14
Besta, T. 45, 47
Bird, S.R. 30
bourgeoisification, of contemporary
    football 21
bromance 30–31
Brøndby Copenhagen 13
brotherhood 2, 26, 34, 107, 153, 165, 171;
    see also fraternity
'brothers in scarves' 165
Bury FC 105
Butler, J. 32

Canada 19
Catholic Church *see* Roman Catholic Church
chivalry: as explanation for male fans'
    behaviour 31, 167–169, 196; place of in
    masculine identity 168–170
Chiweshe, M.K. 14
clothing: club clothing worn by female fans
    131–133; expression of attachment to club
    through 119; match attendance and 109,
    113; political 132; produced exclusively
    for female fans 136–138; sizing issues
    139; use of pink colouring 138